ROUTLEDGE LIBRARY EDITIONS: ETHICS

Volume 23

REASON, ACTION AND MORALITY

REASON, ACTION AND MORALITY

J. KEMP

LONDON AND NEW YORK

First published in 1964 by Routledge & Kegan Paul Ltd

This edition first published in 2021
by Routledge
2 Park Square, Milton Park, Abingdon, Oxon OX14 4RN

and by Routledge
52 Vanderbilt Avenue, New York, NY 10017

Routledge is an imprint of the Taylor & Francis Group, an informa business

© 1964 J. Kemp

All rights reserved. No part of this book may be reprinted or reproduced or utilised in any form or by any electronic, mechanical, or other means, now known or hereafter invented, including photocopying and recording, or in any information storage or retrieval system, without permission in writing from the publishers.

Trademark notice: Product or corporate names may be trademarks or registered trademarks, and are used only for identification and explanation without intent to infringe.

British Library Cataloguing in Publication Data
A catalogue record for this book is available from the British Library

ISBN: 978-0-367-85624-3 (Set)
ISBN: 978-1-00-305260-9 (Set) (ebk)
ISBN: 978-0-367-49865-8 (Volume 23) (hbk)
ISBN: 978-1-00-304793-3 (Volume 23) (ebk)

Publisher's Note
The publisher has gone to great lengths to ensure the quality of this reprint but points out that some imperfections in the original copies may be apparent.

Disclaimer
The publisher has made every effort to trace copyright holders and would welcome correspondence from those they have been unable to trace.

REASON, ACTION AND MORALITY

---

by
J. Kemp

*First published
in the United States of America 1964
by Humanities Press Inc.
303 Park Avenue South
New York 13, N.Y.*

*Published in Great Britain by
Routledge & Kegan Paul Ltd
London*

© *J. Kemp 1964*
Library of Congress Catalog Card No. 64-15248

Printed in Great Britain

TO MY FATHER

CONTENTS

ACKNOWLEDGEMENT	*page*	viii
INTRODUCTION		1

PART ONE

I.	CUDWORTH	7
II.	LOCKE	15
III.	CLARKE	27
IV.	HUME	39
V.	KANT	64

PART TWO

VI.	THE ASSESSMENT AND CRITICISM OF CONDUCT	95
VII.	RULES	112
VIII.	CONSISTENCY	127
IX.	INTELLIGENCE	148
X.	INTUITION	167
XI.	THE LIMITS OF JUSTIFICATION	177
	INDEX	206

ACKNOWLEDGEMENT

I AM grateful to my St. Andrews colleagues, Professor A. D. Woozley and Dr. I. Mészáros, both of whom have read the whole of this book in typescript and have helped me generously with suggestions and criticisms. They have enabled me to remove a number of errors and imperfections and are, of course, in no way responsible for those that remain.

INTRODUCTION

THERE is a traditional belief to the effect that man is a rational animal. Rationality or the ability to reason has often been held to be not merely an essential part of human nature, but also the quality which serves best of all to distinguish man from the rest of the animal creation, and *a fortiori* from the vegetable and mineral kingdoms, the quality which raises him above the beasts of the field and the fowls of the air, and gives him such dignity and worth as he possesses. The outlines of this distinction are today perhaps more blurred than they once were: evolutionary biology and modern experimental psychology have both, in their different ways, stressed the resemblances as well as, if not more than, the differences between man and the other animals. Nevertheless, the belief in the over-riding importance of man's rationality may not unfairly be regarded as one of the most powerful elements in the thought of what is known as Western civilisation.

If man is essentially rational it is natural to suppose that his rationality pervades his whole existence; not merely that he thinks rational thoughts, but that he leads a rational life, or rather, that he should do so. ('Man is a rational animal' implies, not that man always behaves rationally—it is only too obvious that he does not—but that he can behave rationally, and that in doing so he behaves in a distinctively human way.) The concept of reason has therefore often been taken as the key, not merely to man's thinking in a narrow sense, i.e. to what are sometimes called his cognitive capacities, but also to his actions and, though less frequently, to his ability to create and appreciate beautiful things. The purpose of this book is to investigate the function of reason in man's practical life: in the life of action as opposed to that of pure thought or to that of contemplation or imagination, whether aesthetic or religious.

INTRODUCTION

It is notorious that a philosopher's difficulties begin at an earlier stage than those of many other investigators; for he has to spend a great deal of labour in formulating his questions before he can usefully set about answering them. G. E. Moore said, in an often-quoted passage from the preface to *Principia Ethica*, that most of the difficulties and disagreements in which students of ethics and other branches of philosophy are apt to find themselves are due to the fact that they have attempted to answer questions without first making up their minds as to the precise nature of the questions they are trying to answer; and few topics in philosophy provide a clearer illustration of the truth of what Moore says than the problem, or problems, with which we are here concerned. Much time and labour has been wasted, both in earlier periods and more recently, in disputes over such questions as 'Are moral distinctions derived from reason?' or 'Can reason alone move to action?' when the meanings of the questions themselves have not been adequately determined. When the questions are analysed, verbally similar statements are often seen to mean quite different things to different people, while verbal contradictions often conceal identity, or considerable resemblance, of thought. In order to clarify the questions at issue, I shall in the first part of this book examine critically a number of theories that have been put forward concerning the connection between reason and action. The discussion will be confined to what is conventionally known as modern philosophy, i.e. to philosophy since Descartes, and even within this period it makes not the slightest claim to be exhaustive. Some important thinkers find no place in it: other less notable figures are treated at greater length than their abilities might seem to warrant. The principles of selection and treatment have been determined solely by reference to the contribution which this critical section can make to the independent examination of the issues involved.

Descartes is customarily regarded as the founder of modern philosophy; and although we have become much more conscious than we used to be of his debt to his medieval predecessors, it is nevertheless not incorrect to give him much of the credit for a philosophical revolution which is particularly relevant to our subject. For Descartes' philosophical method presupposed the ability of human reason to discover fundamental truths unaided

INTRODUCTION

by divine revelation; and although Descartes himself made little use of this principle in the sphere of practical philosophy, his influence on other thinkers of the second half of the seventeenth century and the first quarter of the eighteenth can hardly be overestimated. As E. C. Mossner has said,

> In the history of modern thought, he [Descartes] is of unparalleled importance in supplying the first philosophical justification of independent reasoning. Descartes distilled the quintessence of abstract reason. Through him, the mathematical method was felt capable of extension over philosophy, ethics and religion as well as over natural science, and its apparent conquest of the last through Newton lent its claims over the others increased plausibility.[1]

According to the rationalism of this period, the proper way for men to live, whether in relation to God or to one another, can be discovered or demonstrated by the use of reason. But this general statement covers a multitude of opinions as to the exact form the discovery or demonstration should take; and I begin by examining some of these differing views.

[1] *Bishop Butler and the Age of Reason* (New York, 1936), p.39.

PART ONE

I

CUDWORTH

THE work of Cudworth with which we are concerned is his *Treatise concerning Eternal and Immutable Morality*, written apparently not long before his death in 1688, but not published until 1731. Cudworth's main object in the *Treatise*[1] was to attack the Protagorean theory of the relativity of all knowledge, and in particular to refute the view that moral good and evil depend on some arbitrary command, human or divine. His chief scorn is reserved for those who, in his opinion, make moral standards depend on arbitrary human wills, notably Protagoras and Epicurus among the ancients and Hobbes among the moderns. But, although he insists that there can be no such thing as morality unless God exists, he is equally opposed to those theists, among whom he mentions especially Ockham and Descartes, who assert that good is simply what God commands, and evil simply what he forbids. The positive side of his philosophy is that moral standards exist in the nature of things eternally and immutably, quite independently of any divine or human will. 'It is so far from being true, that all moral good and evil, just and unjust are mere arbitrary and factitious things, that are created wholly by will;

[1] As J. A. Passmore has pointed out (*Ralph Cudworth* (Cambridge, 1951)), Cudworth differs in many ways from the typical ethical rationalist of the seventeenth and early eighteenth centuries, and the difference becomes more pronounced if we take into account some of his unpublished manuscripts in addition to his published works. But while his detailed views are in many respects unlike those of Locke and Clarke, his whole approach to the subject is rationalistic, as opposed to theological; and his affinities with Descartes, as well as with the much later intuitionists, justify us in devoting some attention to him.

that (if we would speak properly) we must needs say that nothing is morally good or evil, just or unjust by mere will without nature, because everything is what it is by nature, and not by will' (*Treatise*, I. 2. 3; S-B, II, p. 249).[1] Further, 'if there were no natural justice, that is, if the rational or intellectual nature in itself were indetermined and unobliged to anything, and so, destitute of all morality, it were not possible that anything should be made morally good or evil, obligatory or unlawful, or that any moral obligation should be begotten by any will or command whatsoever' (*Treatise*, I. 2. 6; S-B, II, p. 253).

It is not altogether easy to see exactly what Cudworth means by his concept of an eternal and immutable morality existing in nature, mainly because he devotes more time to attacking his opponents' views than to explaining his own. But if we try to state his position in non-technical terms it seems to be something like this. Certain general principles, such as that cruelty and injustice are morally wrong, or that it is morally obligatory to keep just promises, are true or valid everywhere and always, independently of any wish or decision of any being, human or divine, to the effect that men should or should not act in certain ways or that some things or actions are good or evil. Similarly with particular judgements; if it is true that X acted wickedly in stealing a purse from a helpless old lady, it is because such an action is somehow wrong in itself and always has been and always will be wrong, not because it has been forbidden by God or man. Variations of individual character or social organisation may be the source of legitimate differences of opinion as to the best way of creating enjoyment for oneself or for others, or of differences in fashion and custom; but there can be no such variation in moral standards. Where the moral principles of one man or community genuinely contradict those of another, one party, at least, must be in error. In short, if a particular course of action is morally required of me, this is not because God requires it, still less because some man or group of men require it, but because this 'requiredness' is inherent in the nature of things. It follows—though this point is not stressed by Cudworth—that a rule morally binding on one man is also binding on anyone who is placed in a similar situation.

[1] References to the *Treatise* are made by Book, Chapter and Section; also, where possible, to the pages of Selby-Bigge's *British Moralists* (Oxford, 1897).

There is a certain obscurity in Cudworth's notion of moral obligations or principles existing 'in nature' or 'by nature', implying, as it appears to, that statements of moral obligation are, in a way, statements of fact. There is, of course, in Cudworth, no trace of any so-called 'naturalism', if this involves the attempt to derive moral principles from non-moral facts. But his argument requires him to speak of justice and injustice, right and wrong, as 'existing things'. 'Now the demonstrative strength of our cause lying plainly in this, that it is not possible that any thing should be without a nature, and the natures or essences of all things being immutable, therefore upon supposition that there is any thing really just or unjust, due or unlawful, there must of necessity be something so both naturally and immutably, which no law, decree, will nor custom can alter' (*Treatise*, II. 1. 1; S-B, II, p. 258). But although it is perfectly proper to speak of the existence of moral rules or obligations, it does not follow that, in the last analysis, this is philosophically the most accurate or illuminating way of speaking. As far as obligations are concerned, indeed, it seems clear that it is not. For language of this kind is apt to obscure the most important feature of obligation-statements, viz. that what they say is not that something *is* the case, but that something *ought to be* the case; and this 'ought' cannot be treated as a special kind of 'is' without depriving it of half its meaning.

It might, of course, be argued that, even if the ordinary obligation-statements of everyday life do not refer directly to existing facts, they are nevertheless in some way grounded in those facts, i.e. that they depend for their validity on the independent existence of moral principles. But this dependence is illusory. It may indeed be said that a particular moral judgement (e.g. that Jones ought to keep his promise to lend his lawn-mower to his neighbour, even though it will cause him more trouble than he expected) depends for its truth on that of a more general principle (viz. that possible inconvenience to oneself can never justify the breaking of a promise). But it is absurd to say that the truth of the general proposition that promises ought always to be kept depends on the existence of an eternal and immutable obligation to keep promises; for to say that there is such an obligation is just to say 'Promises ought always to be kept' in a different, and perhaps more impressive, way.

Supposing, then, that we leave aside the misleading ontological implications of Cudworth's treatment of obligations as existing things, can we produce an intelligible version of his theory without omitting anything essential? We can at least say this, that the theory maintains that, if a moral judgement to the effect, say, that sexual intercourse outside marriage is morally wrong is true, then it has always been true, and will always be true, in virtue of its own inherent meaning, not of any divine command or legal ordinance to that effect. Its truth is also independent of local conditions or social customs. The traditions of a primitive tribe may allow promiscuous relations between the unmarried of both sexes; but sanctification by tradition and custom does not make the practice any less wrong, although its adherents may be less blameworthy than those who are civilised and educated enough to know better. But Cudworth wishes to do more than assert a merely hypothetical proposition: he states categorically that certain moral judgements are universally and eternally true and certain others universally and eternally false. It is at this point that the need for some justification of his theory becomes pressing.

The justification which Cudworth provides is negative in form. He argues that, if a voluntaristic or legislative ethics is accepted, whether in divine or human terms, there can be no moral standards at all. A command cannot of itself create obligation; there can be an obligation to obey a command only if the person who utters it has the right and authority to utter it, and if what is commanded is obligatory, or at least not forbidden, by the standards of natural justice.

> It is so far from being true, that all moral good and evil, just and unjust (if they be any thing) are made by mere will and arbitrary commands (as many conceive) that it is not possible that any command of God or man should oblige otherwise than by virtue of that which is naturally just. And though particular promises and commands be made by will, yet it is not will but nature that obligeth to the doing of things promised and commanded, or makes them such things as ought to be done (*Treatise*, I. 2. 6; S-B, II, p. 253).

But even if we grant the validity of Cudworth's arguments against voluntarism, we must also point out that he nowhere shows that the postulation of eternal and immutable moral principles is the only alternative which does not implicitly deny the existence of morality altogether. Moreover, the voluntarist might retort that Cudworth has replaced what was at least a clear and intelligible theory by one the central concept of which is obscure and does not receive the explanation which it requires. It is easy to understand what is meant by saying 'This action is required of me by God, that is forbidden by the state'; much harder to understand 'This is morally required of me, but not required by anyone; that is morally forbidden, but not forbidden by anyone'. No doubt people sometimes experience a feeling that some action is required of them without having any clear idea of the origin of that feeling; but it does not follow that the notion can be accepted as it stands without further elucidation and analysis, and, in particular, it does not follow that the existence of such a feeling guarantees the truth of the claim that the action is really required of them—whatever that claim might turn out to mean.

We must now turn our attention to the question how these eternal and immutable moral truths are apprehended or discovered. There are, in Cudworth's view, two 'perceptive powers' in the soul, an inferior, sensation, and a superior, the faculty of knowing or understanding. The senses are incapable of grasping, or giving rise to, either truth or falsity; hence truth and falsity, in morals as in other fields, must be apprehended by the intellect or understanding. The principles of morality are as immutable as those of geometry and, like them, they are discoverable only by rational reflection. We cannot discover moral truth by sensible observation any more than we can in this way prove that the sum of the interior angles of a triangle is two right angles.

On what principles, then, does the intellect proceed? How can it distinguish between true and false ethical judgements? Cudworth's answer to this is to reassert Descartes' dictum that whatsoever the mind clearly and distinctly conceives is true.

> I answer, therefore, that the criterion of true knowledge is not to be looked for any where abroad without our own minds, neither in the height above, nor in the depth beneath, but only in our knowledge and conceptions themselves. For the entity of all theoretical truth is nothing but clear intelligibility, and whatever is clearly conceived is an entity and a truth; but that which is false, divine power itself cannot make it to be clearly and distinctly

understood, because falsehood is a nonentity, and a clear conception is an entity: and omnipotence itself cannot make a nonentity to be an entity.

Wherefore no man ever was or can be deceived in taking that for an epistemonical truth which he clearly and distinctly apprehends, but only in assenting to things not clearly apprehended by him, which is the only true original of all error (*Treatise*, IV. 5. 5).

If the truth of a presumed moral principle is in dispute the cause must be a lack of clearness or distinctness in the perceptions or ideas of at least one party to the dispute. There can be no more difference of opinion over moral questions, once they are clearly understood, than over the theorems of geometry.

Cudworth's defence of this criterion of truth in general and moral truth in particular is unsatisfactory. He is guilty of some looseness of language, and especially of confusing propositions about truth with propositions about being. A judgement which is false, he argues, cannot be clearly and distinctly conceived, because 'falsehood is a nonentity, and a clear conception is an entity'. Unfortunately, however, the sense of the word 'entity' in which falsehood is not one is different from that in which a clear conception is one. A false belief or judgement can be called non-existent only in an indirect way, what is really a nonentity being the state of affairs which is wrongly believed to exist; similarly, a true belief is an entity, in this sense of the word, only in that the state of affairs believed to exist does really exist. In another, more straightforward, sense of 'entity', however, all beliefs, true or false, are 'entities', to the extent that they actually exist in someone's mind, quite independently of the existence of anything to which they refer. Not all false judgements are meaningless—not even all false non-empirical ones. And even if it is perhaps arguable that I can have no clear and distinct idea of what is meant by saying 'The sum of the interior angles of a triangle is 170 degrees', I can understand quite clearly what is meant by saying 'There is no moral obligation on a man to tell the truth if he does not want to', however strongly I may disagree with anyone who says it. Cudworth has in fact tried to assimilate moral judgements too closely to the pattern of mathematical judgements.

Cudworth does attempt to face the possible objection that, since a man may often think he clearly and distinctly conceives something when in fact he does not (indeed, this is, on his view, the only possible source of mathematical or moral error), we can never be sure of the truth of anything. His retort to it is, however, short and unconvincing.

> It cannot be denied but that men are oftentimes deceived, and think they clearly comprehend what they do not: but it does not follow from hence, because men sometimes think they can clearly comprehend what they do not, that therefore they can never be certain that they do clearly comprehend any thing; which is just as if we should argue, that because in our dreams we think we have clear sensations, we cannot therefore be ever sure when we awake, that we see things that really are (*Treatise*, IV. 5. 12).

The analogy with dreaming fails, however, because there are independent, external tests to distinguish between the states of waking and dreaming, quite apart from what may be called the 'feel' of our thoughts and perceptions, whereas, on Cudworth's own showing, there is no such independent method of distinguishing a genuinely clear and distinct idea from an idea that falsely purports to be clear and distinct. And once this is admitted, it becomes pointless to claim that the clearness and distinctness of our ideas provides an infallible criterion of their truth; for where there is disagreement as to which of two conflicting beliefs is true there will arise a corresponding disagreement as to which of them is clearly and distinctly conceived, and the dispute will be no nearer solution. Moreover, like most of those who have tried to assimilate ethical principles to mathematical ones, Cudworth does not accept the possibility that there may be genuine moral disagreement between upright and intelligent people, and he therefore pays little attention to the analysis of the disagreements that do actually exist, thinking apparently that they must be due either to inadequate thought and consideration, like miscalculations in arithmetic, or to deliberate dishonesty. Disputes in which one party is dishonestly concealing his real opinions present no philosophical difficulty; but it cannot be seriously denied that there are some genuine ethical disagreements, just as there are also some cases of genuine ethical perplexity within a single individual, which cannot be resolved by appeal to the principle of clarity and distinctness. If a man makes an arithmetical miscalculation he will, if he is competent, usually recognise his mistake when it is pointed out to him, without the need for any external argument to be brought in to support the objection; but this is obviously not so with serious moral differences. It can, of course, be retorted that, just as some men are more competent mathematicians than others, so some are more competent than others at ethical reasoning and understanding. But this reply is unsatisfactory, for there are no generally accepted tests of moral, as there are of mathematical, competence. If I, making use of some dim memories of my schooldays, try to solve a problem in trigonometry, and obtain a different answer from that unanimously arrived at by six professors of mathematics, I shall be quite certain that I have made a mistake, even before the mistake is pointed out to me, or before I discover it for myself. But I shall have no such certainty of being mistaken over a moral issue, even where I am contradicted by grave and learned men. For, in the first place, it is likely that some equally grave and learned men will share my opinion; and, in any case, morality, unlike mathematics, is a matter on which everyone has to decide for himself. If I am bad at arithmetic, and require to add or multiply large sums of money, I can always give up the attempt to do the mathematics for myself, and use a calculating machine. But there are no calculating machines for solving moral problems; and if there were, they would not all give the same answer. One can, of course, decide to rely for guidance on other people whom one considers wiser and better than oneself; but this decision itself presupposes another moral decision, viz. that these people are, for certain reasons, good guides to follow, i.e. that the moral principles they recommend are, or are likely to be, true or sound.

II
LOCKE

AS Gibson has pointed out, Locke 'does not follow Descartes in proclaiming *a priori* the universal applicability of the mathematical method. The possible extent of demonstrative science should, he holds, be made the subject of a careful enquiry, which must seek to discover the reasons for the present unique position of mathematics and to ascertain what other subject-matters, if any, are intrinsically capable of similar rational treatment'.[1] Moreover, for Locke, unlike Descartes, our purely rational or scientific knowledge is restricted to the study of the relations of our abstract ideas; knowledge of real existence comes only from experience. It is this that distinguishes the mathematical sciences from natural philosophy; the latter, unlike the former, cannot take a strict demonstrative form, because it deals with existents, of the essential nature of which it is impossible to form a clear and distinct idea, and about which universal propositions cannot be formulated. Moral philosophy does not labour under this disability. 'The precise real essence of the things moral words stand for may be perfectly known, and so the congruity and incongruity of the things themselves certainly discovered; in which consists perfect knowledge' (*Essay concerning Human Understanding*, III. 11. 6).[2] Hence there is ground for hope that morality is capable of demonstration; if men would only define the terms they use in their moral discourse, moral truths could be easily understood and proved.

[1] *Locke's Theory of Knowledge* (Cambridge, 1917), pp. 148–9.
[2] References to the *Essay* are given by Book, Chapter, and Section.

> The negligence or perverseness of mankind cannot be excused, if their discourses in morality be not much more clear than those in natural philosophy: since they are about ideas in the mind, which are none of them false or disproportionate; they having no external beings for archetypes which they are referred to and must correspond with. It is far easier for men to frame in their minds an idea, which will be the standard to which they will give the name justice, with which pattern so made, all actions that agree shall pass under that denomination, than, having seen Aristides, to frame an idea that shall in all things be exactly like him; who is as he is, let men make what idea they please of him (*Essay*, III. 11. 17).

Locke thinks, in other words, that the first principles of morality can be formulated with sufficient clarity and precision to admit of clear and precise conclusions being drawn from them.

It might be objected that the reason why the concepts of natural philosophy are as clear as they are is that many, at least, of its branches are, or are capable of becoming, quantitative sciences; that they admit of numerical representation and measurement. And the concepts of moral philosophy are not of this type (unless, of course, one holds, with Bentham, that all moral questions can be reduced to calculations with quantities of pleasure and pain; but this was not Locke's view). The introduction of mathematical reasoning into the physical sciences was fruitful, it might be argued, just because of the peculiar nature of their subject-matter, in particular because they are essentially quantitative sciences. Locke would not have been impressed by this objection.

> They that are ignorant of Algebra cannot imagine the wonders in this kind [*sc.* in finding proofs] are to be done by it: and what further improvements and helps advantageous to other parts of knowledge the sagacious mind of man may yet find out, it is not easy to determine. This at least I believe, that the ideas of quantity are not those alone that are capable of demonstration and knowledge; and that other, and perhaps more useful, parts of contemplation, would afford us certainty, if vices, passions, and domineering interest did not oppose or menace such endeavours (*Essay*, IV. 3. 18).

There are, Locke thinks, two reasons why the ideas of quantity have in the past been considered more capable of demonstration than those of morality. The first is that the former, unlike the latter, can be represented in diagrammatic form.

> Diagrams drawn on paper are copies of the ideas in the mind, and not liable to the uncertainty that words carry in their signification. An angle, circle, or square, drawn in lines, lies open to the view, and cannot be mistaken: it remains unchangeable, and may at leisure be considered and examined, and the demonstration be revised, and all the parts of it may be gone over more than once, without any danger of the least change in the ideas. This cannot be thus done in moral ideas: we have no sensible marks that resemble them, whereby we can set them down; we have nothing but words to express them by; which, though when written they remain the same, yet the ideas they stand for may change in the same man; and it is very seldom that they are not different in different persons (*Essay*, IV. 3. 19).

The second reason is that moral ideas are often more complex than those of ordinary mathematical figures. Some of the disadvantages here referred to could be removed, Locke thinks, if moral philosophers were to make precise definitions of their primitive moral terms, and were to keep steadily to them, using one word always to stand for the same idea. The other disadvantages should not prove fatal.

> And what methods algebra, or something of that kind, may hereafter suggest, to remove the other difficulties, it not easy to foretell. Confident I am, that, if men would in the same method, and with the same indifferency, search after moral as they do mathematical truths, they would find them to have a stronger connection one with another, and a more necessary consequence from our clear and distinct ideas, and to come nearer perfect demonstration, than is commonly imagined (*Essay*, IV. 3. 20).

The formulation of precise definitions of ethical terms, however, and the drawing of strict logical conclusions from first principles containing those terms, will not do as much to resolve ethical disagreement as Locke seems to have thought it would. The initial definitions may not, indeed, be completely arbitrary; but it is unlikely in the extreme that they will coincide sufficiently with the ordinary meanings of the terms they define for the conclusions drawn to be universally acceptable. Almost every man will agree that justice, as he defines it, is better than injustice, as he defines it. But it does not follow that everyone will, or should, agree that justice, as defined by the moral philosopher, is better than injustice, as defined by the same philosopher. We may put the same objection the other way round, and express a doubt whether it is possible to achieve definitions of moral terms that are not only clear and precise, but also consistent with the normal usage of the words corresponding to those terms. Indeed, in a sense, there is no normal usage of ethical words; for in this field connotation tends to vary with denotation, and ethical disagreements are often accompanied by differences in the use of ethical language. The attempt to establish a demonstrative science of ethics thus seems to be open to the objection that the more nearly it approaches to being a strictly demonstrative science with clear and precise definitions and first principles, the less it will deserve the name of moral science. Its conclusions will always be open to a complaint of the type 'You have shown conclusively that the action I propose to perform is morally wrong according to your definition of "morally wrong". But is it *really* wrong? Is it wrong, not on any strict definition of that term, but according to the way in which I, or most people, ordinarily use the word? And if it is wrong in your sense, but not wrong in mine, is there any good reason why I may not perform it?'

A further source of error consists in Locke's comparison between morals and mathematics in respect of their abstractness; here his determination to find resemblances between the two disciplines leads him to overlook an important difference. After arguing that the ideas of morality, like those of mathematics, are non-representative and do not stand for any existing thing, he goes on:

> All the discourses of the mathematicians about the squaring of a circle, conic sections, or any other part of mathematics, concern not the existence of any of those figures: but their demonstrations, which depend on their ideas, are the same, whether there be any square or circle existing in the world or no. In the same manner, the truth and certainty of moral discourses abstracts from the lives of men, and the existence of those virtues in the world whereof they treat: nor are Tully's Offices less true, because there is nobody in the world that exactly practises his rules, and lives up to that pattern of a virtuous man which he has given us, and which existed nowhere when he writ but in idea. If it be true in speculation, i.e.

in idea, that murder deserves death, it will also be true in reality of any action that exists conformable to that idea of murder. As for other actions, the truth of that proposition concerns them not (*Essay*, IV. 4. 8).

Now it is, of course, true, as Kant was later to stress, that the validity of any moral rule is unaffected by the question whether it is actually obeyed or not—indeed, this is true of all kinds of rule, non-moral as well as moral; and it is also true that geometrical truths about squares and circles remain true whether there are in fact such things as squares and circles or not. What Locke fails to see, however, is that actions do not fall into classes and categories as easily and as neatly as do geometrical figures and the rest of the subject-matter of mathematics. Some actions and situations cannot be usefully categorised at all, primarily because they are too complicated; others fall into two or more apparently conflicting categories. An action may, as Locke says, deserve death in that it is a case of murder; another may deserve praise or reward in that it is a case of kind-heartedness or public-spiritedness. But what if the same action is both at once? How, for example, does one decide what is the proper attitude to adopt to a mother who deliberately kills her child because it is suffering from a painful and incurable disease? It is no use saying that *qua* murder the act is wrong and *qua* kind-heartedness it is right; for this is merely another way of saying that there are some reasons why it should have been performed, and others why it should not, and this provides no answer to the question 'Did this woman act rightly or wrongly?' The point is that any particular action takes place in a concrete situation, is performed from concrete motives, and accompanied by concrete feelings. We cannot always abstract from, i.e. ignore, the particular circumstances or motives of an act without impairing our judgement of its moral quality. It follows that moral rules, which are necessarily abstract to a greater or lesser degree, cannot provide a complete answer to the question 'How ought I to act here and now in this particular situation?' It is here that the difference between morals and mathematics becomes clear. The size and shape of a triangle are completely irrelevant to the truth of the proposition that the sum of its interior angles is equal to two right angles. But one can never say in advance that anything is irrelevant to one's moral assessment of a particular action that someone has performed, or to one's decision how best to act in the particular situation in which one finds oneself.

If we ask ourselves how Locke would have tried to deal with such objections as these we are faced with the difficulty that he nowhere discusses this subject in a connected way and at sufficient length. The relevant passages in the *Essay* are more concerned to explain why a demonstrative science of ethics must be possible than to show in detail how such a science can be constructed; nor did the promptings of Molyneux and others ever succeed in persuading Locke to write a systematic ethical treatise of the required kind. He wrote to Molyneux on September 20th, 1692, 'Though by the view I had of moral ideas, whilst I was considering that subject, I thought I saw that morality might be demonstratively made out; yet whether I am able so to make it out, is another question. Every one could not have demonstrated what Mr. Newton's book hath shown to be demonstrable' (*Works* (London, 1801), IX, pp. 294–5). A few years later (March 30th, 1696) he offers further excuses.

> As to a 'treatise of morals', I must own to you that you are not the only persons (you and Mr. Burridge, I mean) who have been for putting me upon it; neither have I wholly laid by the thoughts of it. Nay, I so far incline to comply with your desires, that I, every now and then, lay by some materials for it, as they occasionally occur, in the rovings of my mind. But when I consider, that a book of offices, as you call it, ought not to be slightly done, especially by me, after what I have said of that science in my essay; and that 'nonum prematur in annum', is a rule more necessary to be observed in a subject of that consequence, than in any Horace speaks of; I am in doubt, whether it would be prudent, in one of my age, and health, not to mention other disabilities in me, to set about it. Did the world want a rule, I confess there could be no work so necessary, nor so commendable. But the gospel contains so perfect a body of ethics, that reason may be excused from that enquiry, since she may find man's duty clearer and easier in relevation, than in herself (*Works*, IX, p. 377).

However, from disconnected passages in the *Essay concerning Human Understanding* and *The Reasonableness of Christianity* we can obtain some idea, even though an imperfect one, of the kind of thing that Locke had in mind when he spoke of a demonstrative ethics.

The idea of a supreme Being, infinite in power, goodness and wisdom, whose workmanship we are, and on whom we depend; and the idea of ourselves, as understanding, rational creatures, being such as are clear in us, would, I suppose, if duly considered and pursued, afford such foundations of our duty and rules of action as might place morality among the sciences capable of demonstration: wherein I doubt not but from self-evident propositions, by necessary consequences, as incontestable as those in mathematics, the measures of right and wrong might be made out, to any one that will apply himself with the same indifferency and attention to the one as he does to the other of these sciences. The relation of other modes may certainly be perceived, as well as those of number and extension: and I cannot see why they should not also be capable of demonstration, if due methods were thought on to examine or pursue their agreement or disagreement. 'Where there is no property, there is no injustice', is a proposition as certain as any demonstration in Euclid: for the idea of property being a right to anything, and the idea to which the name 'injustice' is given being the invasion or violation of that right, it is evident that these ideas, being thus established, and these names annexed to them, I can as certainly know this proposition to be true, as that a triangle has three angles equal to two right ones. Again: 'No government allows absolute liberty'. The idea of government being the establishment of society upon certain rules or laws which require conformity to them; and the idea of absolute liberty being for any one to do whatever he pleases; I am as capable of being certain of the truth of this proposition as of any in the mathematics (*Essay*, IV. 3. 18).

Now it is easy to see that, whatever the status of the propositions, 'Where there is no property, there is no injustice' and 'No government allows absolute liberty', and however indubitable they may be, they cannot possibly of themselves function as guides to, or rules of, action. From neither of them does it follow that some action, or type of action, is morally obligatory or morally wrong. Indeed, as Berkeley complained,[1] it is difficult to see how either of them escapes being what Locke himself derogatorily called 'trifling propositions'; and if all the propositions in Locke's ethical system were of this type he would be open to the charge which he himself levelled against certain kinds of metaphysics—'By this method one may make demonstrations and

[1] *Philosophical Commentaries* 691, in *Works* (ed. Luce and Jessop, London, 1948), Vol. I, p. 84.

undoubted propositions in words, and yet thereby advance not one jot in the knowledge of the truth of things' (*Essay*, IV. 8. 9). It is therefore perhaps better to regard them as examples of defining or quasi-defining propositions, expressing 'relations of other modes', i.e. in this case relations between moral or, more generally, practical concepts. In any case, whatever Locke may have thought he was doing, he has not here provided us with any examples of demonstrable rules of action (or, if the expression 'demonstrable rules' seems odd, with demonstrably true ethical propositions from which moral rules can be derived). But it does not follow from this alone, of course, that such rules or propositions cannot be in some way established.

It might be supposed that the most systematic way of exhibiting moral rules in a demonstrative science would be to start with one or more fundamental rules, taken as self-evident (e.g. 'Always try to promote the greatest happiness of the greatest number' or 'Always do as you would be done by'), and to derive other rules, and propositions about the morality of individual actions, from them. For Locke, however, there can be no self-evident practical propositions of this kind.[1] There are, he thinks, no moral rules of which we cannot properly demand a justification, moral rules differing in this respect from theoretical propositions, some of which are self-evident.

> He would be thought void of common sense who asked on the one side, or on the other side, went to give a reason why it is impossible for the same thing to be and not to be. It carries its own light and evidence with it, and needs no other proof: he that understands the terms assents to it for its own sake, or else nothing will ever be able to prevail with him to do it. But should that most unshaken rule of morality and foundation of all social virtue, 'That one should do as he would be done unto', be proposed to one who never heard it before, but yet is of capacity to understand its meaning; might he not without any absurdity ask a reason why? ... So that the truth of all these moral rules plainly depends upon some other antecedent to them, and from which they must be deduced; which could not be if either they were innate or so much as self-evident (*Essay* I. 3. 4).

[1] The desire for happiness and the aversion to misery are admittedly 'innate practical principles' of a sort; but they are, Locke says, 'inclinations of the appetite to good, not impressions of truth on the understanding' (*Essay*, I. 3. 3).

If all moral rules, then, require to be defended by reference to some higher-order principles, what are these principles, and how, if at all, can they in their turn be justified? This question, Locke says, has been answered in a variety of ways.

> That men should keep their compacts is certainly a great and undeniable rule in morality. But yet, if a Christian, who has the view of happiness and misery in another life, be asked why a man must keep his word, he will give this as a reason:— Because God, who has the power of eternal life and death, requires it of us. But if a Hobbist be asked why? he will answer:— Because the public requires it, and the Leviathan will punish you if you do not. And if one of the old heathen philosophers had been asked, he would have answered:— Because it was dishonest, below the dignity of a man, and opposite to virtue, the highest perfection of human nature, to do otherwise (*Essay*, I. 3. 5).

Locke's own answer, of course, is that which he takes to be the Christian answer: the true ground of morality, he says, 'can only be the will and law of a God, who sees men in the dark, has in his hands rewards and punishments, and power enough to call to account the proudest offender' (*Essay*, I. 5. 6). But this, he thinks, is by no means to give up the belief in a rationally based ethics; for, although most men quite properly derive their religious beliefs from divine revelation, not from an intellectual enquiry into natural religion, yet we still need to use our reason in order to decide whether a supposedly revealed truth really comes from God; moreover, the truths of revealed religion can, once revelation has communicated them to us, be shown to be consonant with reason. Locke argues in *The Reasonableness of Christianity* that men needed a divine saviour, both to lead them from superstition to a true knowledge of the one God and to teach them the principles of morality; but he also thinks that, now that these truths and principles have been revealed, it should be possible to show by rational argument why the revealed theology is true and the revealed morality valid. 'It is no diminishing to revelation, that reason gives its suffrage, too, to the truths revelation has discovered. But it is our mistake to think, that because reason confirms them to us, we had the first certain knowledge of them from thence; and in that clear evidence we now possess them' (*Works*, VII, p. 146; and cp. the whole section, pp. 138–47). Locke, that is to say, steers a middle course between an extreme rationalism, which forbids us to believe anything unless we can prove it to be true, and the detested 'enthusiasm', which exalts revelation at the expense of reason, refusing to the latter the right to distinguish between genuine revelations and imagined ones, between divine and diabolic inspiration.

What are we to make of this kind of theologically based ethics? I think we shall have to conclude that, even if we accept Locke's religious premises—whether from genuine agreement or for the sake of argument—the claim to be able to demonstrate certain ethical principles to be valid, or certain ethical propositions to be true, must be rejected. The claim is, roughly, that it is our duty to behave in certain ways because, and only because, God wills us to behave in these ways, will reward us if we do and punish us if we do not. The rewards and punishments may be dismissed at once; however true it may be that the good are to be rewarded and the wicked punished, this cannot function as a *moral* reason in favour of being good or against being wicked. To try to derive ethical principles from considerations of reward and punishment is to give up what purported to be a system of ethics in favour of a system of prudential calculations. But can a series of propositions concerning the nature and will of God function as premises from which ethical rules may be deduced? May we not always ask, '*Why* ought I to obey God's word and keep his commandments?' The only way of answering this question which keeps the matter at an ethical level is to say, in effect, 'Because God is perfectly good (or, perhaps, perfectly wise and good)'; for if there is no ethical term in our premises we cannot deduce ethical conclusions from them, even though we may be able to derive such conclusions from them in a non-deductive way (and this non-deductive derivation would not, of course, amount to 'demonstration', in Locke's sense of the word). A perfectly good being, we must therefore suppose, wills that all men, or all rational beings, should keep promises, love one another, do as they would be done by and so on.

Now if this assertion of the will of a perfectly good being were accepted as true, i.e. if it were agreed that this being did will, or wish, men to behave in certain clearly defined ways, it might be reasonable to conclude that men ought to act in these ways; though we might hesitate to say that this conclusion is demonstrably true. It does not seem self-contradictory, though it may seem queer, to say 'God, who is perfectly wise and good, wills that I should do x, but it is not the case that I ought to do it'. But how do we know that a perfectly good being exists and wills these things? Sooner or later we must come to some premiss or premisses which are not deducible from any higher-order premiss. For it is obvious that we cannot demonstrate everything by deductive methods. By deduction we can show only that A follows from B, which follows from C, and so on; we have demonstrated A, in Locke's sense of the word 'demonstration', only if we have shown that it follows deductively, in the end, from some premiss which is known to be true, though not itself deduced from anything. Now the existence of a God of the kind postulated by Locke is either denied or doubted by millions; and if we are trying to construct a demonstrative ethics on the mathematical model we can hardly leave these fundamental doubts and denials out of our reckoning—i.e. some attempt must be made, by those of Locke's way of thinking, to prove God's existence and to show that his nature is as Locke supposes it to be. Fortunately, however, it is not necessary for us here to enter deeply into theological questions; it is sufficient for our purpose to point out that, even if it could be indubitably established that a perfectly wise and good God existed, the notion of such a being could not possibly fulfil its required function in Locke's system of demonstration. It is an essential part of Locke's case that the God whom it is our duty to obey is a moral being. He does not say, for example, as some theists have done, that we ought to obey God simply because he is all-powerful and will punish us if we do not; to do this would make the moral 'ought' depend on a non-moral 'ought' and would make nonsense of his claim that morality can be demonstrated from the principles of natural religion. It is our duty, he thinks, to act in certain ways, because God, being perfectly good and perfectly wise, wills us so to act. It is only because of God's goodness that his will is morally binding on us. But once this is admitted, the existence of such a God ceases to be a premiss from which moral principles can be validly deduced. The difficulty is not now logical so much as epistemological; i.e. it is not primarily that the ethical conclusion cannot be validly inferred from the theological or ethico-theological premisses, but that we cannot know the premisses to be true without first assuming the truth of some, at least, of the moral principles which we are trying to deduce from them. If we claim that God is good this must be because of our knowledge (or opinion) that God acts in certain ways (e.g. according to the principles of love and justice); hence acting on principles of love and justice must be good independently of and antecedently to anything that God may do or will, and it must be morally fitting that men should act on such principles quite independently of any consideration of the nature and attributes of God. The argument from God's nature to man's duty simply begs the question; if there are good reasons for accepting the theological premisses there are already equally good reasons for accepting the moral conclusions without referring to the premisses at all, and conversely, if we do not accept some moral principles antecedently to any consideration of the nature and attributes of God we shall find no justification for attributing moral characteristics to God, and hence no justification for claiming to be able to demonstrate morality from the truths of natural religion.

III
CLARKE

ALTHOUGH he was not a profound thinker, Samuel Clarke is of some importance for our purpose because he does try to construct, in fairly considerable detail, a demonstrative ethical system of the same general kind as that which Locke had held to be possible. His main theological and moral ideas are contained in the two series of sermons delivered on the Robert Boyle foundation at St. Paul's Cathedral in 1704 and 1705. The first series is entitled 'A Demonstration of the Being and Attributes of God', and the second 'A Discourse concerning the Unchangeable Obligations of Natural Religion and the Truth and Certainty of the Christian Revelation'.[1] The object of the *Demonstration* was to refute atheism, and its arguments are directed largely against Hobbes and Spinoza. In the *Discourse* Clarke set out to refute deism, and it is in this context that most of his observations on ethics occur. The deist, he maintains, cannot hold his position consistently. Most kinds of deism issue logically in atheism: the one kind which does not—the best kind—issues logically in true Christianity. Although we are not directly concerned with Clarke's arguments against deism as a theological doctrine, it is important to remember that, for him, morals and religion are inseparably linked, and to understand the context in which his moral philosophy is placed.

The outline of his argument is as follows:

[1] References to the *Discourse* will be made to the pages of the original edition (London, 1706), and also, where possible, to the pages of Selby-Bigge's *British Moralists*, which contains extracts from it.

(1) Anyone who believes, as all but out-and-out atheists do, that God exists and that he is an eternal, infinite, omnipresent, omnipotent and intelligent being must acknowledge God to be also infinitely good, just and truthful. (This argument, and the proofs of God's existence, appear in the *Demonstration*.)

(2) Anyone who acknowledges these moral attributes of God must accept the obligations of morality and natural religion as binding on men.

(3) Once we have gone thus far we must, in order to support those obligations and to ensure their fulfilment, believe in a future state of rewards and punishments.

(4) But once (2) and (3) have been granted, there is no longer any good reason for rejecting the Christian revelation.

The question we have to ask is, 'What is the general nature of these moral rules or principles which are exemplified in God and which, in the form of obligations, are binding upon men?' It will be best first to quote Clarke's own statement of the proposition he sets out to prove.

> That the same necessary and eternal different relations, that different things bear to one another; and the same consequent fitness or unfitness of the application of different things or different relations one to another; with regard to which, the will of God always and necessarily *does* determine itself to choose to act only what is agreeable to justice, equity, goodness and truth, in order to the welfare of the whole universe; *ought* likewise constantly to determine the wills of all subordinate rational beings, to govern all their actions by the same rules, for the good of the public in their respective stations: that is, these eternal and necessary differences of things, make it fit and reasonable for creatures so to act; they cause it to be their duty, or lay an obligation upon them, so to do; even separate from the consideration of these rules being the positive will or command of God; and also antecedent to any respect or regard, expectation or apprehension, of any particular private and personal advantage or disadvantage, reward or punishment, either present or future; annexed either by natural consequence, or by positive appointment, to the practising or neglecting those rules' (*Discourse*, pp. 45–6; S-B, II, p. 3).

Moral obligations, according to Clarke, owe their existence to the fact that certain kinds of conduct are fitting or suitable, unfitting or unsuitable, to certain situations; and this fittingness or unfittingness depends on certain necessary relations which exist independently of any divine or human regulation. One of these necessary relations is God's infinite superiority to man: hence it is fitting that men should honour, worship and obey him, unfitting that they should despise and disobey him. The nature of men and the relations between them being what they are, it is fitting that each should endeavour to promote the general welfare, unfitting that a man should work for the unhappiness of his fellows; fitting that a man should conduct himself in a just and equitable manner, unfitting that he should cheat and lie for his own supposed advantage. Such moral truths as these cannot be denied by any reasonable man; the fundamental rules of morality are self-evident. To say that an action is fitting, or unfitting, to a situation is, for Clarke, another way of saying that it is a reasonable, or unreasonable, action, as the case may be. He agrees with Locke, however, in holding that a man's unaided reason will not enable him to discover all his duties—to allow otherwise would be to concede too much to the deists—but the validity even of those principles which revelation is needed to show us can, once they have been revealed, be demonstrated on purely rational grounds.

That there are 'eternal and necessary differences of things' which result in the moral suitability of certain kinds of conduct and the unsuitability of others is, Clarke thinks, perfectly obvious to any fairly intelligent and unbiased observer.

> These things are so notoriously plain and self-evident, that nothing but the extremest stupidity of mind, corruption of manners, or perverseness of spirit, can possibly make any man entertain the least doubt concerning them. For a man endued with reason, to deny the truth of these things; is the very same thing, as if a man that has the use of his sight, should at the same time that he beholds the sun, deny that there is any such thing as light in the world; or as if a man that understands geometry or arithmetick, should deny the most obvious and known proportions of lines or numbers, and perversely contend that the whole is not equal to all its parts, or that a square is not double to a triangle of equal base and height (*Discourse*, pp. 50-1; S-B, II, p. 6).

In other words, not merely do these moral rules, these 'fitnesses and unfitnesses', exist antecedently to all divine command or human convention, they are also recognised by the reason or understanding of any man who is neither extremely stupid nor extremely depraved. By his faculty of reason man is enabled to know what he ought to do; by his faculty of will he is enabled to choose the good and avoid the evil. It follows that there are two sorts of moral error. The first is the theoretical error of mistakenly believing a wrong course of action to be right, or vice versa; the second is the practical error of doing something one knows to be wrong. But both these errors are instances of irrationality and are thus on a level with mathematical or logical absurdities, even though the second of them has the peculiar property of being an error or absurdity which we can deliberately choose to commit.

> He that wilfully refuses to honour and obey God, from whom he received his being, and to whom he continually owes his preservation; is really guilty of an equal absurdity and inconsistency in practice, as he that in speculation denies the effect to owe anything to its cause, or the whole to be bigger than its part. He that refuses to deal with all men equitably, and with every man as he desires they should deal with him, is guilty of the very same unreasonableness and contradiction in one case, as he that in another case should affirm one number or quantity to be equal to another, and yet that other at the same time not to be equal to the first (*Discourse*, p. 65; S-B, II, p. 14).

To act in a way one knows to be wrong is to try 'to make things be what they are not, and cannot be', which is to act 'contrary to that understanding, reason and judgement, which God has implanted in their natures on purpose to enable them to discern the difference between good and evil' (*Discourse*, pp. 66–7; S-B, II, p. 15).

'In a word; all wilful wickedness and perversion of right is the very same insolence and absurdity in moral matters, as it would be in natural things, for a man to pretend to alter the certain proportions of numbers, to take away the demonstrable relations and properties of mathematical figures, to make light darkness and darkness light; or to call sweet bitter or bitter sweet' (ibid.).

It is important to distinguish these two kinds of 'absurdity' or irrationality, viz. (1) the having of mistaken or absurd moral beliefs, and (2) having correct moral beliefs but failing to act on them. It will be convenient to consider each kind separately.

(1) Clarke seems to be saying that all true moral propositions

are either self-evident or can be inferred from self-evident propositions, and that all false moral propositions are self-contradictory. It follows that there can be no genuine moral disagreements, at least as far as general and fundamental principles are concerned. Some backward communities may perhaps be completely ignorant of moral good and evil; but this ignorance no more invalidates moral truth than their ignorance of geometry invalidates Euclid. And ignorance apart, disagreement in morals, as in geometry, must spring from error, and error, in matters so plain, can be due only to 'negligent misunderstanding'. It is impossible to understand a moral truth and at the same time not see it to be true.

Clarke is not always careful enough to distinguish the absurdity of denying that there are any moral principles 'in nature' (as he thinks Hobbes does) from the absurdity of actually believing in some erroneous principles. In fact, he underestimates the extent to which this latter type of error must, on his theory, occur, and tends always to try to reduce it to the first kind. He admits that men often disagree on matters of right and wrong, but insists that these disagreements occur genuinely only in complicated situations, where the inferences which have to be made before the correct decision is reached are many and difficult. And therefore, since there is no uncertainty concerning the fundamental principles of morality, even the most minute moral problems must admit of only one correct solution, even if they are as difficult to solve as problems in advanced mathematics.

> Though it may perhaps be very difficult in some nice and perplext cases (which yet are very far from occurring frequently) to define exactly the bounds of right and wrong, just and unjust; and there may be some latitude in the judgement of different men, and the laws of divers nations; yet right and wrong are nevertheless in themselves totally and essentially different; even altogether as much as white and black, light and darkness (*Discourse*, p. 58; S-B, II, p. 10).

But differences of principle do occur now, as they did in Clarke's day. A sincere Nazi or Communist might believe that the putting to death of his political opponents is morally justified if it is required by the interests of his country or of the political movement to which he owes allegiance; a liberal democrat might dispute this strongly. This is certainly what Clarke would have called a flagrant case; whether one speaks of murder or judicial execution, there is nothing trivial about the taking of men's lives. It is immaterial which side in the dispute Clarke, or anyone of Clarke's philosophical views, might take; the point is that Clarke's opponent is, on his view, not simply mistaken, but contradicting himself. Clarke sometimes expresses this by saying that such a man is implicitly stating that wrong is right or that right is wrong; and this, if true, would support the charge of self-contradiction. But there is a confusion of thought here. If I have a strong opinion on some moral issue I may perhaps say indignantly of an opponent, 'He is saying that wrong is right and right wrong.' But this is only a picturesque exaggeration; all that I am entitled to mean by it is, 'He is saying that action x (which is, in fact, wrong) is right, and that action y (which is, in fact, right) is wrong.' He is, no doubt, contradicting me, but he is not—or at least he has not been shown to be—contradicting himself, any more than the colour-blind man who 'says that red is green' contradicts himself.

Clarke's view is a plausible one if we restrict our attention to the moral properties of certain classes of action or types of conduct, the names for which have a strongly eulogistic or dyslogistic flavour. As ordinarily understood, for example, the statement 'Murder can never be morally justified' has an analytic air about it; and, more generally, words such as 'murder', 'stealing', 'adultery' and 'treason' are often used to imply that the actions to which they refer are morally wrong. Often, though not always, a man would say, not 'Yes, I murdered Jones, but I was morally justified in doing so', but 'Yes, I killed Jones, but it was justifiable homicide, not murder'. The apparent illogicality or self-contradiction involved in trying to justify murder is due, in such a case, to the fact that 'murder' is being used as an evaluative word, as well as a descriptive one: 'A murdered B' means 'A deliberately killed B, and acted wrongly in doing so'.

But some people might behave differently; they might admit that they had committed murder, and still seek to justify themselves. One may, that is to say, use the word 'murder' in a purely neutral sense, without any moral implications or overtones. Moreover, terms that are susceptible of the treatment described in the last paragraph do not by any means cover the whole field of morality. It is not enough for Clarke to show that the proposition 'Murder may sometimes be morally justified' is self-contradictory; this, given the morally dyslogistic use of the word 'murder', is easy, but futile. He needs to demonstrate the self-contradictoriness of some such proposition as 'Deliberately killing another man, not in self-defence, not as an enemy in wartime, nor in any other legally permitted way, may sometimes be morally justified'; and this clearly cannot be done, since it makes perfectly good sense to assert the proposition.

It might still be argued, however, that the truth or falsity of any moral judgement can be validly inferred from certain fundamental principles which are themselves self-evident. The 'valid inference' here could include inductive as well as deductive inference, and empirical facts might be included among the premises from which the inferences were drawn.[1] The basic principles of moral obligation, according to Clarke, can be reduced to three heads, laying down our duty to God, to our fellow-men and to ourselves. Our duty to God is to worship, honour, obey, serve and pray to him; our duty to our fellow-men is, first, to treat them justly and fairly and, secondly, to promote their welfare and happiness; our duty to ourselves is to preserve our lives and keep ourselves in such a condition that we are capable of properly fulfilling all our other duties. If we could accept these as certainly true principles could we not, using them as premises, develop a set of more specific moral rules which would serve as a guide to the moral rightness or wrongness of any proposed or actual course of action? Could we not, for example, say something like this? 'I ought, provided I can do so consistently with my other obligations, to promote the happiness of my fellow-men. But, of all the actions open to me, action x, which is perfectly just and consistent with my duty to God and to myself, best promotes that happiness; therefore I have a positive duty to perform action x.' Or again, 'Actions y and z are equally consistent with my duty to God and to myself and will, as far as I can see, produce equal happiness; but y is an unjust, z a just action, and therefore z is a morally preferable action to y'.

---

[1] Cp. *Discourse*, p. 17, where Clarke contrasts the mathematical certainty of the proofs provided in the *Demonstration* with the 'mixt proofs from circumstances and testimony' with which in the *Discourse* he has sometimes to be content.

There are two comments to be made on this view. First, it assumes that the fundamental moral principles can never conflict with one another, e.g. that injustice can never in the long run produce more happiness than justice, or that God will never command us to act unjustly. Such an assumption is not necessarily a mistaken one; but if the reliance on reason is to be maintained it needs to be justified. Secondly, these fundamental moral principles are far too vaguely formulated to provide an adequate guide to action. It is, in fact, only because of this vagueness that they may appear as unexceptionable and as obvious as they do. Take the case of justice. Anyone who accepts any moral principles will agree that, other things being equal, it is better to behave justly than unjustly (even if he does not agree that justice cannot conflict with benevolence, or that, if it does, it is necessarily the overriding duty); but the difficulties and disagreements, which seem to have been ruled out if the deductive–inductive method is properly used, are bound to reappear as soon as we are asked to provide a definition or criterion of justice. The rule of justice, for Clarke, is that 'we so deal with every man as in like circumstances we could reasonably expect he should deal with us' (*Discourse*, p. 86; S-B, II, p. 23). This has an appearance of circularity, seeming to say, in effect, that the just way for me to behave towards a fellow-man is the way in which it would be just for him to behave towards me; and it is perhaps because he fails to see this that Clarke insists that unjust behaviour is somehow self-contradictory.

> Iniquity is the very same in action as falsity or contradiction in theory; and the same cause which makes the one absurd makes the other unreasonable. Whatever relation or proportion one man in any case bears to another; the same that other, when put in like circumstances, bears to him. Whatever I judge reasonable or unreasonable that another should do for me; that, by the same judgement, I declare reasonable or unreasonable that I in the like case should do for him. And to deny this either in word or action is as if a man should contend that, though two and three are equal to five, yet three and two are not so (*Discourse* pp. 86–7; S-B, II, pp. 23–4).

Clarke overlooks the fact that the unjust man does not always, and certainly need not, believe that those who behave unjustly towards him are acting unreasonably, however annoyed he may be at their conduct. A tyrant who practises cruelty towards his subjects may very well believe that any of his subjects would be quite as sensible and reasonable if they were to treat him with equal cruelty, given the opportunity; all that need concern him is to see that the opportunity never arises. Moreover, it is arguable that people find themselves in exactly similar circumstances far less often than this account presupposes, and that an attempt to define justice and injustice in defiance of this fact is an example of the error, already noted in the chapter on Locke, of treating ethics as if it were as abstract a subject as arithmetic or geometry. Human beings and human situations can never resemble one another as closely as do triangles and squares.

But even if we replace Clarke's account of justice with a less objectionable one, the fundamental difficulty remains. All the while our definition of justice remains vague, it may be unexceptionable, but it will also be unhelpful in providing a definite rule of conduct. Every sensible man may agree that an action is just if it fulfils certain conditions; but the conditions will have been insufficiently specified to enable him to decide, in many cases at least, whether a given action is just or not. On the other hand, if the definition or criterion of justice is made so specific that no doubt on this question is left, disagreement of a higher order will express itself, viz. as to whether it is always one's duty to act justly. Still, no doubt, one of the parties to the dispute may be mistaken; but it is impossible to maintain that it is a mistake in logic.

One may still go on to query the status of the fundamental ethical principles from which, however unsatisfactorily, Clarke tries to derive particular moral rules or criteria of the morality of particular actions. How do we know that it is our duty to obey God, to act justly and benevolently, to look after ourselves? Clarke's answer, as we have seen, is that these principles follow from certain necessary relations inherent in the nature of things, i.e. that they are themselves deduced from higher, not specifically moral, principles. Briefly, we ought to obey God because he is good and just and infinitely superior to ourselves; we ought to act justly because, if $A = B$, then $B = A$; we ought to act benevolently because (i) since what is good is fitting and reasonable, the greatest good must be that which is most fitting and reasonable—hence the production of the greatest good ought always to be aimed at, and (ii) men are so constituted as to need one another's help; and we ought to preserve our own lives and capacities as far as is consistent with our other obligations, because God has sent us into the world, and it is for him to say when we shall leave it.

Our concern is with the general status of these arguments rather than with their detailed content; though it should be pointed out that there is a serious mistake in the first part of the argument for benevolence, caused by Clarke's failure to distinguish between 'doing a good action' and 'doing good', in the sense of acting benevolently.

> (Cp. *Discourse*, p. 92; S-B II p. 25 : For if (as has been before proved) there be a natural and necessary difference between good and evil; and that which is good is fit and reasonable, and that which is evil is unreasonable to be done; and that which is the greatest good is always the *most* fit and reasonable to be chosen: then, as the goodness of God extends it self universally over all his works through the whole creation, by doing always what is absolutely best in the whole; so every rational creature *ought* in its sphere and station, according to its respective powers and faculties, to do all the good it can to all its fellow-creatures. To which end universal love and benevolence is . . . plainly the most direct, certain and effectual means.)

More generally, it must be stressed that these arguments have not the compelling force of strictly logical proofs, however sound they may be as proofs of some weaker kind. It sounds sensible to say 'I ought always to obey God, because he is infinitely wiser and better than I', but the 'because' here cannot be held to indicate a relation of logical entailment or deducibility; for it makes sense to say, even if it happens not to be true, that, even though God is infinitely wiser and better than I, I may nevertheless sometimes legitimately disobey him. Such a conjunction of propositions cannot be self-contradictory, as Clarke's theory requires it to be.

(2) We must now consider what Clarke has to say about the second sort of moral 'absurdity', viz. that which consists in failing to do what one knows to be one's duty.[1] This failure can, he thinks, be caused only by the influence of 'wilful passions or

---

[1] Is the behaviour of a man who acts contrary to his own *erroneous* moral principles *ipso facto* illogical? Clarke never asks himself this question. Hence it is not clear whether it is failure to live up to one's own beliefs as such that he considers logically absurd, or failure to live up to one's true beliefs.

lusts'. 'The eternal reason of things' would of necessity be strong enough to determine men's actions were it not for 'inexcusable corruptions and depravations' (*Discourse*, p. 63; S-B, II, p. 13). To act in defiance of one's knowledge of right and wrong is as illogical and absurd as to believe, say, that murder and theft are morally permissible.

Clarke's attempt to explain failure to live up to one's moral beliefs in the same way as he explains the holding of mistaken moral beliefs—in terms, that is, of a kind of contradiction—does not stand up to examination. For actions cannot be self-contradictory in the same way as can propositions or beliefs; if they are to be called self-contradictory or logically absurd it must be in an extended, perhaps metaphorical sense. Nor is the relation between a belief and an action which conflicts with it identical with that between two conflicting beliefs. We may, of course, say of a man whose actions do not square with his beliefs that he is guilty of inconsistency; and inconsistency of behaviour is often, if not always, a sign of irrationality or unreasonableness. But the inconsistency here is not a purely formal, logical one, as it would be in the case of a man who believed, or claimed to believe, both that all men are mortal and that Socrates is a man and immortal. It might be a reasonable extension of the basic meaning of the expression 'logically absurd' to apply it to any action which is the result of logically absurd beliefs. A mathematician may make a mistake in calculation, with the result that the conclusion he arrives at is an illogical one; and if his calculations have been made with a view to working out a plan for the construction of a bridge, then the plan, if based on his calculations, might be called, in a sense, an illogical one. But the behaviour of an engineer who constructs a bridge by reference to incorrect calculations, which he nevertheless believes to be correct, is essentially different from that of one who constructs a bridge on principles that he knows to be mistaken (his purpose in doing so being perhaps to ensure a larger profit to the contractors by the use of cheap materials). The conduct of the latter, though it is certainly immoral and though there may be some grounds for calling it, in a wide sense, unreasonable, is not in any way logically absurd or self-contradictory.

A similar distinction has to be made in the case of moral principles. To act on mistaken beliefs as to what is right or wrong might conceivably be regarded as illogical if we were to accept, for the sake of argument, Clarke's contention that mistakes in moral belief are, in effect, mistakes in logic. But to act deliberately in a way one knows to be wrong is not to act illogically, even in this extended sense of the word. For when I act in so reprehensible a way as this all my beliefs may be perfectly true, and all the inferences I have made before acting may be perfectly valid. To put it perhaps rather crudely, it is the link between thought, or belief, and action that is at fault, not the thought or belief itself. Thus, although it is no doubt *prima facie* unreasonable to act in a way contrary to one's beliefs about right and wrong—and doubly so, perhaps, when those beliefs are true—this 'unreasonableness' cannot be reduced to, or explained in terms of, any kind of logical error or absurdity. And it is not obvious, even though it may turn out on investigation to be true, that it is absolutely, as opposed to *prima facie*, unreasonable so to act—for example, if one's duty seems to conflict with considerations of one's future happiness.

IV

HUME

IN this chapter I have for the most part restricted my discussion of Hume to the arguments of the *Treatise of Human Nature*; and this procedure may require a word of justification. It is true, of course, that Hume maintained the *Enquiry concerning the Principles of Morals* to be 'incomparably the best' of all his writings, and came in his later years to be more and more dissatisfied with the *Treatise*. But on the particular question of the function of reason in morals, the essential doctrine of the *Treatise* is not altered or added to in the *Enquiry*. There is, however, a considerable change of emphasis in the later work, and a noticeable tendency to soften the tone of the argument. Hume would not have written a sentence of this kind in the *Treatise*: 'These arguments on each side (and many more might be produced) are so plausible, that I am apt to suspect, they may, the one as well as the other, be solid and satisfactory, and that *reason* and *sentiment* concur in almost all moral determinations and conclusions' (E. 172).[1] Indeed this sentence, when taken out of its context and without reference to Appendix I of the *Enquiry*, is positively misleading, since it suggests a radical change in Hume's philosophy, whereas the change is in fact rather one of literary method and tactics. Since I am not in any case here concerned with the development of Hume's ideas, I have thought it better to concentrate on the work in which his views (on this subject, at least) are most trenchantly and vigorously stated.

[1] References to the *Treatise* and the *Enquiry* are given by the letters 'T.' and 'E.' respectively, followed by the page numbers of the Clarendon Press editions, edited by Selby-Bigge.

Hume's discussion in the *Treatise* of the problems which arise concerning the connection between reason and action falls into two main parts. The first part occurs in Book II (entitled 'Of the Passions') and is, *prima facie* at least, a purely psychological account of various types of behaviour and the feelings which accompany or give rise to them. The second part occurs in Book III ('Of Morals') and consists mainly of a criticism of those theories which assert that moral distinctions are founded on reason.

In Book II Hume refers to the commonly held belief that, when we act, we ought to obey the dictates of reason rather than yield to the demands of passion, and he points out that if it is taken strictly it implies both that reason alone can be a motive for action and that reason and passion can be opposed to one another as potential directing motives of the will. He proceeds to argue that neither of these assumptions is true.

According to Hume, there are only two kinds of reasoning, demonstrative and probable. His first concern, therefore, is to show that neither of these two types of reasoning can by itself provide a sufficient motive for action. Demonstrative reasoning, he admits, is of great use in planning certain kinds of undertaking, but it can never of itself produce action. The engineer, for example, needs to make use of abstract, demonstrative reasoning in his calculations; but his machines will never be built unless there is something besides his reasoning to spur him to action.

> I believe it scarce will be asserted, that the first species of reasoning [*sc.* demonstrative] alone is ever the cause of any action. As its proper province is the world of ideas, and as the will always places us in that of realities, demonstration and volition seem, upon that account, to be totally remov'd, from each other. Mathematics, indeed, are useful in all mechanical operations, and arithmetic in almost every art and profession: but 'tis not of themselves they have any influence. Mechanics are the art of regulating the motions of bodies *to some design'd end or purpose*; and the reason why we employ arithmetic in fixing the proportions of numbers, is only that we may discover the proportions of their influence and operation.... Abstract or demonstrative reasoning, therefore, never influences any of our actions, but only as it directs our judgement concerning causes and effects (T. 413–14).

A similar argument is used for probable (or empirical) reasoning. Experience, like abstract reasoning, may help us to decide what the results of alternative courses of action are likely to be. A man may decide, on inductive grounds, that a certain course of action will cause more happiness to his friends than will any other open to him. But this decision, Hume insists, will not be enough to make him act accordingly unless the thought of his friends' happiness is more pleasant to him than the thought of the states of affairs that would result from pursuing alternative ends.

> 'Tis from the prospect of pain or pleasure that the aversion or propensity arises towards any object: And these emotions extend themselves to the causes and effects of that object, as they are pointed out to us by reason and experience. It can never in the least concern us to know, that such objects are causes, and such others effects, if both the causes and effects be indifferent to us. Where the objects themselves do not affect us, their connexion can never give them any influence; and 'tis plain, that as reason is nothing but the discovery of this connexion, it cannot be by its means that the objects are able to affect us (T. 414).

The argument, then, is: there are only two kinds of reasoning; neither of these can by itself be the cause of action (nor—though Hume does not make this point explicitly—can the two kinds in conjunction); therefore reason alone cannot be the cause of action.

Hume now proceeds to argue that, since reason alone cannot cause action, it cannot oppose passion in the direction or influence of the will. The vulgar may talk of the conflict between reason and passion, especially in connection with the contrast between action which is motivated by a powerful and immediate impulse and that which proceeds from a considered judgement of what will conduce to the agent's overall advantage; but this way of speaking is mistaken if it is meant to imply that reason by itself could ever be powerful enough to prevent an action, to the performance of which a man was initially inclined by some desire, however weak.

> But if reason has no original influence, 'tis impossible it can withstand any principle, which has such an efficacy, or ever keep the mind in suspence a moment. Thus it appears, that the principle, which opposes our passion, cannot be the same with reason, and is only call'd so in an improper sense. We speak not strictly and philosophically when we talk of the combat of passion and of reason (T. 415).

Hume allows that in certain circumstances we are justified in speaking, by extension, of a passion as unreasonable; but he insists that such language can legitimately refer only to the falsity of the beliefs which accompany the passion. We may say that it is unreasonable to be afraid of mice; but the correct interpretation of this sort of statement is, first, that to be afraid of something implies a belief that the object feared is liable to cause one harm and, secondly, that this belief, as far as mice are concerned, is false. Again, we may say that it is unreasonable for a man to eat and drink too much if he wants to remain healthy; but this means only that the fact that he indulges himself as he does involves the belief that his excesses will do him no harm, and that this belief is false.

> Where a passion is neither founded on false suppositions, now chuses means insufficient for the end, the understanding can neither justify nor condemn it. 'Tis not contrary to reason to prefer the destruction of the whole world to the scratching of my finger. 'Tis not contrary to reason for me to chuse my total ruin, to prevent the least uneasiness of an *Indian* or person wholly unknown to me. 'Tis as little contrary to reason to prefer even my own acknowledg'd lesser good to my greater, and have a more ardent affection for the former than the latter. A trivial good may, from certain circumstances, produce a desire superior to what arises from the greatest and most valuable enjoyment; nor is there any thing more extraordinary in this, than in mechanics to see one pound weight raise up a hundred by the advantage of its situation. In short, a passion must be accompany'd with some false judgement, in order to its being unreasonable; and even then 'tis not the passion, properly speaking, which is unreasonable, but the judgement (T. 416).

Hume is, of course, far from wanting to deny that psychological conflicts of the type here referred to often occur; his point is that they have nothing to do with reason, properly so-called. His own account of them is in terms of a distinction between calm and violent passions. Violent passions are violently felt; they cause 'disorder in the soul'. Calm passions, on the other hand, are not associated with strong feelings of any kind. They are of two types, 'either certain instincts originally implanted in our natures, such as benevolence and resentment, the love of life, and kindness to children; or the general appetite to good, and aversion to evil, consider'd merely as such' (T. 417). The same emotion may often be either calm or violent, according to circumstances; resentment, for instance, as a calm passion, may give rise to a carefully planned course of action directed against a man whose behaviour towards us we have had occasion to dislike, while as a violent passion it may be nothing more than a sudden feeling of annoyance, which will pass away as quickly as it came. Calm passions, unlike violent ones, may involve thought and the calculation of causes and effects.

Strictly speaking, then, strength of mind consists not in reason prevailing over passion, but in calm passions prevailing over violent ones. The failure of many philosophers to see this is attributed by Hume to the fact that calm passions, like the operations of reason, are accompanied by a tranquillity in the mind which makes the difference between them imperceptible to a casual introspection. 'Their nature and principles have been suppos'd the same, because their sensations are not evidently different' (T. 417). But the confusion can be made only by those 'who judge of things from the first view and appearance' and who do not 'examine objects with a strict philosophical eye'.

Moral judgements are, according to Hume, 'perceptions' of the mind and must therefore, in accordance with his general theory of knowledge, be either impressions or ideas. The question at issue with regard to the origin of moral judgements is accordingly formulated in these terms: 'Whether 'tis by means of our *ideas* or *impressions* we distinguish betwixt vice and virtue, and pronounce an action blameable or praise-worthy?' (T. 456). The theories of those who hold that 'virtue is nothing but a conformity to reason' imply 'that morality, like truth, is discern'd merely by ideas, and by their juxtaposition and comparison'. In order to assess these rationalistic theories, therefore, we must ask whether it is possible to distinguish between moral good and evil by means of reason alone, or whether some other principle is required. Hume's answer to this question is, of course, that moral distinctions cannot be derived from reason; and he justifies this answer in the first place by referring to his earlier discussion of the part that reason plays in action. His argument is briefly this. It is obvious that moral precepts and judgements can influence men's actions; indeed, the desire to produce such an influence is the main occasion for the making of such judgements. But it has been shown that reason alone cannot originate or influence action. It follows that moral judgements cannot be based on reason alone. 'Morals excite passions, and produce or prevent actions. Reason of itself is utterly impotent in this particular. The rules of morality, therefore, are not conclusions of our reason' (T. 457). In fact, just as reason plays a subsidiary part to that of the passions in the origination of conduct, so also it plays a subsidiary part to that of emotion and feeling in the origination of moral judgements.

Hume regards this argument as conclusive; but he has a good deal more to say in support of his view. Two specific contentions are worth mentioning here. Reason can, in Hume's opinion, pronounce only as to relations between ideas or as to matters of fact. In neither of these functions, he maintains, is it capable of giving rise to moral judgements. To prove his point as far as judging of relations between ideas (demonstrative reasoning) is concerned, Hume puts forward the examples of ingratitude (and especially a particular form of ingratitude, viz. parricide) and incest. A tree may produce from its seed a sapling which eventually smothers and destroys it; the relations between the sapling and the parent tree are exactly the same as those between a young man and his father, whom he has murdered. Yet we regard only one of these situations as an instance of immorality; to the other the notions of morality and immorality are simply irrelevant. Since the relations are the same, it follows that the immorality of the parricide cannot be due merely to the relations involved in his action; therefore his immorality cannot be judged to be such by means of demonstrative reasoning. Similarly with incest; if the immorality of the incestuous conduct on the part of human beings consisted solely in certain relations which could be discovered by pure reasoning it would follow that incestuous behaviour in animals is equally immoral and 'criminal'; and this, Hume thinks, is obviously not true.

As to the ability of reason to pronounce concerning matters of fact, consider any action which we call immoral—say a wilful murder. What, Hume asks in effect, is the moral, or other, fact to which, on this theory, I am supposed to be referring when I say that the action is immoral?

> Examine it in all lights, and see if you can find that matter of fact, or real existence, which you call *vice*. In which-ever way you take

it, you find only certain passions, motives, volitions and thoughts. There is no other matter of fact in the case. The vice entirely escapes you, as long as you consider the object. You never can find it, till you turn your reflection into your own breast, and find a sentiment of disapprobation, which arises in you, towards this action. Here is a matter of fact; but 'tis the object of feeling, not of reason. It lies in yourself, not in the object. So that when you pronounce any action or character to be vicious, you mean nothing, but that from the constitution of your nature you have a feeling or sentiment of blame from the contemplation of it (T. 468–9).

It follows that, in so far as reason is concerned with matters of fact, a moral judgement can be untrue, and so contrary to reason, only when the person who makes it is mistaken or lying about the nature of his own feelings.

In assessing these views of Hume's it is important to remember that he uses the word 'reason' in a very narrow sense. Hobbes, and many writers between Hobbes and Hume, had used it to mean simply 'reasoning' or 'ratiocination', and Hume follows in this tradition. His own definition of 'reason' seems to be 'the discovery of truth or falsehood' (T. 458); but truth and falsehood are discovered only by reasoning—there is for Hume no easy, non-ratiocinative, way to the truth. Hence a superficial reading might lead us to conclude that his only quarrel is with those who, like Locke and Clarke, thought that moral truths could be discovered by ratiocination alone, and with those who, like Wollaston (if indeed there were any others like him), held that actions could be literally true or false in the same way as beliefs or propositions, thus making them conformable to reason in the very strictest Humean sense of that expression.[1] But this conclusion would fail to do justice to an important feature of Hume's argument. He is not merely saying that reason, in his sense of the word, does not do certain things that others had said it did; he is also maintaining that his sense of the word 'reason' is the only strict and proper sense it can have. In common speech, of course, 'reason' and its derivatives have other, wider, senses, and some

---

[1] Wollaston maintained this view in his *The Religion of Nature Delineated* (London, 1725). Hume rejects it in a scathing footnote, not deigning to mention Wollaston by name, but referring to him as 'a late author, who has had the good fortune to obtain some reputation' (T. 461 n).

of these senses can be accommodated to Hume's views with only minor modifications, as when an unreasonable fear is explained as a fear associated with, or caused by, some false belief (though this explanation is not always as plausible as Hume thought—I may sometimes fear or worry, even though I know that there is nothing in the situation to justify my fear or worry, which thus becomes even more unreasonable). Other senses Hume makes no attempt to explain, and would doubtless be content to dismiss as vulgar errors. For example, the common practice of describing a human being as a reasonable or an unreasonable man does not solely refer, if indeed it refers at all, to the extent to which the more reasonable man knows more facts and is a better reasoner than the less reasonable; it must, therefore, on Hume's view, be an improper practice.

Of these two aspects of Hume's thesis the first (viz. that reason, in the sense of the discovery of truth and falsehood by means of ratiocination, cannot by itself lead to action or be the sole source or justification of moral distinctions) has been by implication discussed, and largely endorsed, in the preceding chapters. But before we proceed to discuss the second aspect there is one point that needs stressing. When Hume says that reason cannot of itself function as a guide to conduct he does not mean, although he has sometimes been taken to mean, that demonstrative and empirical reasoning are of no value to a man who is trying to make up his mind what to do. On the contrary, he agrees that such things as ignorance of the relevant facts and of the probable effects of one's actions are frequently the cause of serious mistakes in one's behaviour, even though the mistakes are not necessarily blameworthy unless the ignorance is so itself. In stressing the impotence of thought without emotion or feeling, he is not recommending men to act according to the feelings of the moment without stopping to think—no out-and-out rationalist could object more strongly to conduct of this type than Hume. Locke, for example, regarded the principle that alleged revelation must be judged by reason as a necessary safeguard against enthusiasm and extravagancy in religion. Hume, of course, denies reason some of the functions ascribed to it by Locke; but he is no less opposed to enthusiasm than Locke, and holds no brief for unbridled or unregulated emotion—unregulated, that is to say, by knowledge of the facts and of the likely consequences of one's actions, and by the ability to set aside consideration of one's selfish interests and to take a sober, impartial view of things.[1]

We have now to consider Hume's claim that some commonly held opinions, in the form in which they are usually stated, involve an unphilosophical and inexact use of words. I shall refer in particular to three such opinions:

(*a*) that reason alone can move a man to act, or oppose passion in the influencing of the will;

(*b*) that a man ought to live in accordance with reason; and

(*c*) that moral judgements have their origin in, or are based on, reason.

(*a*) Hume is clearly right in his contention that a process of reasoning can never of itself lead a man to perform any action. We may, of course, say that a certain man's discovery, made as the result of a process of reasoning, that something was the case, led him to perform a certain action; but in saying this we are leaving out of account some factor which must have been present in the situation before the action could occur—an enormous number of statements we make in our ordinary everyday life are elliptical in this way, since there is no need to make express mention of something that both the speaker and his hearers take for granted. For example, a man who wants, or who has decided, to instal in his house that form of central heating which will incur the lowest running costs may examine all the possible alternatives and discover by exact mathematical calculation that an oil-fired system will be more economical to run than any of the others. We may subsequently say that his reasoning, or his calculations, led him to instal an oil-fired system. But we quite clearly do not mean that his reasoning alone would have been sufficient to cause him to do this: it is the reasoning, taken in conjunction with the desire or decision to instal the most economical type of system available, that leads to action.

However, some of those who have claimed that reason alone can move a man to act have not meant to assert, as against Hume, that reasoning alone can do so; they have held, rather, that there is

---

[1] It is worth noticing that Francis Hutcheson, the first systematic expositor of a moral sense theory, also devised a kind of moral arithmetic or algebra to help men to ratiocinate, or even calculate, about moral problems.

another, perfectly proper, sense of the word 'reason' in which reason alone can be said to lead a man to act. Thomas Reid, for example, maintained, in explicit opposition to Hume, that it is possible for a man to act on the principle of pursuing what is good for himself on the whole, and that this principle is justly called 'reason' to contrast it with acting in accordance with the appetite or 'passion' of the moment. 'Reason' and 'passion' can conflict, in the sense that a general determination to pursue what we know to be in our own interest can conflict with a strong, though perhaps transitory, desire or appetite. 'Reason' is a correct, and 'calm passion' an incorrect, way of referring to this general determination, because the very existence of a general idea of what is good for me on the whole requires the exercise of reason and intelligence. 'I shall endeavour to show that, among the various ends of human actions, there are some, of which, without reason, we could not even form a conception; and that, as soon as they are conceived, a regard to them is, by our constitution, not only a principle of action, but a leading and governing principle, to which all our animal principles are subordinate, and to which they ought to be subject' (*Essays on the Active Powers of Man*, in *The Works of Thomas Reid*, ed. Sir William Hamilton (Edinburgh, 1895), Vol. II, p. 580). (There are, in Reid's view, two such ends, a man's general good and his duty, but we are at the moment concerned with the first of these only.) Man differs from other animals, Reid thinks, in that by the use of memory and reflection he can learn that yielding to the impulse of the moment will often give him less satisfaction than resisting it. Man does not merely desire particular objects, though he does of course do this; he can also form a conception of what will be good for him on the whole, in the sense of what will most conduce to his happiness and perfection, and as soon as he has formed this conception, he immediately comes to desire his own good.

> We learn to observe the connexions of things, and the consequences of our actions; and, taking an extended view of our existence, past, present, and future, we correct our first notions of good and ill, and form the conception of what is good or ill upon the whole; which must be estimated, not from the present feeling, or from the present animal desire or aversion, but from a due consideration of its consequences, certain or probable, during the whole of our existence (ibid., pp. 580–1).

Now it cannot be denied, and Hume would certainly not have wished to deny, that a man can form this general notion of what will be for his own good on the whole, and that he can sometimes act in accordance with it even when he has some strong particular appetite which is tending to influence him in the opposite direction. But this is not enough to show that Hume was mistaken in his refusal to regard such a situation as an example of reason alone influencing the will. For it is necessary to distinguish two different factors, the decision that a certain course of action will best promote one's own good or advantage and the decision (in another sense of the word 'decision') to act in a certain way because it will best promote one's own advantage. The first decision may well be arrived at through the use of intelligence and experience alone, provided that one has a clear conception of the state of affairs referred to as one's own good on the whole (one's own greatest pleasure, for example, or one's maximum monetary enrichment), and a knowledge, based on experience and thought, of how this state of affairs may best be achieved. But it is possible to reach the conclusion that a certain course of action is best on the whole, and yet not to act in accordance with this conclusion; and, Hume might well say, no amount of reasoning or factual knowledge, nor the exercise of intelligence in a wider sense, will suffice to produce such action unless, besides the operation of reason, there is also a desire to do whatever will make me happiest, or richest, in the long run. In other words, whatever is lacking in the man who knows what is good for him on the whole, but who acts instead according to some strong contrary impulse, it is not anything that can properly be called 'reason'.

Reid claims that there is a contradiction in supposing an intelligent being to have the notion of what is good for him on the whole without also having the desire for that good. This is, however, a mistake, springing from a double ambiguity in Reid's terminology. In the first place the expression 'an intelligent being' is ambiguous. It may mean either a being possessed of the capacity for intelligent thought and action, as opposed to one not so possessed—a man, for example, as opposed to a fish—or, within the category of intelligent beings in this sense, one whose capacity of intelligence is of a high order and is frequently, perhaps usually, evinced by his thoughts and actions—an intelligent man as opposed to a stupid one. If the first interpretation is adopted there is clearly no contradiction of the sort envisaged by Reid; a stupid man can perfectly well see that some action will be good for him, and yet have no desire whatsoever to perform it. But if we adopt the second interpretation the statement no longer contradicts Hume, for it amounts merely to saying that an intelligent man cannot but choose what he thinks will be best for him on the whole in preference to yielding to the strongest impulse of the moment. As long as, in common with many people, we regard the readiness to choose in this way as one of the main criteria whereby we can distinguish intelligent men from stupid ones, this statement is doubtless true; but it is true only because the intelligent man, on this criterion of intelligence, is the man who both desires to do what will be good for himself on the whole and knows what will be good, not the man who merely knows.

Secondly, there is an ambiguity in the word 'good' in this context, which also lends some plausibility to Reid's argument. The expression 'one's own good' can be used to refer to some more or less definite concept. For example, a man may be said to be seeking his own good on the whole if he is trying to discover what will give him the most pleasure in the long run, or what will make him richest. Alternatively, a man may be said to be seeking his own good on the whole in the more abstract sense that he is trying to discover that action which will in the long run best satisfy his desires. (Hobbes's account of the relation between 'good' and desire is an example of this usage: cp. *Leviathan*, ed. Oakeshott, p. 32, 'Whatsoever is the object of any man's appetite or desire, that is it which he for his part calleth good.') In the first sense of the expression a man may perhaps discover by the use of reason that a certain course of action will make him, say, richer than any other; but this discovery will not by itself provide a sufficient motive for performing this action—the action will be performed only if he also desires, above all relevant desires, his own enrichment. One may, in much the same way, contrast the man who impulsively realises an investment in order to take a quick profit with the man who leaves his money invested because he thinks this will in the long run prove to be the more profitable course. It is possible to say that, while the former acts on impulse, the latter is influenced by rational considerations; but this does not alter the fact that the latter would not have acted at all but for his desire to make as much money as possible. In the second sense, on the other hand, a man's knowledge that a certain course of action will be best for him on the whole (meaning, as it now does, that it will lead to the state of affairs he most strongly desires) will certainly provide a sufficient motive for his performing the action; but this knowledge cannot be attained by the use of reason alone apart from the 'passions', for the simple reason that one cannot know that a certain course of action will lead to the achievement of what one most desires without having at least one desire that is not dependent on or derived from that knowledge. Reason, in short, can suggest to a man possible ends or objectives which would never have occurred to him otherwise; but it is not reason that gives him a desire for those ends once he has conceived them.

(*b*) In common speech we distinguish rational behaviour from irrational, and reasonable behaviour from unreasonable. Both these pairs of words are used with many different shades of meaning, but there is one use of the rational/irrational distinction that can be quite easily explained on Humean lines. Irrational behaviour, in this sense, is behaviour to which the agent has not given enough thought or consideration, while rational behaviour is behaviour which is preceded by the requisite amount of thought. Irrational behaviour is so called, not because it possesses the quality of being irrational, but because it has not been preceded by thought, although it ought to have been so preceded; behaviour not preceded by thought where thought is not considered necessary would be called non-rational rather than irrational. There is a sense in which a man may be said to approach a situation rationally if he thinks about it before he decides what to do, even if his thinking contains serious mistakes of fact or of logic.

But this is not the only way in which the words 'rational' and 'irrational' are used, and it is certainly not what is meant by the distinction between reasonable and unreasonable behaviour. Here an assessment of the conduct itself is involved, not a description of its antecedents. The question we have to ask is, what account can Hume give of the distinction between reasonable and unreasonable behaviour, and how far can he allow that 'reasonable' and 'unreasonable' are appropriate words for marking the distinction? Hume, as we have seen, takes the view that a passion can be called unreasonable only on the ground that it is accompanied by a false judgement (it would be more accurate to say that it must be dependent on, or connected with, a false judgement); and even then the passion is called unreasonable only by extension—it is, strictly speaking, the judgement, not the passion, that is untrue, and therefore contrary to reason. The same restriction applies to the assessment of actions. A man may act foolishly, in taking what he thinks is the best, but what is in fact the worst, means to a given end, and we may loosely call his action unreasonable; but what is meant is that the action is connected with an untrue belief. 'These false judgements may be thought to affect the passions and actions, which are connected with them, and may be said to render them unreasonable, in a figurative and improper way of speaking' (T. 459).

Hume has often been criticised on the ground that his standards of propriety and correctness in speech are excessively rigorous, and there is some plausibility in this criticism. If it is 'proper' or 'correct' to call a belief unreasonable the extension of this epithet to an action connected with the belief is not improper, if by this it is meant that any such extension should be avoided by those who wish to speak correct English. For correct English is full of such extensions; there is nothing improper, in the ordinary sense of that word, in speaking of a Foreign Secretary who is not foreign, or of a walking stick that does not walk. But to suppose that Hume can be refuted in this way shows a complete misunderstanding of the point he is trying to make. He is not saying that people who want to speak correct English should not call actions reasonable or unreasonable; the impropriety he is alleging is a philosophical one, not one of linguistic usage. It is not the plain man's use of the phrase 'unreasonable action' to which Hume is objecting, but the philosopher's use of it, and in particular his use of it to suggest that there are certain connections and affinities between actions, on the one hand, and judgements or propositions, on the other, when in Hume's view these connections do not exist. Hence Reid's criticism, like most of his criticisms of Hume's moral philosophy, misses the point.

> To act reasonably [Reid says] is a phrase no less common in all languages, than to judge reasonably. We immediately approve of a man's conduct, when it appears that he had good reason for what

he did. And every action we disapprove, we think unreasonable, or contrary to reason.

A way of speaking so universal among men, common to the learned and unlearned in all nations and in all languages, must have a meaning. To suppose it to be words without meaning, is to treat, with undue contempt, the common sense of mankind (*Works*, Vol. II, p. 579).

Reid here confuses two quite different questions, the question whether a certain belief is one of those widely held beliefs which go to form what he calls the common sense of mankind and the question whether a commonly used verbal formulation of such a belief is a satisfactory formulation. Hume is concerned with a question of the second type, not, as Reid supposes, with one of the first. Hume does not have to deny that there is a real distinction between actions commonly called reasonable and those commonly called unreasonable; his point is, in effect, that it is misleading to use the words 'reasonable' and 'unreasonable' to make this distinction. (Similarly, he does not deny that the expression 'We ought to obey reason rather than passion' has a meaning, in the sense that it expresses a genuine opinion; his point is that the opinion is, for the philosopher, better, because less misleadingly, expressed by the words 'We ought to obey our calm passions rather than our violent ones'.)

However, the fact that Hume could easily dispose of an objection of this type does not mean that his views are above criticism. The words 'reasonable' and 'unreasonable' apply strictly, he argues, to judgements or beliefs; a reasonable belief, or a belief in accordance with reason, is true, and an unreasonable belief, or a belief contrary to reason, is false. But actions cannot be true or false; therefore they cannot, in that sense, be reasonable or unreasonable, in accordance with or contrary to reason. Now it is possible to use the expressions 'in accordance with reason' and 'contrary to reason' as periphrastic equivalents for 'true' and 'false', as applied to beliefs, though it is doubtful whether this is their most natural meaning; but 'reasonable belief' certainly does not mean the same as 'true belief', nor 'unreasonable belief' the same as 'untrue belief'. A reasonable belief, in the commonest use of that expression, is one which is probably true on the evidence at our disposal, and an unreasonable belief one which is probably untrue on that evidence. In both cases the degree of probability may be extremely high, so high indeed that the evidence may be conclusive; the point is, however, that the reasonableness or unreasonableness of a man's beliefs depends on the evidence he has for or against them, or, alternatively, on the evidence he might have if he looked or reflected more thoroughly—it is not simply a matter of their truth or falsehood. A reasonable belief—a belief which it was reasonable for him to hold on the evidence before him, or available to him—may turn out to be false, and an unreasonable belief—one held in spite of the evidence—may turn out to be true. In short, the reasonableness or unreasonableness of a belief is not a matter of its truth or falsity, but a matter of whether there are good reasons for holding or for rejecting it. Is it not possible, then, we may ask, to give a comparable account of the reasonableness or unreasonableness of actions, in terms of the existence of good reasons for performing, or for not performing them? And if this could be done, would it not suggest that Hume was over-hasty in his rejection of the claim that actions can be reasonable or unreasonable, in a strict and philosophical sense?

There is, however, Hume might reply, an important difference between the two cases to which this suggestion fails to do justice. Granted that 'reasonable belief' does not mean the same as 'true belief', nevertheless the reasonableness of a belief has to be defined in terms of the reasons a man has, or is entitled to have, for believing it; and 'reasons for believing that p' is equivalent, logically, to 'reasons for believing that p is true'—i.e. we are still concerned with questions of truth and falsity, even though the concern is indirect. When, on the other hand, we talk about the reasons for or against performing a certain action, this is not equivalent to talking about the reasons for or against believing that something is the case. Reasons for acting, it may be said, are not reasons in the same sense of the word as reasons for believing; even if we allow it to be said that a reason for acting is a reason why someone should act in a certain way,[1] and a reason for believing a reason why someone should believe something, the word 'should' is clearly being used very differently in the two expressions.

[1] A reason for acting is sometimes, of course, a reason why someone is acting, has acted or will act in a certain way; but we are not here concerned with reasons of this kind.

It might perhaps be suggested, in reply to someone who tried to defend Hume in this way, that to give reasons for performing a certain action is, in effect, to give reasons for holding a certain belief, viz. the belief that the action in question is the right one for the agent to perform in the circumstances (the word 'right' not being restricted in meaning to 'morally right', of course). An action would then be reasonable if there existed good reasons for thinking it to be right, and unreasonable if there existed good reasons for thinking it to be wrong. But, apart from the difficulty of fitting beliefs of this kind into Hume's epistemological framework, a difficulty which might be overcome by arguing that the framework itself was defective, the parallel between the two types of reason is still by no means exact. For the question whether an action is right, in this sense, is not independent of the question whether there are good reasons for performing it, nor is the fact that it is right a reason why it should be performed. We do not first discover that an action is the right action in the circumstances, and then regard this factual discovery as providing us with a reason why the action should be performed; on the contrary, to say that it is the right action is just another way of saying that it should be performed. In spite of this lack of symmetry, however, it is clearly absurd to rule out in advance as improper all talk of reasons as applied to conduct. Although a reason for acting is not precisely the same kind of thing as a reason for believing something, there are no good grounds for objecting to the use of the word 'reason' in the former context which would not apply equally to its use in the latter. (Similarly, in the expressions 'reasons why one should believe, or conclude, that...' and 'reasons why one should perform a certain action', the word 'should' is perhaps being used in two different ways or senses; but it does not follow that either use is in any way improper.)

We seem, then, to be left with a situation in which the differences and resemblances between two types of reason, reasons for believing something and reasons for doing something, are being stressed in such a way as to yield contradictory accounts of their nature. Hume is saying, in effect, that the differences are so great that the words 'reasonable' and 'unreasonable', which are properly used in connection with beliefs, ought not to be used in connection with actions; an opponent of Hume, on the other hand, is not committed to denying or belittling the differences, though some of his opponents have done these things, but merely to asserting that the resemblances or affinities are important enough to justify the application of the same terms to both. Now, interpreted simply as linguistic recommendations, neither of these theses is particularly important. A philosopher cannot always avoid the use of language that may perhaps mislead; and he should not worry too much about claims that something he says is misleading, provided that he somewhere furnishes the necessary correction to this tendency to mislead. It may be claimed, on the one hand, that it is misleading to speak of actions as being reasonable or unreasonable, because it leads people to suppose that the reasonableness or unreasonableness of actions is exactly on a par with that of beliefs; or, on the other hand, that it is misleading to argue that it is improper to call actions reasonable or unreasonable, because the argument suggests that all one can ever do is act according to the impulse of the moment. But any statement about anything can mislead us, if we are not careful enough in our examination of it, and especially if we fail to consider it in its context—we cannot restrict every word in a language to one, and only one, use. What is important is that the nature and possible extent of what is ordinarily called reason-giving and justification in respect of actions should be discussed and analysed; and Hume's contribution to this discussion is of inestimable value mainly because he is the first modern philosopher to draw attention in a systematic way to the fact that the justification of actions differs in important respects from logical proof and inductive argument, even though it may at times make use of these.

(c) In our examination of Hume's views we have so far considered the motivation and justification of action in general. We have now to discuss what he has to say about moral judgements. Much of the discussion in the preceding section will be applicable to this topic also; for the moral justification of actions is merely one aspect of their justification in general, so that the giving of reasons, and the distinguishing of good from bad reasons, why a certain action should be performed, where the 'should' is a moral 'should', will have obvious affinities with the giving and distinguishing of reasons in non-moral practical contexts. But certain additional points have to be made.

To begin with, Hume's account of the nature of moral judgements has a positive, as well as a negative, side. He does not merely claim that moral distinctions are not derived from reason alone, in his strict sense of the word 'reason'; he asserts that they are, in fact, derived primarily from feeling or sentiment. Reason may, of course, enter into the making of any moral judgement in a subsidiary way, just as it may play a subsidiary part in the formation of decisions and the motivation of actions; for example, my moral disapproval of anything that harms the well-being of my country may have to be supplemented by much factual enquiry and logical thinking before it can issue in the judgement that a certain aspect of the government's foreign policy is morally wrong. We may approve of A, and approve of B as a means to A, and of C as a means to B, and so on; or disapprove of P, and disapprove of Q because it will lead to P, and of R because it will lead to Q, and so on. But such processes as these must, logically, have a termination. There must be at least one thing of which we approve directly, and at least one thing of which we disapprove directly; and this approval and disapproval are, in Hume's view, straight sentiments, unmixed with any ratiocinative element.

Our present approach to Hume now leads us to pose the question whether reason, in some other sense than his 'strict philosophical sense', may properly be said to have something to do with the making of moral judgements, even with those supposed final, direct moral judgements, which cannot be, even in part, the product of reason in Hume's sense of the word. But it is necessary first to say something in elucidation of the question whether moral judgements and distinctions have their origin in sentiment or reason. Much that Hume says lends itself to the conclusion that what he is providing is a piece of descriptive psychology or phenomenology; i.e. he is saying that a correct account of what happens in a man's mind when he makes a moral judgement necessarily includes a reference to a feeling or sentiment of approbation or disapprobation, and that anything else is incidental to the particular moral judgement being made. We may also take note of the mental processes which were the immediate antecedents of the judgement, and say, as Hume said of the antecedents of an action, that, although some ratiocination may have occurred, there must also have been some element of feeling or 'passion', since the approbation or disapprobation could not have been produced by an act or acts of reasoning alone. Unfortunately for Hume, however, an account of this kind, even if it were adequate as psychology, would not justify the conclusion that moral judgements are not, in any sense, connected with or dependent on reason.

If we consider any particular act of judging, whether moral or non-moral, we can, given sufficient information, provide a description both of the nature and content of the judgement and of the way in which it was arrived at. Take first a simple non-moral judgement. If I judge that it is going to rain shortly, there may have been some ratiocination in the process which led up to the making of this judgement (e.g. inferences from the weather forecast or from the height and type of the clouds); but there must in addition have been belief in, or knowledge of, some propositions from which the ratiocination began, for a judgement or belief can be derived only from another judgement or belief, not from reasoning alone. But it would be absurd to conclude from this that the belief that it is going to rain shortly is not in any sense a matter of reason. It may be a matter of reason in at least two ways: (i) in that it has been arrived at as the result of a correct or incorrect process of reasoning from premisses which are true or false, and (ii) in that it is open to be checked and criticised in a rational way by reference both to the facts and to the normal rules of logic and evidence. In (i) we are still concerned with the particular act of judging by a particular person; but in (ii) we have made the vitally important step from considering the act of judging to considering the content of that act, and of any other act which has the same content (the step is important because we are no longer tied to the particular individual and the particular act, and can consider the truth or falsity of the judgement in abstraction from any actual making of it).

When we turn to moral judgements, it should be equally clear that, even if we accept, for the sake of argument, Hume's account of them, to the effect that their central element or primary causal antecedent is a feeling or sentiment of approbation or disapprobation, it does not follow that moral judgement is not in any respect a matter of reason. For in the same sort of way, it is still open to an opponent of Hume to claim that a particular moral judgement has been arrived at as the result of a correct or incorrect process of reasoning from true or false premisses and, more important, that any moral judgement is open to criticism and checking in a rational way. The claims may conceivably be unjustified; but it does not follow from Hume's arguments that they are. We must distinguish the claim that the use of our reasoning powers gives us the best chance of arriving at factual or logical truth from the proposition that factual or logical beliefs can be correct or incorrect, or reasonable or unreasonable; similarly, we must distinguish the claim that the use of reasoning gives us the best chance of arriving at correct moral judgements or of acquiring knowledge of how we ought to act, from the proposition that beliefs or judgements as to how we ought to act can be reasonable or unreasonable, in the sense that they can be checked and criticised, that reasons can be given for and against the holding of such beliefs or the performance of such actions, and that of these reasons some may be characterised as good, others as bad. Hume says a great deal about the first proposition, but far too little about the second.

It is worth noticing here one respect in which Hume's use of words varies according to the point he is trying to make. Throughout Book III of the *Treatise* he links together demonstrative and probable reasoning, the making of logical and of causal inferences, and he does not suggest that one is any more or less rational than the other; his aim is to show that they both admit of a certain kind of rationality, of which reflection about moral matters does not. But in Book I, where his aim is not to compare but to contrast logical with causal reasoning, his language is very different; indeed, what he there says about reasoning concerning causes and effects has some important resemblances to what he says about moral reasoning in Book III. It is quite clear that probable reasoning is, for Hume, when he is discussing it in detail, in some way less rational than logical reasoning—so much so that he sometimes speaks as though 'reasoning' was an improper appellation for it.

> Thus all probable reasoning is nothing but a species of sensation. ... When I give the preference to one set of arguments above another, I do nothing but decide from my feeling concerning the superiority of their influence. Objects have no discoverable connexion together; nor is it from any other principle but custom operating upon the imagination, that we can draw any inference from the appearance of one to the existence of another (T. 103).

And he refers later to his hypothesis 'that all our reasonings concerning causes and effects are deriv'd from nothing but custom; and that belief is more properly an act of the sensitive, than of the cogitative part of our natures' (T. 183). But the fact that, in Hume's view, my judgement that malaria is caused by an infection transmitted by the bite of a mosquito is brought about by the operation of custom on the imagination does not prevent him from counting such judgements (in Book III) as springing, in a sense, from reason and as capable of being true or false. Now he is, of course, quite right in refusing to allow his theory to prevent him from doing this; for a judgement to the effect that X causes Y can, indeed must, be either true or false, however it may have been arrived at. What Hume does not see is that, in a precisely similar way, the fact that a moral judgement may have been produced by the operation of a feeling or sentiment does not of itself rule out the possibility of the judgement's being true or false, and to that extent, at least, a matter of reason. In Book I he is stressing the differences between demonstrative and probable reasoning, and in Book III he is stressing the resemblance or connection between them (both perfectly proper activities); but while, in Book III, he engages in the equally proper activity of stressing the differences between the making of moral judgements, on the one hand, and the making of logical and factual judgements, on the other, it is still open to us to consider, at least, whether there are not also some important resemblances or connections between logical, factual and moral judgements, as contrasted in particular with the expression of many kinds of feeling or of liking and disliking. And one way of indicating the possibility of such connections would be to suggest that there is room for the application of the word 'reason', or some of its derivatives, to all three, instead of to the first alone (*Treatise* Book I) or to the first and second alone (*Treatise* Book III).

Now what sort of reply could Hume make to the objection that he overlooks certain respects in which the making of moral judgements may properly be described as a matter of reason? He could, of course, perfectly well admit that any ratiocination that takes place before the making of a moral judgement may be carried out correctly or incorrectly according to the normal rules of logic; and he could admit also that any purely factual beliefs or propositions involved may be either true or false in the ordinary way. But he would presumably question the implied claim that any moral judgement, whether original or derived, could be true or false in any important sense. Indeed, he thinks that the word 'judgement' may here be misleading: 'morality is more properly felt than judg'd of' (T. 470), and we think that we are judging only because the moral sentiment is 'commonly so soft and gentle, that we are apt to confound it with an idea, according to our common custom of taking all things for the same, which have any near resemblance to each other' (ibid.). Of course, we could define truth or falsity here in purely subjective terms, according as the speaker did or did not genuinely have the relevant feeling or sentiment; my statement that adultery is wrong would then be true if I do feel disapproval of adultery, but false if I am only pretending to feel it. But apart from the well-known difficulties of this type of subjectivism, it is clear that the truth and falsity here referred to are of a subsidiary nature, being concerned only with the correctness or incorrectness of the account which a man gives of his moral sentiments and attitudes, whereas what we are discussing is the possibility of assessing their appropriateness or relevance. Hume pays little attention to this possibility, assuming that his previous arguments have ruled it out. But this, as we have seen, is not so; whatever terminological decision we eventually arrive at about the application of such words as 'reasonable' and 'unreasonable' to moral judgements, it is clear that some kind of criticism and checking of such judgements is possible—I can both criticise the judgements of others and ask myself whether a previous judgement of my own is correct or whether I should change my mind. It is a serious defect in Hume's account of moral judgements that he gives no consideration to the forms which such criticism can take and to the question whether it has any important limitations and, if so, what those limitations are. Hume's talk about morality being a matter of feeling and sentiment is, of course, sound enough up to a point, for feeling does enter into the making of many, if not of all, moral judgements; but it ignores an important feature of moral feelings which distinguishes them from many, though by no means all, other types of feeling, viz. the fact that such feelings may be, and often are, judged appropriate or inappropriate to the action or object to which they are directed, and that the question whether the feeling is appropriate or inappropriate is one that may be publicly discussed, with reasons given on either side. In many kinds of non-moral feeling, on the other hand, the question of the appropriateness or inappropriateness of the feeling does not arise. If a man at one time felt moral disapproval of all kinds of war, but now disapproves more strongly of failure to fight in some circumstances than he does of fighting, he will generally be prepared to say that his earlier feeling was wrong or inappropriate or unjustified—he will not as a rule be content to say that his feelings have altered. If, on the other hand, he once liked sugar in his tea and now no longer does so, there is no question, for a sensible person at least, of justifying his likes or dislikes, or of saying that his taste has improved—it has just changed. Now Hume can to some extent account for our tendency to defend, as opposed to reporting merely, changes in our moral feelings, to the extent, that is, that these changes are the result of our discovery of new facts or of mistakes in the arguments which had led up to the earlier feelings; but it requires to be argued, not merely stated, that all revision or criticism of moral thinking must be of these purely factual or logical kinds.

There is one apparent exception to Hume's lack of concern for the possibility of a criticism of moral judgements which is not limited to criticism of purely factual judgements or of deductive or inductive arguments. I refer to his attempt to explain how feelings of moral approval or disapproval can be distinguished from similar non-moral feelings. Moral approval is a feeling of pleasure derived from the contemplation of a certain action or character; but it is, Hume insists, a special kind of pleasure that is involved, viz. the pleasure that arises from a consideration of the action or character from which all thought of our own personal advantage or interest is withdrawn.

> Nor is every sentiment of pleasure or pain, which arises from characters and actions, of that *peculiar* kind, which makes us praise or condemn. The good qualities of an enemy are hurtful to us; but may still command our esteem or respect. 'Tis only when a character is considered in general without reference to our particular interest, that it causes such a feeling or sentiment as denominates it morally good or evil (T. 472).

It follows that a Humean might criticise one man's statement or judgement to the effect that a certain action was morally wrong, on the ground that the judgement was, at least in part, motivated by considerations of self-interest, and was therefore not properly speaking a moral judgement at all. But it is clear that criticism of this kind, though often of great importance, forms only a small part of the criticism of moral judgements, as indeed of any other judgements; it is quite possible to admit that an opponent is impartial, while still insisting that he is wrong.

We seem therefore to be justified in concluding that Hume has not established his claim that the theory according to which moral judgements have their origin in, or are based on, reason, makes an improper use of the word 'reason'. The possibility of criticism and assessment of moral judgement leaves open the question whether some use of the word 'reason' or of its derivatives may not be illuminating and therefore proper (rather than misleading and therefore improper), to the extent that it expresses some connection or resemblance between such criticism and the criticism of factual beliefs and logical arguments, to which last the term 'reason' may, in Hume's view, be properly applied. Similar or connected, though not identical, procedures in different fields may properly be called by the same name to indicate the similarity or connection, just as they may properly be called by different names to indicate the difference.

In our next chapter we have to examine an elaborate attempt to give the word 'reason' a wider meaning without committing the errors of which Hume accused, and, on the whole, justly accused, his rationalist predecessors.

V
KANT

KANT'S examination of the concept of reason and of its speculative and practical working is one of the greatest achievements of modern philosophy, and an adequate discussion of it would require a book to itself, at the very least. Both in expounding Kant's views and in criticising them, I have therefore concentrated on those features which are most immediately relevant to my subject, while recognising that much more could be said, and perhaps should be said if a properly balanced assessment is to be achieved.[1]

Superficially, Kant's view of the relation between reason and action appears to be totally at variance with Hume's. He refers to Hume as the man 'who can be said to have begun the assault on the claims of pure reason which made a thorough examination of them necessary' (KPV, A88, Ak50); and where action, as opposed

---

[1] References are made to Kant's works as follows:

Critique of Pure Reason (KRV): to the pages of the first (A) and second (B) editions.

Critique of Practical Reason (KPV): to the pages of the first edition (A), and of Volume V of the Prussian Academy edition (Berlin: 1913) of Kant's works (Ak).

Critique of Judgement (KU): to the pages of the first edition (A), and of Volume V of the Academy edition (Ak).

Groundwork of the Metaphysic of Morals (G): to the pages of the first edition (A).

Quotations are taken for the most part from the following translations:
    KRV: N. Kemp Smith (London, 1950)
    KPV: L. W. Beck (New York, 1956)
    KU: J. H. Bernard (London, 1931)
    G: H. J. Paton (London, 1958)

to speculation, was concerned, Kant was at least as determined to defend 'the claims of pure reason' as Hume was to attack them. It must be remembered, however, that Hume's attack on the view that moral distinctions have their foundation in reason is in part an attack on an intellectualist ethics of a kind which Kant was in no way anxious to defend. He agreed with Hume that moral excellence is neither the same as, nor directly derived from, intellectual excellence; and although they often contradict one another verbally when talking about the function of reason in action, many of the contradictions would disappear if for Hume's word 'reason' we substituted 'intellect' or 'understanding'. Kant would doubtless have endorsed Hegel's criticism of Clarke and his fellow-rationalists, to the effect that they 'carry on their speculations within forms such as belong to a very commonplace metaphysic of the understanding' (*History of Philosophy*, English translation (London, 1896), Vol. III, p. 320). But for Kant, unlike Hume, there is more to reason than mere intellect or understanding.

Kant's debt to Rousseau for some of the leading principles of his moral philosophy has often been stressed, and was acknowledged by Kant himself.[1] One feature of Rousseau's thought is especially important in this connection. He had argued that, as far as the possession of understanding is concerned, man is superior to the rest of animal creation only in degree. Yet there is still a difference in kind between man and beast; and the definition of man is now no longer 'rational animal', but 'animal capable of freedom' (and an animal capable of freedom is an animal capable of self-improvement).

> Every animal has ideas, since it has senses; it even combines those ideas in a certain degree; and it is only in degree that man differs, in this respect, from the brute. Some philosophers have even maintained that there is a greater difference between one man and an-

[1] The following fragment (Academy edn., Vol. XX, p. 44) is interesting and important. 'I am myself by inclination an enquirer. I feel the universal thirst after knowledge, and the passionate urge for further advance in it or the joy at every acquisition of it. There was a time when I thought that this alone could confer honour on men, and despised the masses who know nothing. Rousseau has set me right. This deluding preference vanishes; I learn to honour men, and I should regard myself as more useless than the common labourer if I did not believe that this study, the establishing of the rights of mankind, can bestow a value on all others.'

other than between some men and some beasts. It is not, therefore, so much the understanding that constitutes the specific difference between the man and the brute, as the human quality of free agency. Nature lays her command on every animal, and the brute obeys her voice. Man receives the same impulsion, but at the same time knows himself at liberty to acquiesce or resist: and it is particularly in his consciousness of this liberty that the spirituality of his soul is displayed. For physics may explain, in some measure, the mechanism of the senses and the formation of ideas; but in the power of willing or rather of choosing, and in the feeling of this power, nothing is to be found but acts which are purely spiritual and wholly inexplicable by the laws of mechanism (*Discourse on the origin of Inequality*, Everyman edn., p. 170).

Now there is much in this doctrine that Kant simply adopted for himself; but, unlike Rousseau, he adopted it as a starting-point for philosophical investigation and analysis, rather than as an ultimate and inexplicable fact. Kant insists as strongly as Rousseau that it is man's freedom, not his intellect, that distinguishes him from the rest of creation. Indeed, as he tries to show in the *Critique of Judgement*, it is because of this freedom, this ability to conceive purposes for himself and to act in accordance with them, that man must be regarded as the final purpose of creation. But Kant, unlike Rousseau in the passage I have just quoted,[1] does not contrast man's freedom with his rationality; on the contrary, he holds that man is free by virtue of his rationality. 'Everything in nature works in accordance with laws. Only a rational being has the power to act *in accordance with his idea* of laws—that is, in accordance with principles—and only so has he a *will*' (G A36). But man does not owe his freedom to his intellectual powers, i.e. to his ability to form concepts and make inferences; it is in those aspects of rationality which go beyond mere passive intellectual ability and speculation that the source of man's freedom, and hence of his status as a moral agent, is to be found.[2]

[1] Elsewhere Rousseau does anticipate Kant in giving a wider meaning to the concept of rationality; but it is difficult, if not impossible, to make a consistent theory out of his various comments on the subject of 'entendement' and 'raison'. For discussions of this problem see the important works of E. Cassirer (*The Question of Jean-Jacques Rousseau*, translated by P. Gay (New York, 1954)) and R. Derathé (*Le rationalisme de J-J. Rousseau* (Paris, 1948)).

[2] Cp. KRV, B167 n. 'The use of reason is not always directed to the determination of the object, that is, to knowledge, but also to the determination of the subject and of its volition.'

Man is not, of course, a purely rational being; he has impulses and desires which often seduce him from the path which reason traces for him. But he can act rationally if he chooses; and in so doing, and only in so doing, he lives up to his high status.

Kant saw clearly, what Rousseau had dimly grasped, that if the rationality of human conduct were to be set up as an ideal, the word 'reason' would have to be given a wider meaning than it had had in the narrowly intellectualistic theories of his predecessors; and our examination of his views must be directed primarily towards his attempt to provide this wider meaning. Two distinctions are especially important, that between Vernunft (reason) and Verstand (understanding), and that between speculative and practical reason.

(i) *Reason and Understanding.* Kant uses the word 'Vernunft' (and his expositors have to use the word 'reason') in two senses, a wide and a narrow. In the wider sense it covers the whole field of the *a priori*, including the understanding and, sometimes, the *a priori* elements in sensibility. It stands, that is to say, for the source of all that is non-empirical in our knowledge or in our thought. An example of this sense occurs in a well-known passage in the second Critique, where Kant is speaking of the attempt to prove that there can be no such thing as *a priori* knowledge: 'It would be like proving by reason that there is no such thing as reason; for we only say that we know something through reason when we know that we could have known it even if it had not actually come within our experience. Thus knowledge through reason and *a priori* knowledge are the same thing' (KPV, A23–4, Ak 12). But it is the narrower sense of the word 'reason', in which it is distinguished from understanding, that is especially characteristic of Kant's philosophy. Hume, following Hobbes, regarded reason as the making of, or the faculty of making, inferences. Kant distinguishes two types of inference, immediate inference, which is the business of the understanding, and mediate inference, which is the business of reason in the narrow sense of the word. (From 'All men are mortal' we can immediately infer 'Some men are mortal'; but from 'All men are mortal' we can infer 'All learned beings are mortal' only through the mediation of a third proposition 'All learned beings are men'.) But reason, in the narrow sense, has also what Kant calls a 'pure employment' in addition to this 'logical employment', that is to say the function of originating certain concepts and principles, viz. the transcendental ideas. 'Reason, like understanding, can be employed in a merely formal, that is, logical manner, wherein it abstracts from all content of knowledge. But it is also capable of a real use, since it contains within itself the source of certain concepts and principles, which it does not borrow either from the senses or from the understanding' (KRV, A299, B355). Kant later expresses this more accurately when he points out that reason does not strictly generate any concept, since its ideas are nothing but concepts of the understanding extended beyond their usual limitations. 'Reason does not really generate any concept. The most it can do is to *free* a concept of *understanding* from the unavoidable limitations of possible experience, and so to endeavour to extend it beyond the limits of the empirical, though still, indeed, in terms of its relation to the empirical' (KRV, A409, B435). The idea of God as First Cause, for example, is simply the category of cause extended beyond the limits of all experience.

In Kant's view, reason shares with the understanding a connection with the notions of universality and necessity; its distinction from the understanding is based ultimately on the fact that it is concerned always with that which is unconditioned, whereas the working of the understanding is confined to the field of the conditioned. These somewhat obscure statements require a certain amount of elucidation.

A strictly universal judgement, according to Kant, is not derivable from experience, which can tell us only that, so far as our observation has extended, we have come across no exception to this or that particular rule; it cannot assure us that no such exception exists. Thus, all universal judgements must be *a priori*, and have their origin in reason or understanding. The proposition 'Every event has a cause' must be derived from the understanding, if the word 'every' is to be taken as implying strict universality. It is, in fact, a rule which the understanding supplies for the organisation or interpretation of sense-experience, and cannot, as Hume thought, be itself derived from sense-experience alone.[1] Reason, in its turn, is the source of the universal principles according to which the understanding works; it is because of this that it can be called the highest of the faculties of the mind.

[1] I do not wish to commit myself to agreeing with this Kantian interpretation of Hume.

Judgements which are necessarily, as opposed to contingently, true are all, in Kant's view, *a priori*; for experience can tell us only that something is the case, never that it must be the case. Causal laws, for instance, are not just empirical generalisations, stating that something often happens, or that it has always happened in the past and will probably happen in the future; they state that, under certain conditions, something necessarily happens. 'Appearances do indeed present cases from which a rule can be obtained according to which something usually happens, but they never prove the sequence to be *necessary*. To the synthesis of cause and effect there belongs a dignity which cannot be empirically expressed, namely, that the effect not only succeeds upon the cause, but that it is posited *through* it and arises *out of* it' (KRV, A91, B124).

Now if we take any empirical judgement, or any *a priori* judgement of the understanding, we shall find that it is true only subject to certain conditions, and in particular, to the condition that it is about, or relevant to, some possible experience. Reason, as opposed to the understanding, seeks to penetrate beyond these conditioned, hypothetical truths to the unconditioned, categorical truth on which they depend. 'What necessarily forces us to transcend the limits of experience and of all appearances is the *unconditioned*, which reason, by necessity and by right, demands in things in themselves, as required to complete the series of conditions' (KRV, B, xx). In short, what Kant says about the logical employment of reason is true of reason in general, namely that its principle is 'to find for the conditioned knowledge obtained through the understanding the unconditioned whereby its unity is brought to completion' (KRV, A307, B364).

There is one further characteristic of reason on which Kant lays considerable stress, namely the fact that it is, or tries to be, systematic. It is not content to establish the truth, even the necessary truth, of a number of independent and unrelated principles, but seeks always to combine the truths it has established into a systematic unity. 'Human reason is by nature architectonic. That is to say, it regards all our knowledge as belonging to a possible system, and therefore allows only such principles as do not at any rate make it impossible for any knowledge that we may attain to combine into a system with other knowledge' (KRV, A474, B502). It is the task of reason to arrange the phenomena of human experience and the workings of the human mind (including, of course, the activities of reason itself) into a coherent and systematic whole. And if the whole of our experience is to be susceptible of such an arrangement it must in every one of its aspects contain some element of order and intelligibility. Sense-experience itself contains *a priori* elements, and would be nothing but a meaningless chaos if it did not: and our moral experience, Kant would conclude, could not be rendered systematically intelligible if, as some appear to have thought, it consisted simply of brute feeling uninformed by any rational element.

(ii) *Speculative and practical reason*. Reason works according to these principles, in Kant's view, in the field of practice as well as in that of speculation; in fact, the practical employment of reason[1] has advantages not possessed by the speculative. Kant thought that the speculative employment of human reason, with its attempts to go beyond the limits of any possible experience, was bound to give rise to error and illusion, whereas its practical employment was fruitful in the highest degree. As long as we confine ourselves to metaphysical speculation on such transcendent topics as God, freedom, and immortality, we shall be involved in sophistry and error; but the fact that we can implement, as well as contemplating and determining, our ideas has important implications even in these fields. A theoretical proof of God's existence and of a future life is impossible, but a practical 'proof' is not.

In Kant's account of moral experience and its presuppositions we can distinguish three main types or levels of moral proposition. There is the singular judgement which refers to one particular action[2] exemplifying duty or its neglect (e.g. 'You ought not to

---

[1] The convenience of the terms 'practical reason' and 'speculative reason' should not blind us to the fact that, for Kant, they are not the names of two separate faculties, but of two ways in which the single faculty of reason works. 'If pure reason of itself can be and really is practical, as the consciousness of the moral law shows it to be, it is only one and the same reason which judges *a priori* by principles, whether for theoretical or for practical purposes' (KPV, A218, Ak 121). It is because of this that we can usefully preface our examination of Kant's specifically moral philosophy with a discussion of the activity and function of reason in general.

[2] It is important to realise that, when Kant talks about the morality of actions, he is usually thinking not, in the manner of many more recent

have taken that money'); there is the general moral rule, binding on all men who find themselves in the circumstances to which it refers, but still dependent to some extent on empirical facts (e.g. 'Telling lies is morally wrong'—a rule which, though not itself derived from sense-experience, nevertheless presupposes the existence of a state of affairs in which communication is possible); and finally, there is the moral principle, determined wholly *a priori* and applying to all rational beings simply in virtue of their rationality (e.g. 'Act as if the maxim of your action were to become through your will a universal law of nature'). Since morality is discovered or established through reason, it should be possible to show how all true singular moral judgements are derivable from moral rules, and these in their turn derivable from the fundamental principle or principles of morality.[1]

We shall be concerned mainly with what Kant has to say about the fundamental principle of morality and the way in which it can be established, and to a somewhat lesser extent with the derivation of moral rules and judgements from this principle. In view, however, of the objection that is commonly made to Kant's ethics on the grounds of their abstractness and remoteness from human affairs, it may be worth pointing out that making the correct moral decision, or making a true singular moral judgement, is not, for him, simply a matter of making rational inferences from rational first principles, but involves also the vitally important exercise of judgement as to the particular circumstances of each case. This judgement is required in the application of any rules, whether theoretical or practical, and the power of judging correctly, in this special sense of 'judging', cannot itself be learnt by rule, although it can be improved by experience and the judicious use of examples.

[1] In fact, Kant thinks, there is only one such principle, though it may be formulated in various ways.

---

philosophers, of actions in abstraction from their motives or maxims, but of the whole which consists in the action-performed-from-this-motive, or action-on-this-maxim. When he argues that failure to develop a talent through self-indulgence is wrong he is not arguing or implying that failure to develop a talent is always wrong, no matter what the reason for the failure: a man with a talent for music may well be justified in neglecting it if he does so because he sees that its development would interfere with his activities as, say, a doctor or a priest.

> If understanding in general is to be viewed as the faculty of rules, judgement will be the faculty of subsuming under rules; that is, of distinguishing whether something does or does not stand under a given rule ... Judgement is a particular talent which can be practised only, and cannot be taught. It is the specific quality of so-called mother-wit; and its lack no school can make good. For although an abundance of rules borrowed from the insight of others may indeed be proffered to, and as it were, grafted upon, a limited understanding, the power of rightly employing them must belong to the learner himself; and in the absence of such a natural gift no rule that may be prescribed to him for this purpose can ensure against misuse (KRV, A132–3, B171–2).

Kant adds in a footnote that deficiency in this power of judgement is just what is ordinarily called stupidity (Dummheit). In other words intelligence (or rationality in a wide sense) and its opposite are manifested not only in the discovery of universal principles but also in their application to concrete cases. Accordingly, the decision whether a particular action ought or ought not to be performed by me here and now requires the exercise of judgement as well as of the power of abstract reasoning. The moral rules which are given *a priori* to a man as a rational being require, Kant says, 'a power of judgement sharpened by experience, partly in order to distinguish the cases to which they apply, partly to procure for them admittance to the will of man in influence over practice; for man, affected as he is by so many inclinations, is capable of the Idea of a pure practical reason, but he has not so easily the power to realise the Idea *in concreto* in his conduct of life' (G, A vii).

The fundamental principle of morality must, because of its connection with reason, be a necessary principle, a universal principle, and an unconditioned principle; and one of Kant's problems in the *Grundlegung* and the *Critique of Practical Reason* is to see whether the content of this principle can be discovered simply by reference to these purely formal aspects of it. We saw earlier that in the theoretical sphere universality and necessity might belong to the deliverances of the understanding, as well as to those of reason; and a similar situation exists as far as action is concerned. Not all necessary or universal propositions about actions are moral propositions; for a proposition to be a moral proposition, its necessity or universality must be an unconditioned necessity or universality, or, as Kant also puts it, the imperative of morality is categorical, not hypothetical.

How, Kant asks, is the consciousness of the moral law possible? His answer is this: 'We can come to know pure practical laws in the same way we know pure theoretical principles, by attending to the necessity with which reason prescribes them to us and to the elimination from them of all empirical conditions, which reason directs' (KPV, A53, Ak30). Moral rules are necessary rules, in the sense that no conceivable change of circumstances, no alteration in the nature of man or of the universe, could make them different from what they are. Of course, all rules, with the exception of permissive rules, might be said to involve necessity of a sort, since they provide that certain people must act in certain ways, and the word 'must' could be taken as expressing necessity; but this is not what Kant has in mind. The rules of a club may provide that its members must pay their subscriptions before March 31st, but this is a contingent, as opposed to a necessary, rule because, although the rule does actually exist, it might not have existed; a club perhaps has to have some rules, but it need not have precisely the rules it has. The moral law, on the other hand, in the sense of the sum total of moral rules, is a necessary law because it simply could not be, or have been, other than what it is. Bishop Butler said in the preface to his *Sermons* that moral principles may be derived in either of two ways, from propositions about 'the nature and reason of things', or from propositions about the nature of man. Kant insists, in effect, that both these methods are inadequate, and that no propositions about the nature of anything can give rise to that necessity which belongs to moral rules.

> Everyone must admit that a law has to carry with it absolute necessity if it is to be morally valid—valid, that is, as a ground of obligation; that the command 'Thou shalt not lie' could not hold merely for men, other rational beings having no obligation to abide by it—and similarly with all other genuine moral laws; that here consequently the ground of obligation must be looked for, not in the nature of man nor in the circumstances of the world in which he is placed, but solely *a priori* in the concepts of pure reason; and that every other precept based on principles of mere experience ... can indeed be called a practical rule, but never a moral law (G, A vi).

For much the same reason, we cannot obtain our knowledge of moral laws from the notion of the will of a supreme being; from the merely contingent will of God, it is impossible to derive necessary laws of morality.

> For it is these very laws that have led us, in virtue of their *inner* practical necessity, to the postulate of a self-sufficient cause, or of a wise Ruler of the world, in order that through such agency effect may be given to them. We may not, therefore, in reversal of such procedure, regard them as accidental and as derived from the mere will of the ruler, especially as we have no conception of such a will, except as formed in accordance with these laws (KRV, A818–9, B846–7).

For perfectly rational beings, the necessity of the moral law is both objective and subjective; i.e. they necessarily fulfil what it necessarily ordains. For human beings, however, the law is not subjectively necessary; i.e. it is possible for us to disobey it. Because of the limitations of human nature, the objective necessity (Notwendigkeit) of the law appears to us as necessitation (Nötigung), the necessitation to place our inclinations under the control of reason.

That a rule should exhibit necessity in this way, however, is by no means a sufficient, even though it is a necessary, condition of its being a moral rule; there are other types of rule or precept besides moral ones which are necessary, as opposed to contingent, rules. The distinguishing feature of moral rules is that their necessity is unconditioned and absolute, not merely conditioned and relative. It is a necessary rule that if a doctor wishes to cure a patient who is suffering from pneumonia he must make him rest, and it is a necessary rule that a man who wants to lead a happy life must keep himself as physically and mentally fit as he can—these rules, unlike the rules of a club, cannot be changed at will. Their necessity, however, is not absolute, but relative to a certain end which may be (or, in the case of happiness, which is) desired. But the rule that we must not tell lies is subject to no such limitation; it is binding on us, no matter what we may happen to desire. Kant suggests that a terminological distinction might appropriately be made between rules of skill, counsels of prudence, and laws (or commands) of morality.

> For only *law* carries with it the concept of an *unconditioned*, and yet objective and so universally valid, *necessity*; and commands are

laws which must be obeyed—that is, must be followed even against inclination. *Counsel* does indeed involve necessity, but necessity valid only under a subjective and contingent condition—namely, if this or that man counts this or that as belonging to his happiness. As against this, a categorical imperative is limited by no condition and can quite precisely be called a command, as being absolutely, although practically, necessary (G, A43–4).

A hypothetical imperative, that is to say, expresses a relative or conditioned necessity: if you want X, you must do A, or, since you want to be happy, you must do B. A categorical imperative, or an imperative of duty, alone expresses a necessity which is subject to no condition at all—whatever you may or may not want, you must do C.

It is man's possession of a reason which can be practical that enables him to formulate laws having this absolute necessity; and, as Kant maintains in the *Critique of Judgement*, it is this ability to legislate unconditionally that gives man his unique status in the universe. 'Only in man, and only in him as subject of morality, do we meet with unconditioned legislation in respect of purposes, which therefore alone renders him capable of being a final purpose, to which the whole of nature is teleologically subordinated' (KU, A394, Ak435–6). Man's happiness, on the other hand, is only a conditioned happiness; i.e. a rational man can desire happiness only subject to the condition that it is attained by methods which are in accordance with the laws of morality (whereas the rational man does not seek to do what is morally right only on condition that it will bring him happiness).

We must now turn our attention to the way in which Kant links the notion of universality with the moral law. All deliberate action, he thinks, is action in accordance with a maxim, or subjective principle. This does not imply that the maxim of every action is necessarily before the agent's mind as he performs it, but only that the maxim can be extracted, as it were, from the action and used as some kind of explanation of it. If I, on one particular occasion, stop and buy a flag from someone who is collecting for charity, my maxim may be 'Whenever there are officially organised charity collections in my neighbourhood, I will contribute to them'. I do not necessarily say this to myself before buying the flag; but if I ask myself, or am asked, for an explanation of my action, a reference to some such maxim as this is one kind of explanation that might be given. There is a degree of universality about this and about every maxim, their expression requiring the use of some such word as 'whenever' or 'all', and consequently a certain measure of system and rule is involved. Because of this it may be said that every deliberate action is up to a point an example of rational behaviour (as opposed to behaviour on instinct or impulse, like that of a woman who buys a hat which she sees in a shop window, on a sudden whim, just because she likes the look of it. She is not acting on the principle of buying every hat she likes the look of, for she is not acting on a principle at all.)

But mere acting on principle, though expressing a higher level of rationality than the inability or unwillingness to act on any principle, is not by itself enough to satisfy moral requirements. 'Those men who act according to principles are very few in number. This is an exceedingly good thing, for it can so easily happen that people's principles are mistaken; and when this occurs, the damage that arises therefrom increases in extent in proportion to the generality of the principle and the steadfastness of the person who has adopted it.'[1] We need, then, a way of distinguishing morally legitimate or binding maxims from illegitimate ones; and Kant tries to meet this need with his conception of the universality of the moral law. Morally legitimate maxims—i.e. those which can be adopted consistently with one's duty—must be capable of functioning, not merely as general rules, but as absolutely universal laws. This distinction is not merely a matter of extending the application of a maxim from one particular agent to all those agents who are members of a certain class; just as we had to distinguish unconditioned from conditioned necessity, so we must now distinguish absolute or unconditioned universality from a generality or universality that is merely relative and conditioned. An example of conditioned universality would be 'All soldiers must obey orders'; and of unconditioned 'All rational beings must treat themselves, and all other such beings, as ends in themselves'.[2] We have in fact four

---

[1] *Observations on the feeling of the beautiful and the sublime*, Academy edn., II, 227. This is a comparatively early work, and later in his life Kant would not perhaps have expressed such gratification at the scarcity of men of principle; but the distinction between good and bad principles is one from which he never departed.

[2] It might be objected that both these rules are conditioned, the first being rendered 'If x is a soldier he must...', and the second 'If x is a rational

stages of generality or universality: (i) that of the maxim of an action which, although it is particular inasmuch as it is the action of a particular man performed at a particular time, has nevertheless a general or universal reference, inasmuch as it commits the agent to similar action whenever similar circumstances recur; (ii) the generalisation of such a maxim to apply, not merely to one particular agent in a particular situation or type of situation, but to all agents of a certain class in situations of a similar type; (iii) the universality of a maxim which is taken as applying to all agents whatsoever in situations of a similar type;[1] and (iv) the ultimate, absolute universality of a principle that applies to all agents whatsoever in any situation whatsoever. The only such principle, in Kant's view, is, of course, the categorical imperative, which in its simplest and most abstract form says 'Act only on that maxim through which you can at the same time will that it should become a universal law' (G, A52); and this amounts to the requirement that all maxims in stage (i) should be in some sense capable of extension to the further stages without contradiction.

But Kant does not merely claim that the ability of my maxim to function as a universal law is a necessary condition of the moral legitimacy of any action or volition based on that maxim; he also asserts that, from this purely formal claim, we can derive specific moral rules and judgements which are not themselves purely formal. (This is why, of the various distinguishing characteristics of rationality, universality is perhaps the one which provides the best entry to a study of the details of Kant's moral philosophy.) 'A rational being either cannot think of his subjectively practical

---

[1] Kant does not always distinguish between (ii) and (iii) as carefully as he might. The importance of the distinction lies in the fact that some duties depend on a man's special status or position, whereas others are binding quite irrespective of any such considerations. A civilian generally may, whereas a private soldier may not, refuse to obey an order given to him by an army officer; here the difference in status leads to a difference in duties. But the prohibition of lying and the duty to respect the personality of others apply to all beings to whom any sort of moral prohibition or duty can apply—i.e. to all rational beings.

---

being he must . . .'. The objection, however, fails to take account of the fact that, for Kant, the class of rational beings is necessarily coextensive with the class of beings about whom moral judgements can be made—if 'x' is not the name of a rational being, then no such word as 'must', in this sense, can be applied.

principles (maxims) as universal laws, or he must suppose that their mere form, through which they are fitted for being *universal* laws, is alone that which makes them a practical law' (KPV, A49, Ak27). If a practical law were such in virtue of its content, this would imply that the will was subject to some condition, whereas in Kant's view moral willing, if there is such a thing, must be completely unconditioned. Most theories which involve what Kant calls heteronomy of the will place the ground of morality in some empirical concept, such as happiness; and to this Kant objects on the ground that moral principles must be *a priori* and necessary, not empirical and contingent.

> The principle of happiness can indeed give maxims, but never maxims which are competent to be laws of the will, even if universal happiness were made the object. For, since the knowledge of this rests on mere data of experience, as each judgement concerning it depends very much on the very changeable opinion of each person, it can give general but never universal rules; that is, the rules it gives will on the average be most often the right ones for this purpose, but they will not be rules which must hold always and necessarily. Consequently, no practical laws can be based on this principle (KPV, A63, Ak36).

But even an *a priori* theory of morality can commit the same error. Suppose that we have a correct, *a priori*, definition of the *summum bonum*; we must not make the mistake of treating this as the fundamental principle of our moral system, but must realise that any such concept owes what validity it has to its agreement with, and dependence on, the universal moral law.

> The moral law is the sole determining ground of the pure will. Since it is merely formal, requiring only that the form of the maxim be universally legislative, as a determining ground it abstracts from all material and thus from every object of volition. Consequently, though the highest good may be the entire *object* of a pure practical reason, i.e., of a pure will, it is still not to be taken as the *determining ground* of the pure will; the moral law alone must be seen as the ground for making the highest good and its realization or promotion the object of the pure will (KPV, A196, Ak109).

Some maxims, in Kant's view, are illegitimate because they cannot function as universal laws; others are illegitimate because, although they could function in this way, they cannot be willed so to function.[1] Since all illegitimate maxims fall into one or other of these classes, it should be possible to discover some concrete moral rules, not by strict logical deduction from the principle of universality, but by using the principle to assess the validity of any action or maxim of whose moral status we may be in doubt. Kant adds a further refinement: since, as far as human beings at least are concerned, all actions take place in, and have effects in, nature, the criterion of universality is easier to apply if we consider the fitness or unfitness of a maxim to function as a universal law of nature, that is to say, if we consider what it would be like for there to be a natural law to the effect that everyone always and inevitably acted in accordance with that maxim.

Making a promise which one does not intend to keep, for the purpose of obtaining a loan, is morally wrong because the maxim of such an action cannot be expressed in a universal form without contradiction. The maxim would be 'Whenever I believe myself short of money, I will borrow money and promise to pay it back, though I know that this will never be done' (G, A54). If it is to be one of which the critical judgement of reason can approve it must be capable of universal application to all rational beings, and thus to all human beings in virtue of their rationality. But the maxim in question will, if universalised, inevitably contradict itself; 'for the universality of a law that everyone believing himself to be in need can[2] make any promise he pleases with the intention not to keep it would make promising, and the very purpose of promising, itself impossible, since no one would believe he was being promised anything, but would laugh at utterances of this kind as empty shams' (G, A55). Kant is not, of course, saying here, as some of his critics have maintained, that if I continually make false

---

[1] The former give rise to duties of perfect obligation, the latter to duties of imperfect obligation. This distinction, to which Kant devotes a good deal of attention in the *Grundlegung*, is made much less of in the *Critique of Practical Reason*. In the latter work Kant tends to treat maxims which cannot be conceived as universal laws as forming merely a sub-class of those which cannot be willed as universal laws—naturally enough, since if we cannot conceive a particular end or purpose, it is logically impossible for us to will it.

[2] The notion of a universal law of nature to the effect that everyone *can* act in a certain way is strange, since it is difficult to see where the universality, in Kant's absolute sense of the term, comes in; one would expect a reference to a law of nature according to which everyone invariably does act in a certain way.

promises, sooner or later people will refuse to believe me (this would not be a moral consideration at all, but a prudential one, and Kant is the last philosopher to try to reduce morality to a matter of prudence). Nor does he mean that, if this maxim were universally adopted, a causal consequence would be that the practice of promise-making (or at least of promise-making in connection with loans) would die out because it would soon become pointless. The time-lag ensures that there is no contradiction here; similarly, the universal adoption by rich people of the practice of giving generously to the poor is not rendered self-contradictory by the fact that it would eventually lead to a state of affairs in which no one was poor any longer. Kant is, clearly enough, finding some difficulty in the very concept of a state of affairs in which it is possible for everyone to act on the maxim; he is not objecting merely that the state of affairs could not last for long. The exact nature of this difficulty, however, is not so clear. Some commentators, noticing such phrases as 'would make promising, *and the very purpose of promising*, itself impossible' (G, A55, my italics), have suggested that, when Kant speaks of the universalised form of a maxim contradicting itself, what he really means is that action on such a maxim would be self-defeating. For example, it might be said, the whole purpose of making a false promise is to gain some advantage; but if the maxim became a universal law no one would believe the promise, and so no advantage would be gained by making it. Now there is no doubt that this is part of what Kant means; but there is more to his thought than this notion of self-defeat. (If there were not, his continual use in these discussions of such formal expressions as 'sich widersprechen' would be extraordinarily careless, even by Kant's own rather careless standards of writing. Moreover, there are an immense number of maxims which would be self-defeating if they were universally adopted and which are obviously not morally wrong. The maxim 'Whenever I want an hour's relaxation, I will visit the National Gallery' would be self-defeating if adopted by all Londoners, and still more so if adopted by all rational beings; but this does not make it wrong for me to act on it. In cases of this kind I am clearly entitled to assume that the maxim in question will not in fact be universally adopted.) Kant, I suggest, does believe that the universalisation of morally wrong maxims involves a contradiction, in a strict sense of that word. The universalisation of the false promise maxim would entail, according to Kant, that there would be no such things as promises, or at least no such things as believed promises.[1] But it is a requirement of the original maxim (and *a fortiori* of its universalised form) that there are such things as believed promises; for (and this is where the reference to purpose comes in) the whole point of making the false promise was to acquire some money, and this end could be achieved only if the promise was believed. The universalised form of the maxim is self-contradictory, therefore, because there is a direct contradiction between the propositions 'There are no such things as believed promises' and 'There are some believed promises'.

There are two comments to be made on this argument: first, it applies, if at all, to a very limited class of examples. Suppose that I have promised to visit a sick friend in hospital, but when the time comes there is an interesting programme on the wireless, and I ask myself whether I need go. My maxim might be 'Whenever I can obtain more enjoyment or amusement from breaking a promise than from keeping it, I will break it'. When this maxim is considered as a possible universal law of nature there is no question of any purpose of mine being thereby defeated, and therefore no formal contradiction. For, although we might for the sake of argument concede that the universalisation of the law would entail the non-existence of promises, the existence of promises is not required by the original maxim in the same way as it is in Kant's own example. It is, of course, presupposed in a purely logical sense, since I could not be in a position to break a promise unless there were such things as promises; but it is not a necessary condition of the attainment of my objective as it was in the earlier case. There, as Kant himself explains, the success of my making a false promise depends on the fact that most other people will not make false promises, for I require the existence of at least one believed promise in order to achieve my financial objective; in our present example, however, there is no such requirement, since my purpose could perfectly well be achieved even if there were no such things as promises. In short, not all promises are made from a self-centred motive; and, in most cases,

[1] Not all promises are believed by the person to whom they are made, but the promise in the example under discussion obviously has to be thought of as believed.

if not in all, the motive from which I made a promise is irrelevant to the question how stringent is my obligation to keep it. Kant's argument, on the other hand, relies in part on the claim that my purpose, as stated in the maxim, could not be achieved if the maxim became a universal law of nature.

The second comment I wish to make is this. It is possible to think of examples which present a formal similarity to that discussed by Kant, but in which it would be generally agreed that a different view had to be taken on the question whether or not it is our duty to act in a certain way. And, of course, if the formal resemblance is exact, and not merely close, there could, for Kant, be no moral difference, since he insists that our maxims must be good or bad solely in virtue of their form.[1] The closest analogy is that between promises and threats. Suppose that I wish to rob a bank, and that the method I propose to adopt involves my threatening to shoot the cashier if he does not hand me some money; and suppose also that I am too considerate or too timid to consider killing him, and that I therefore decide to enter the bank with an unloaded weapon. The maxim of my action might be 'Whenever I think that I can gain some financial advantage by threatening someone, even though I have not the slightest intention of fulfilling the threat, I will do so'. And, Kant would have to say, the attempt to conceive this as a universal law of nature would lead to contradiction, for if it were a universal law 'it would make threatening, and the very purpose of threatening, impossible, since no one would believe he was being threatened, but would laugh at utterances of this kind as empty shams' (cp. G, A55), whereas the maxim also obviously requires there to be at least one threat that is believed. But something has clearly gone wrong here. For although it is, of course, wrong to rob a bank by any method, it can hardly be claimed that the offence is made worse if it is accompanied by a threat which the agent does not intend to fulfil—indeed, in this particular case, the offence would surely be worse if the agent did intend to fulfil the threat.

Perhaps Kant might say of this example that, since it was wrong to make the threat in the first place, as it was made for a criminal

---

[1] Cp. KPV, A58, Ak33: 'The sole principle of morality consists in independence from all material of the law (i.e., a desired object) and in the accompanying determination of choice by the mere form of giving universal law which a maxim must be capable of having.'

purpose, no question of being obliged to fulfil it could arise, and consequently the question whether the agent intended to fulfil it is morally irrelevant. Even this defence is not altogether convincing; for if I had made a promise, not a threat, as part of my criminal enterprise it might be my duty to keep it, and my offence might be made morally worse by the fact that I did not intend to keep the promise. For a promise is not necessarily void because it ought not to have been made; a bigamist, for example, who promises at the marriage service to look after his 'wife' has some moral obligation to her in virtue of the promise, even though the marriage itself is null and void from the start. But, in any case, it is easy to think of examples of threats which are morally legitimate, but which nevertheless give rise to a similar difficulty. Suppose I discover my office-boy in the act of committing a petty theft, and say to him, 'If I catch you stealing again, I shall report you to the police', but that I intend to give him still one more chance, since I am a kind-hearted person, though hoping that the threat, which I do not intend to carry out, will deter him from further offences. It cannot, I think, be seriously maintained that my action is wrong, just because I have made a threat that I do not intend to carry out. (It might, of course, be held that I acted wrongly, in that I ought to have reported him without giving him another chance; but then the fact that I made a threat which I did not intend to fulfil is not held to be the ground of the wrongness of the act.) Equally, if I make the same threat with the intention of keeping it, but when the boy commits a second offence I relent and decide to give him one more chance, it cannot be said that what I have done is wrong just because I have failed to fulfil a threat—forgiveness is doubtless contrary to the canons of strict justice, which require that a man should receive his deserts, good or bad, but it cannot always be morally wrong. Yet there is no purely formal difference between making a promise, in itself legitimate, which one does not intend to keep and making a threat, in itself legitimate, which one does not intend to fulfil, nor between breaking a legitimately made promise and failing to fulfil a legitimately made threat. If we apply Kant's formal principle or test of universalisation to threats we get the same results as when it is applied to promises; yet people's ordinary moral judgements about threats differ in important respects from their judgements about promises. Hence, either people's ordinary moral judgements on such matters are wrong (and the error would be a considerable one) or Kant's claim that the principle of duty is 'Act as if the maxim of your action were to become through your will a universal law of nature' is, in his own interpretation of it, at least, invalid.

We must now consider what Kant has to say about duties of imperfect obligation. If the maxim of an action of mine is a morally legitimate one it must be legitimate for everyone in a similar situation to mine to act on it. But if I believe that it is legitimate for everyone in a certain type-situation to act on a certain maxim I am committed, in Kant's view, to a willing acceptance of life in a world in which everyone in similar situations inevitably did act on that maxim or, at least, in a world in which it was possible that everyone in such situations should act on it. If it can be shown that the world I am committed to accepting could not conceivably exist, my maxim, and consequently any action based on it, is in Kant's view clearly shown to be contrary to reason, and therefore wrong. (This is part of what he means in the passages we have just been discussing.) But there are many maxims which are wrong, in spite of the fact that the world to which they commit the agent could conceivably exist; in these cases, Kant argues in effect, the world, or 'nature' is one which he could not will to exist. This notion of a maxim which could, perhaps, exist as a universal law of nature without contradiction, but which could not be willed by the agent as a universal law without contradiction, is at first sight obscure, and needs elucidation. Kant himself provides us with some help in a passage in the *Critique of Practical Reason* (KPV, A122–3, Ak69):

> The rule of judgement under laws of pure practical reason is: Ask yourself whether, if the action which you propose should take place by a law of the nature of which you yourself were a part, you could regard it as possible through your will. Everyone does, in fact, decide by this rule whether actions are morally good or bad. Thus people ask: If one belonged to such an order of things that anyone would allow himself to deceive when he thought it to his advantage, or felt justified in shortening his life as soon as he was thoroughly weary of it, or looked with complete indifference on the needs of others,[1] would he assent of his own free will to being a member of such an order of things?

[1] Strictly speaking, mention of the first two of these three examples is out of place in this context. For Kant has argued in the *Grundlegung* that

However, the notion of 'assenting of one's own free will' to being a member of such an order is itself not altogether clear; and it will be best to examine one of Kant's own examples to see what light it may throw on the problem.

The example is of a prosperous man who sees others struggling with hardships which he could, if he wished, help to make less burdensome, but who refuses his aid because he cannot see what business it is of his. A system of nature in accordance with a maxim of neither helping others nor expecting help from them could indeed exist, Kant thinks:

> But although it is possible that a universal law of nature could subsist in harmony with this maxim, yet it is impossible to *will* that such a principle should hold everywhere as a law of nature. For a will which decided in this way would be at variance with itself, since many a situation might arise in which the man needed love and sympathy from others, and in which, by such a law of nature sprung from his own will, he would rob himself of all hope of the help he wants for himself (G, A56).

Using Kant's own interpretation of the expression 'willing that such a principle should hold as a law of nature', we can explain this as meaning that no one who found himself a member of an order of nature in which nobody either received or demanded help from others could of his own free will remain a member of it; for he would be freely depriving himself of all help from others, and this is something he cannot do. It is important to realise that this is in no sense a prudential argument: Kant is not saying that it is imprudent to refuse to help others because, if you do, they will probably refuse to help you when you are in need. Nor, when Kant refers to the impossibility of a man who finds himself in such a world remaining in it of his own free will, is he thinking of a psychological impossibility. A foolish man, for example, who did not reflect sufficiently about the nature of the world he was in, might well be able to bring himself to remain in it voluntarily. Kant's point is that it would be impossible for a rational will to decide to remain—the rational will being, for him,

---

the very notion of such an order of things is self-contradictory and inconceivable; and if one cannot conceive the possibility of such an order of things it is impossible to ask oneself whether one would willingly remain a member of it, and *a fortiori* impossible to decide that one could.

the only free will. In other words, it is contrary to reason to refuse to help others and yet at the same time to expect to receive help from others, since this combination of attitudes is not expressible in universal form, when the distinction of person disappears. The wrongness of refusing to help others depends on the irrationality that is involved in willing a universal extension of such refusal. As far as mere consistency goes, we can will either that we should help others and that others should help us or that no one should help anyone else; and if a man could do without the help of others this latter rule might be quite legitimately adopted. In point of fact, however, Kant seems to think that no man can do without help from others at some time in his life[1] (or at least that man cannot avoid wanting others to help him). It follows that he cannot reasonably refrain from helping others, and therefore that he cannot do so legitimately as far as the moral law is concerned.

How would Kant reply to someone who claimed that, in spite of these arguments, he would be able of his own free will to remain a member of a world in which no one helped anyone else? So long as the man was consistent and agreed that no one should help him why could he not will the relevant maxim to be a universal law? The obvious answer would seem to be that, whatever a man may verbally agree to, he cannot in fact do without some sort of help from others; his agreeing to remain is therefore irrational, not, on this occasion, because it involves him in inconsistency, but because it can have occurred only as a result of his ignorance or misunderstanding of his own nature. But to use the fact, if it is a fact,[2] that men cannot do without the help of others as part of the ground of a moral judgement seems to be contrary to Kant's insistence that moral philosophy must be based entirely on that part of it which is *a priori* (G, A vii) and that it must not be derived in any way from our knowledge of human nature; we cannot be sure that the impossibility of doing without the help of

---

[1] Kant's apparent contradiction of this in the footnote on p. 68 of the *Grundlegung* is, I think, only a verbal one ('Many a man would readily agree that others should not help him if only he could be dispensed from offering help to them'); Kant is thinking there of particular occasions, not of a man's life as a whole.

[2] There might conceivably be a community so organised that help beyond the limits of the legally obligatory was not needed by any of its members. In such a community there would be no duty to help others, considered as a duty of imperfect obligation.

others applies to all rational beings. However, I do not think that this is a serious difficulty. Kant does not need to eliminate all factual knowledge from the determination of particular duties, which would, in any case, be obviously impossible. The importance of the *a priori* foundation of moral philosophy for Kant is that its first principles must be derived, not from our knowledge of the nature of man, but from the concept of a rational being as such. So, the relevant *a priori* conclusions in respect of the duty of helping others are: (*a*) 'If there are rational beings who do not need the help of others, they may legitimately refrain from helping those who are in need', and (*b*) 'If there are rational beings who need the help of others, they may not refrain from helping those who are in need'. So far, no factual knowledge has been employed. Now, however, we may make use of our knowledge of human nature (of the science of anthropology) in order to give these principles concrete application; and in doing so we conclude that since man is a being of the type referred to in principle (*b*), the rule embodied in that principle must be observed by all men.[1]

Throughout this discussion of Kant's moral philosophy I have tried to interpret what he says as generously and sympathetically as possible. There is no point, as far as we are concerned, in any other kind of interpretation, since it is the essential defects, if any, in his theories that need to be exposed, not minor and easily corrigible faults. But however sympathetic our interpretation, and however ready we may be to grant that many of the stock criticisms of Kant's ethics are due to a failure to understand him, we must in the end, I think, admit that there are difficulties in the way of accepting what he has to say as a full and final account of the nature of morality and duty and their connection with reason. In the rest of this chapter I shall mention briefly some of the most important of these difficulties.

(i) Kant seems at times, especially when he is talking about duties of perfect obligation, to confuse two different levels of universality, viz. what may be called universality in respect of persons and universality in respect of circumstances. In the first kind of universality I include the principle that what is right or wrong for one person must be right or wrong for anyone else in

[1] On the need of anthropology for the application of *a priori* moral principles, see G, A35.

the same circumstances, and the assertion that I must not make exceptions in my own selfish interest to moral rules that I require other people to observe. In the second kind I include Kant's tendency to assume that, if he has shown a certain type of action to be wrong for all people in some circumstances, he has thereby shown it to be wrong for all people in any circumstances whatever. In claiming that moral principles must be universal if they are to deserve the name of either principle or law, he argues primarily for the first type of universality, but often speaks as if the need for the second type had been established as well. In the *Grundlegung*, for example, he argues only for the view that false promises may not be made in order to obtain a loan which could not be obtained in any other way. Now we might perhaps generalise this into the principle that false promises ought not to be made for purely selfish reasons; but we are not entitled to generalise it into the principle that false promises ought never to be made in any circumstances. Kant argues for the wrongness of making a false promise in order to get a personal advantage on the ground (in effect) that it is wrong to act in a way in which you could not regard it as legitimate that all men should act. But the rule he is entitled to draw from this is 'Do not make a false promise unless you agree that a false promise may be made by anyone in circumstances similar to your own'. And we cannot conclude from this 'Never make a false promise'; for we may excuse or justify a man who made a false promise (or performed any other action thought by some to be wrong) by saying 'I should (or any sensible man would) have done the same in his place'.

Now it might be said that the moral rigorism involved in the view that we ought never, in any circumstances, to make false promises, tell lies or break promises is just a personal idiosyncrasy of Kant's, and that we do not have to treat it as an integral part of his moral philosophy. But a serious dilemma faces the Kantian, whether he accepts the rigorism or not. If he wishes to maintain, as Kant himself did, that moral principles must be universal in the second sense, and not merely in the first, he is open to the objection that, whatever plausibility there may be in Kant's arguments for universalisability of the first type as a necessary condition of morally legitimate behaviour, there is none whatever in the claim that universalisability of the second type is required. It is one thing to argue that if everyone made false promises whenever they thought it to their advantage there could be no such thing as a promise: quite another to argue that there is a contradiction in conceiving, or permitting, the universal making of false promises under certain clearly and strictly stated conditions. A universal law that everyone may make a false promise, or tell a lie, if he is required to do so by some other, more important, moral principle is obviously quite conceivable; and, moreover, a man who found himself in a world in which this law was followed might well choose of his own free will to remain in it, in Kant's own sense of that expression. However, if a Kantian were to admit this, and to insist only on universalisability in the first sense, he would be faced with another, equally serious, difficulty—that of formulating valid rules for determining the conditions under which false promises may, or may not, be made (and similarly with exceptions to other moral rules). For while it is indeed possible to claim that one moral rule is, in a particular situation, more stringent than another, or that one duty is more important than another, it is impossible for these differing degrees of stringency and importance to be explained by any theory which remains, as Kant's claims to do, at a purely formal level. His ethical theory puts all breaches of any one moral rule, if not all breaches of the moral law in general, on the same level of importance; the idea that it might be more important to keep one promise than another, or to save a large number of lives than to tell a lie, is not merely foreign to Kant's own personal way of thinking about moral issues, but is also inevitably ruled out by his philosophical principles. On those principles, an action or a maxim is either in accordance with reason or contrary to it; it is not possible for one action to be more, or less, contrary to reason than another.

(ii) Another difficulty (or perhaps it is another aspect of the same difficulty) is that Kant's account of moral judgement by reference to the principle of universality does not take into account any cases of serious moral perplexity—indeed, it is hard to see how he could have much to say about this, starting as he does from 'common rational knowledge' about morality. He deals, in effect, only with those cases of wrong conduct in which a man can be expected to see, on reflection, that what he thought of as a genuine moral judgement, to the effect that a certain action was permitted or obligatory, was in fact the product, at least in part, of his personal inclinations and desires; two genuinely moral judgements about the same issue cannot conflict with one another. This view has often been held by rationalists; but, whatever our criteria for distinguishing moral from non-moral judgements may be, it is absurd to deny that there are conflicts of opinion and judgement about many moral issues in which the conflict is not due simply to the fact that at least one party is, with or without his own knowledge, being swayed primarily by non-moral considerations. There are those who believe that capital punishment ought to be (*a*) abolished or (*b*) retained and even, perhaps, extended in its application; those who believe that homosexual behaviour is (*a*) wicked or (*b*) not wicked but the socially undesirable result of a sort of disease which can be cured by treatment; those who believe that sexual intercourse outside marriage is (*a*) always or (*b*) only sometimes wrong; those who believe (*a*) that it is wrong to consider using or threatening to use nuclear weapons for any cause whatever, or (*b*) that a country may legitimately be prepared, and perhaps ought to be prepared, to use them, in spite of the appalling consequences of so doing, if the only alternative open to it is to submit to conquest and tyranny. On both sides in these disputes there are doubtless some whose views are more emotional or prudential than genuinely moral; but there are also many opinions on the opposing sides that are genuinely moral, in the sense that the people who hold them are not adopting a purely selfish attitude, are not merely evincing emotions such as fear or hate disguised as moral principles, and are prepared to act according to their views even if it is inconvenient or unpleasant for them to do so. The Kantian principle of universality does not seem to be relevant to the resolution of moral conflicts of this type.

(iii) Kant's insistence on the universalisability of maxims as a test of their accordance with reason and, hence, of their moral legitimacy, amounts to saying that we may not act on maxims which, if universally acted on, would involve us in contradiction or inconsistency, and, conversely, that we may legitimately act (not, of course, that we must act) on any maxim which does not lead to such inconsistency. I shall have more to say in a later chapter about the necessary shortcomings of any attempt to use the concepts of consistency and inconsistency as criteria of the moral rightness and wrongness of actions; but there is one limitation in particular to which Kant's account of the matter is subject. Whatever we may think of the details of his argument, there is no doubt that his description of certain types of wrongdoer is psychologically accurate. There are many people who behave wrongly towards their fellow-men, but who disapprove strongly of similar conduct in others, especially if their own interest or well-being are seriously impaired by it. But even if Kant had given a completely satisfactory explanation of this type of wrongdoing (and I have already given some reasons for thinking this not to be the case), a large part of the field of morality falls outside this category altogether—not all morally wrong conduct is unjust or unfair conduct, still less is it unjust or unfair in this rather special way. An habitual liar is indeed dependent for the success of his lying on the fact that most people tell the truth, and a thief may feel indignant at those who try to steal from him (though he need not, and it is not clear how Kant would deal with a man who stole whenever he thought it to his advantage, but who agreed that others might legitimately steal from him under the same condition). But a man who engages in sexual promiscuity (to take one example of what Kant would certainly have regarded as morally wrong conduct) does not have to depend or rely on the chastity of others for the success of his activities; and a man who commits suicide because life is too much of a burden to him is not open to the complaint 'But what would happen if everyone did as you are doing?' (Kant, of course, produced a different argument to show the wrongness of suicide, but even the most devoted of Kantians find it difficult to accept. Apart from anything else, it makes use of a teleological assumption about the function of self-love which cannot be justified merely by referring to the principle of universality, or to any other principle that is purely rational or formal.)

PART TWO

VI
THE ASSESSMENT AND CRITICISM OF CONDUCT

THE preceding critical discussion has of necessity worked largely within the general framework, and with the terminology, of the theories criticised; it has for the most part dealt with the questions at issue as they were formulated by the authors concerned. Any attempt to provide our own positive solution of the problem or problems at issue must begin by trying to ensure that there is nothing obscure or confused in our formulation of the problems themselves; and this immediately raises some important doubts and difficulties. In the first place, much that has been written on this subject, even by the most careful writers, is highly metaphorical: we read of the part played by reason in action and in moral judgement, of actions or decisions being based or founded on reason or revelation, of moral beliefs having their origin in reason or sentiment, and so on. Secondly, a good deal of the pre-Kantian treatment rests uncritically content with a faculty-language which seems at times almost to personify such concepts as reason, understanding, emotion, and the like; as if reason, for instance, were an independent agent within a man's mind which, according to Clarke but not according to Hume, ought always to be supreme over the other agents contained therein. Now there is, of course, no harm in metaphor in itself, nor in the faculty-language in itself, and I shall use both from time to time in the remaining chapters of this book; the danger is that their repeated use may obscure the fact that a philosopher must at least try to be literal at some time or other in the expression of his views, and that in the context of this particular family of problems he must make certain distinctions which cannot be formulated without a change in terminology and approach. The first question before us is no longer 'What did Clarke, Hume, Kant and the rest mean by their talk about "reason", and how far is what they said true?' but 'What, in as literal and precise a form as possible, are the philosophically important questions which the metaphorical language about reason as the guide of conduct sometimes conceals?' When people speak of the need to defend reason against the rising tide of irrationalism and claim that the good life is the life of reason, what precisely do they mean—or rather, what precise meaning, if any, can be given to their words? (for whether some particular person has or has not meant anything precise by such language is, for our purposes, relatively unimportant).

We must begin with some preliminary distinctions. If we consider any factual belief held by a certain person—say John Smith's belief that the Conservatives will win the next general election—there are a number of different types of question which we can ask about it.

(i) We can ask for a description of the mental acts or processes which led up to or accompanied the formation of the belief. This description might include an account of the way in which Smith had studied the political situation and the present state of public opinion, and of the views he had formed of them.

(ii) We can ask for a causal explanation of the belief. This might take the form of a general statement to the effect that people of Smith's education and social class naturally tend to hold beliefs of this kind.

(iii) We can ask what are Smith's reasons for holding the belief. This question can be asked either of Smith himself or of a third party; in the former case, we are asking Smith to explain or justify his belief, and in the latter we are asking someone else to give a report of the way in which Smith would explain or justify it. To some extent these reasons may have been formulated by Smith after he first came to hold the belief; for to ask a man why he believes something will often stimulate him to try to provide an explanation or justification which he had not previously thought necessary.[1] Questions of this type are not, therefore, a mere

---

[1] They must, however, have been reasons which he could have given at the time. A justification based on subsequently discovered facts could not form

variant of type (i); indeed, types (i) and (iii) are logically quite distinct, although any statement made in reply to a type (iii) question may often contain a good deal of the same material that would also appear in an answer to a question of type (i).

(iv) We can ask whether Smith's belief is a reasonable one for him to hold in the circumstances; which is roughly equivalent, in this example, to asking whether a Conservative victory is probable on the evidence at Smith's disposal.

(v) We can ask whether Smith's belief is true, and how it can be proved or disproved, or what good reasons there are for accepting or rejecting it.

The important thing to notice is that questions of types (iv) and (v) are radically different from questions of the other three types. They ask for assessments, not descriptions, and, in particular, for assessments of the reasonableness or truth of what is believed, not for descriptions of an act of believing, or of anything connected with it. They do not even ask for assessments of the way in which the belief was arrived at. We can, of course, assess, and not merely describe, a man's thinking as careful, methodical or well-organised and, conversely, as slipshod or slovenly; but such comments function essentially as answers to questions of type (i). To a large extent in questions of type (iv), and to an even larger extent in those of type (v), we are no longer concerned with Smith as an individual; we are interested in assessing the reasonableness or truth of the belief no matter who happens to hold it.

Now we can ask a roughly corresponding series of questions about any action or decision to act (the difference between the two is not important in the present context). Let us take as an example Albert Brown's decision to commit suicide.

(i) We can ask for a description of the ways, relevant to the decision, in which his mind was working before, and at the time of, the decision.

(ii) We can ask what was the cause of the decision; a possible answer would be depression at the death of his wife.

(iii) We can ask what were his reasons for making the decision. This is asking, not for a report on the mental antecedents or

---

part of his reasons for holding the belief, though it could state reasons for holding it, and provide an answer to a question of type (iv) or (v).

accompaniments of Brown's decision, but for information about the way in which he justifies, or would have justified, it. (The justification here in question is not necessarily a moral one, of course.) It should be noticed that the question 'What was Brown's motive for committing suicide?' could be either of type (ii) or of type (iii), or a combination or confusion of the two.

(iv) We can ask whether the decision was a reasonable one on the facts at Brown's disposal; i.e. whether it was the sort of decision a reasonable man would have taken, had his knowledge and opinions about the relevant circumstances been the same as Brown's.

(v) We can ask whether his decision was correct, or whether his belief, actual or implied, that he was doing the right thing was true. In both cases we are concerned with the decision in relation to the situation as it actually was, not as Brown thought, or might have thought, it to be.

With decisions as with factual beliefs, questions of types (iv) and (v) are radically different from the others; they ask for assessments of the decision, not for descriptions of the way in which it came to be made or of the reasons which Brown gave, or might have given, for it. One form of this general difference is especially important: we must distinguish[1] the questions 'Was his decision reasonable or unreasonable?' and 'Was his decision correct or incorrect?' from the question 'Was his decision a reasoned, thoughtful one?' It is obvious that a man may think for a long time about a practical problem and in the end take an incorrect decision; equally obvious that he may sometimes take a correct decision without thinking at all, or after thinking for only a short time. It is not merely that the correctness of one's thinking does not necessarily vary in direct proportion to the amount of time one has devoted to it—though this is both true and important—but also that, even when a man's thinking has been properly performed, his subsequent decision or action is not necessarily correct. Men sometimes fail to abide by the conclusions they have, either correctly or incorrectly, reached; it is one thing to decide that one ought to perform a certain action, quite another actually to set oneself to perform it. Such situations are doubtless less common than their converse; for the most part, we are more

[1] I have already referred to this distinction in the chapter on Hume; see above, p. 51.

likely to act correctly if we think correctly, and more likely to think correctly if we think carefully and hard. But these are both contingent propositions, and the qualification 'for the most part' is important.

The questions about reason and action with which we are primarily concerned in this book are questions of types (iv) and (v), and especially of type (v); but some philosophers have not always been careful enough to avoid confusing them with some of the other types. The uncritical use of the words 'rational' and 'irrational' is particularly liable to give rise to this confusion. They are sometimes used to indicate, respectively, that a man has, or has not, thought about the situation before making up his mind that something is the case, or before deciding to do something. Failure to think, provided at least that one has time to do so, is an obvious sign of irrationality, in this sense of the word, while the fact that one has thought is equally a sign of rationality, in this sense, i.e. a sign of a rational approach to the problem. Yet, however carefully one may have thought, one may still arrive at an irrational belief, in another sense of the word 'irrational', if one's thinking has been faulty in any way; and one may act irrationally, either because one's thinking has been faulty or because one's eventual action is not in accordance with the result of one's thinking. The words 'reasonable' and 'unreasonable' also have different senses, which do not by any means always coincide with the various senses of 'rational' and 'irrational'. It might perhaps be thought appropriate, and it would certainly be in accordance with some contemporary philosophical practice, to preface our enquiry with an investigation into the various ways in which these four words are ordinarily applied to actions, possibly extending our attention to such allied words as 'absurd', 'sensible', 'stupid' and 'intelligent'. We could then deal with the question of the relation between the rationality of conduct and its moral rightness by examining the nature and extent of the correlation between the 'rational' group of epithets and the 'moral' group. Now I should not wish to deny that a linguistic investigation of this kind might prove to be of considerable interest, both for its own sake and for the correction which it might provide to some fairly common philosophical confusions; indeed, I have myself from time to time tried to illustrate certain points by drawing attention to the way in which a particular word is used. But a thoroughgoing, undirected, linguistic investigation, as opposed to the occasional directly relevant reference to usage, although it would possess considerable intrinsic interest, would not, in spite of the enormous length to which it would extend, provide us with the material we require, for two reasons. In the first place, the common use of such terms as 'rational' and 'reasonable' often rests on no rational grounds itself. For example, 'reasonable' is often used as a laudatory, and 'unreasonable' as a derogatory, term; and many people often use them as nothing but laudatory and derogatory terms, respectively, so that in calling a man's conduct reasonable they are doing little, if anything, more than indicating their approval of it, and in calling it unreasonable they are doing little, if anything, more than indicating their disapproval of it. The ordinary use of such terms is so chaotic that, while a careful analytic investigation might have some value, it would not provide nearly enough data to enable us to arrive at reliable philosophical conclusions. Secondly—and this is perhaps a more important objection—the claim that one's conduct, or the conduct of others, is rational or irrational, reasonable or unreasonable, in some of the most important senses of those words, may be made in many ways which do not require the actual use of the words. To give reasons for a belief, or to justify one's conduct—these are common everyday activities, which may imply that the belief and the conduct are rational or reasonable in one or more senses of those terms, and which are highly relevant to a philosophical enquiry into the relations between reason and action, but which do not necessarily include any explicit statement to that effect. Indeed, one can go further than this, and say that the holding of any belief, or the taking of any decision, is more often than not accompanied by the belief that good reasons could be found for the belief or the decision, even if one has not found them, or could not find them, oneself. (In a rather similar way, in making an assertion one implies[1] that what one asserts is true, even though the word 'true' has not been used in the making of the assertion.) Completely capricious assertions or actions are rare.

The general distinction between describing an action and its antecedents and accompaniments, on the one hand, and criticising and assessing it, on the other, is of such importance that it needs further discussion. In saying that a certain decision was a rational

[1] 'Implies' is, of course, not used here in its strict logical sense.

one, we may mean that it was arrived at by some sort of rational procedure; for example, my decision to back a horse called Man Friday in the 2.30 might be called a rational one in the sense that it was arrived at after a careful examination of such causally relevant factors as form and weather conditions, as contrasted with an irrational decision arrived at by shutting my eyes and jabbing a pin into the list of starters. Yet the latter decision, however irrationally arrived at, might be called reasonable, in a sense, if it could be somehow supported on rational grounds, i.e. if it could be shown that there were good reasons for making it, even if those reasons had never entered the head of the person who made it. Moreover, in some cases it may be more sensible and, in that sense, more reasonable[1] to adopt the less rational procedure. If one's information about the current form of the horses is of doubtful accuracy it may be just as sensible to use a pin as to rely on the evidence; and, to give a more realistic example, if a man has a certain gift for playing chess but is not very good at holding a long piece of complicated analysis in his head, it may well be more sensible for him to trust to his insight (or guess) that a certain move is good than to try to work out in detail the consequences of the half a dozen plausible moves that are open to him. But in chess, and with practical problems in general, we can still go on to ask whether the move or the decision, however irrationally[2] arrived at, was a sensible or reasonable one—whether, as one might say, it showed a genuine insight into the situation or was a mere guess, either inaccurate or, if accurate, owing its accuracy entirely or largely to chance. How one would answer this question would depend on the context in which the decision was made; for the way to test the correctness of a move in chess is not the way to test the correctness of a political decision. But in no case would the testing of its correctness require any reference to the procedure by which it was arrived at; for one can arrive at correct decisions by faulty, even crazy, procedures, or at incorrect decisions by entirely rational procedures (the word 'rational' implying here not only that the procedure consisted of, or

---

[1] We might even say, by a deliberate paradox, that it is sometimes more rational to adopt the less rational procedure.

[2] 'Irrationally' means here simply 'non-rationally'. The word is, of course, often used derogatorily to imply that a non-rational procedure was used when a rational one was required.

included, thinking but also perhaps that the thinking was correct thinking, as far as it went).

It may accordingly be possible to justify[1] an action, in the sense of supporting it with reasons or by rational argument, even though the agent himself could not at the time, and after the event perhaps still cannot, justify it or give reasons for it (except possibly to say 'Well, it works, doesn't it?'). If we examine the various ways in which such verbs as 'reason', 'think' and 'deliberate' can be qualified we can distinguish two especially important categories. We may say, on the one hand, that someone thought about a problem diligently, or intermittently, or that he deliberated carefully, or for a long time. All these are what might be called psychological statements about the man's thinking behaviour. But we may also say of a man that he reasoned correctly, or thought sensibly, about something; and these are not psychological statements but assessments, and refer, not to any concurrent features of the man's thinking activity, but to the success or failure of his thought. Of course, to say that statements of the first group are psychological statements does not mean that the philosopher need pay no attention to them; on the contrary, the psychology of thought and action is of great philosophical importance. But it is essential that he should not confuse his activity in discussing the diligence or casualness, say, of a man's thinking with his activity in discussing its correctness or incorrectness, validity or invalidity. Indeed, a man may think correctly or reasonably, in the sense of having a correct or reasonable belief or opinion, without having thought at all; and correspondingly a man can behave correctly or reasonably without having reasoned or thought about his behaviour.

However, the extent to which a man can achieve correct or reasonable opinions or correct or reasonable behaviour without thinking for himself is subject to certain limitations; for there are some situations in which unthinking reliance on the advice or

[1] We must distinguish two different senses of the word 'justify'. In one sense, the giving of any reasons for a belief or an action can be called justifying it, without any implication as to the satisfactoriness or unsatisfactoriness of the reasons given; in this sense almost anything can be justified. But in the other, more common, sense of the word 'justify' the reasons given must be good ones; its use indicates success, not merely attempt, and implies that the reasons offered in support of the belief or action really do support it, and support it adequately.

authority of others is inappropriate. If I want to multiply £7456 10s. 11½d. by 5977 I shall do best, unless I am a mathematician (and perhaps even if I am), to consult a ready reckoner. The fact that the answer I get will not have been thought out by myself will not put me at any disadvantage. But if I am trying to construct a rigorous proof of a theorem in geometry it is no use my relying for proof of one of my statements on the fact that some other mathematician has claimed to have demonstrated it. In this type of situation authority is no substitute for proof or evidence; I must show, or be able to show if asked, that his demonstration is valid, and to do this I must make his reasoning my own. I am entitled to say 'Euclid argued, or tried to prove, that the sum of the interior angles of a triangle is 2 right angles' if I have seen in my copy of Euclid a series of arguments with this as their conclusion; but I am not logically entitled to say 'Euclid proved that the sum of the interior angles of a triangle is two right angles' unless I have followed the steps of his proof and have seen for myself that they are valid. For to say 'X has proved, or shown, that p' is, as it were, to give a guarantee of the truth of p; and the guarantee is worthless if, either from carelessness or by way of deception, I fail to make sure of the value of that which I am purporting to guarantee.

A parallel situation may be found in the field of morality. A man can act rightly, i.e. in a way that is not morally wrong, without having thought for himself and without, in particular, any thought of his moral duty. But for behaviour to be a genuine mark of the excellence of the agent's moral character, not only must it be correct, appropriate or fitting, but the agent must have seen this for himself and, in addition, he must either have understood why it was appropriate or have been able to see why it was so after the reasons for its appropriateness were pointed out to him. In some contexts, that is to say, and for some purposes, it is not enough that one's behaviour *could* be shown to be appropriate; one must know, or have good reason for believing, that it is appropriate before one acts, even though it is not necessary to reflect on these reasons on every occasion of acting. We may call to mind in this connection Aristotle's remark about the dependence of moral virtue on practical wisdom: it is not enough to define virtue as a state of character in accordance with practical wisdom, for the virtuous man must possess practical wisdom himself, and not be content to rely on the wisdom of others.[1] The regular performance of good acts is a necessary, but not a sufficient, condition of being a good man; for we may perform good or right acts from bad or morally neutral motives and, more important in this context, we may perform good or right acts without understanding that, or why, they are good or right.

The distinction between the antecedents or accompaniments (and in particular the psychological or mental antecedents or accompaniments) of a decision or action, on the one hand, and its correctness, appropriateness or reasonableness, on the other, does not, in spite of its fundamental importance, take us very far. For within this latter category there are many complications and subdivisions. (In what follows I make only those distinctions which are necessary for my particular purpose.) The first and basic notion is that of correctness itself, a notion which may be expressed in a number of different ways. We may ask simply 'Is this the correct thing to do?' or say that someone acted incorrectly or improperly: or we may use the adjectives 'right' and 'wrong' as equivalents of 'correct' and 'incorrect'. But because actions always take place in the context of an actual or imagined situation we often use relational words, and speak of conduct as being appropriate or fitting to the situation, or as being inapposite or unsuitable. (These related notions of correctness and appropriateness are, of course, employed in both moral and non-moral judgements. In them there is no reference to reason, rationality or reasonableness in any sense of those words.)[2]

But a person who claims that an action is correct or incorrect, appropriate or inappropriate, is generally prepared to offer reasons in support of his claim; one may sometimes say 'I'm sure this is wrong, though I don't know why', but no one could get away with this every time. Hence there is a class of words which refer to the procedure of giving reasons for or against the performance of certain actions (reasons why they are right or wrong, appropriate or inappropriate), and to the success or failure with which

---

[1] Cp. EN 1144b26 (Ross's translation): 'It is not merely the state in accordance with the right rule, but the state that implies the *presence* of the right rule, that is virtue; and practical wisdom is a right rule about such matters.'

[2] But notice the phrases 'avoir raison' and 'avere ragione', meaning to be right, or correct.

this procedure is or might be conducted in any particular case. We may say, for example, that an action was unexceptionable, or justified by the facts of the situation, or conversely that it was indefensible, objectionable or questionable. The words 'reasonable' and 'unreasonable' are sometimes used in this general sense, to indicate that there are, or are not, good reasons which might be given in support or justification of the action. (Note also the expression 'a reasonable man', which sometimes means 'a man *with* whom it is possible to reason'—i.e., in this context, a man who is prepared to give reasons for his conduct and to listen to, and critically examine, objections which may be brought against it.)

The two notions of correctness and justification are, of course, closely connected, the connection being analogous in many respects to that between the truth of a factual belief and the testing of that belief, and also to that between the guilt or innocence of a prisoner and the proof, in court, of his guilt or innocence. This latter analogy is illustrated by the common metaphorical use of such legal words as 'justify' and 'defend' in discussion of conduct in general, as well as in lawyers' or judges' discussion of it in court. It should be noticed that the very concept of justification involves the notion of argument, or the giving and considering of reasons; so that if one is prepared to admit that actions, conduct and policies can be defended or attacked in what may be called a dialectical way one is already committed in some sense to the view that reason has some part to play in action, or at least in its assessment—'non-rational justification' is, if not formally self-contradictory, a very odd phrase. But this does not by itself show that *moral* judgements about actions are matters of reason in this or any other sense; this is a question which has still to be discussed.

The justification, and in general the assessment and reasoned criticism, of actions, take many forms; but there are four especially important types which it will be necessary to consider separately, and at some length. First, however, I shall make some general remarks about the concept of a reason, which is central to the notion of justification, of whatever type. In matters of fact or theory we may sometimes speak of having, or giving, absolutely conclusive reasons for a belief or an assertion; indeed, if we have absolutely conclusive reasons for making an assertion we should usually call this a case of knowledge rather than belief. But reasons more often vary in excellence; some are better than others, some are so unconvincing that they might be considered completely irrelevant to the belief or assertion in support of which they were adduced. Now suppose that I am trying to defend my assertion that it will rain tomorrow. If, in answer to the question 'What grounds have you for saying that?', I say 'Rain is forecast for this district by the Meteorological Office', this may well be accepted as a good, even though not a conclusive, reason for holding the belief or making the assertion. And if instead I say 'My joints ache' it might perhaps be retorted that this is not a good reason, because, although such aches are sometimes caused by factors which are signs of incipient weather changes, they have in my case been brought on by excessive and unaccustomed exercise; nevertheless, the aching of one's joints is the sort of fact that might on occasion be considered a good reason for asserting that it was going to rain, even if it is not a good reason on this occasion. But if I answer the question by saying 'Arsenal beat Manchester United last week' the retort might well be not merely that this was not a good reason for my assertion, but that it was not a reason at all, because, however true the statement might be, it was completely irrelevant to the assertion it purported to justify. The claim of irrelevance would be defended, if defence were thought necessary, by pointing out that there could be no possible causal connection or correlation between the result of last week's football match and tomorrow's weather (whereas in the previous example it was agreed that a causal connection might exist between people's aching joints and the weather, although it did not happen to exist in the particular case under discussion). And if I wanted to defend my claim that I had given a good reason (and to give a reason is usually to claim implicitly that it is a good reason) I should have to show that, contrary to appearance, some such causal connection did exist.

An analogous, though not entirely similar, situation exists in practical matters. If I am asked to justify my action in refusing to give money to a beggar in the streets I might say that I could not afford to, or that the man was not really as poor as he looked, or that giving money to beggars tends to weaken the moral fibre of the community. It might be disputed whether any of these were good reasons, or just how good any one of them was, but there would be no dispute that the reasons offered were at least relevant to the question at issue. But if, when asked to defend my refusal, I say that Glasgow is west of Edinburgh nobody would accept this as in any way relevant to my lack of generosity; it is no reason at all, not even a bad one. Moreover, it would be pointless for me to say that it might conceivably be relevant in some way, even though I do not know how. For if I offer some fact or statement as a reason, whether for an assertion or an action, I am clearly claiming that it is relevant; it would be absurd for me to meet the challenge by saying 'Well, how do you know it isn't relevant?', for the onus of proof is clearly on me, since it is I that am making the claim. Now if the point at issue in justifying or criticising a certain action were whether or not it contributed to a particular end (say, the safety of pedestrians crossing Piccadilly Circus) the difference between a totally irrelevant remark and one which offered a very poor reason would be that the former would be recognised by even the stupidest person as doing nothing to prove that the action contributed to the required end, whereas the latter, although in fact it did nothing to prove this, might be the subject of a more or less intelligible and natural mistake—a man who accepted it might be stupid, but not outrageously stupid.

But not all attempts to justify actions or decisions seem to be of this simple means-end kind; if they were, all practical issues could be reduced in the end to issues of fact. Many practical arguments, especially those on moral questions, seem to be more complicated than this, and to involve something more than a combination of logical rigour and the establishment of empirical facts. Must we then suppose that there exists a special set of rules for practical, or at least for moral, discussion, over and above the normal rules of deductive and inductive logic? C. L. Stevenson has argued that, apart from appeals to logic or to fact, the reasons which support or attack ethical judgements do so psychologically rather than logically, even in the widest sense of that term—their primary function is to influence attitudes. In this they resemble the reasons offered in support of 'imperatives', i.e. commands or requests. 'Reasons support imperatives by altering such beliefs as may in turn alter an unwillingness to obey' (*Ethics and Language* (New Haven, 1944), p. 28). For example, if I tell a student to work harder and support my instruction or advice by saying that if he does not he will fail in his examinations, what happens is that I point out certain facts of which he was previously ignorant or to which he was not paying sufficient attention. My intervention may cause him to work harder: alternatively, if his desire for leisure is stronger than his desire to pass his examinations, it may not. Stevenson proceeds to give a similar psychological account of the relation between ethical judgements and the reasons given by way of support or criticism of them. For the most part, he agrees, they do not remain within the framework of deductive or inductive argument; but this does not mean that we have to postulate a further kind or kinds of logical or quasi-logical argument over and above these two. The function of ethical reasons is to influence attitudes; in them questions of truth and validity, other than the truth of non-ethical, factual assertions and the validity of ordinary deductive or inductive arguments, do not arise. The support which such reasons give to the original judgement is psychological, not logical. The conclusion is '*If* any ethical dispute *is* rooted in disagreement in belief, it may be settled by reasoning and inquiry to whatever extent the beliefs may be so settled. But if any ethical dispute is *not* rooted in disagreement in belief, then no *reasoned* solution of any sort is possible' (ibid., p. 138).

Now it is, of course, true that the giving of reasons in ethical contexts does have a psychological function of this kind. We do often offer reasons in order to make our moral utterances more acceptable or convincing to others. But this happens also in purely factual contexts, where the disagreement is clearly one of belief, in Stevenson's sense of the term. I may, for example, produce reasons in order to try to convince someone that he is mistaken that it will rain tomorrow. The point which Stevenson seems to overlook is that two quite distinct types of question may be asked about such reasons: (i) 'Do they, on this particular occasion, convince the person to whom they are offered?' (i.e. do they succeed in altering his beliefs?), and (ii) 'Are they *convincing* reasons, good reasons, reasons by which a sensible man *ought* to be convinced?' Now about ethical reasons we can obviously ask question (i), with the proviso that its second formulation in Stevensonian terminology would have to be 'Do they succeed in altering his attitudes?'; but it should not be assumed from the start that question (ii) is in some way improper. Stevenson would, of course, agree that ethical reasons may be bad reasons in the sense that they involve logical fallacies or mistakes of fact; but he seems to have been led to reject any other kind of non-psychological meaning for the expressions 'convincing reason', 'unconvincing reason', 'good reason' and 'bad reason' because of his belief that this would presuppose the existence of a third, independent, type of reasoning, over and above logical and inductive. This, however, is a mistake. If one considers ethical discussions from a purely psychological point of view one naturally sees only psychological factors; but we do from time to time assess the arguments used and the reasons offered in such discussions, not merely according as they succeed or fail in their purpose of convincing a particular person or group of persons, but on the basis of their being arguments such as would, or would not, convince a sensible, reasonable man.[1] We use such words as 'reasonable' and 'sensible' in this type of context with a reference that is not restricted to the ability to understand or propound logical or factual considerations; a reasonable man is one who can be relied on in practical (including ethical) as well as in logical and factual matters. One task of the moral philosopher in dealing with this group of problems is to examine the ways in which reasonable and unreasonable conduct and discussion are, and can be, distinguished; the fact that the word 'reasonable' occurs in ethical as well as in non-ethical contexts may be seen in the end to be misleading or unfortunate, but it must not be assumed from the outset to be so.

We cannot, however, simply define or explain the notion of justification by reasons in terms of the judgement or the behaviour of the reasonable man—we cannot say, for example, 'X is a good reason if and only if it is a reason that would be offered or approved by a reasonable man'. For this would involve us in a vicious circle, since we cannot know whether someone is a reasonable man without first knowing something about the reasonableness or appropriateness of the conduct which he displays or approves. It is true that the concept of the reasonable man is frequently and usefully employed in legal contexts; but it is used there more as a practical criterion for the making of certain kinds

---

[1] This is true also of many reasons offered in support of non-moral 'imperatives'. 'Because there's a draught' is a good reason for 'Shut the door' (assuming that there is in fact a draught): 'Because I say so' is not (unless I have authority to order you to shut it, and even then it is not so much a reason as a suggestion that the request for a reason is improper).

of legal judgement than as a theoretical justification of them. We cannot elucidate the notion of a correct judgement, either in law or in morals, by saying that it is one that would be made by a reasonable man; for, since even a reasonable man can make mistakes, we could preserve the correlation between the correctness of the judgement and the notion of the reasonable man only by saying 'A correct judgement is one that would be made by a reasonable man judging (on this occasion) reasonably', and it is this very notion of judging correctly or reasonably that requires to be elucidated.

What kinds of fact or other consideration, we must then ask ourselves, are relevant to the justification or, more generally, to the criticism and assessment of actions, and to their moral justification, assessment or criticism in particular? I have already suggested (above, p. 105) that there are four especially important types or methods of assessment.

(i) We may say of an action that it is lawful, proper or just, or, conversely, that it is unlawful, improper or unjust, meaning that it conforms, or does not conform, to some law or rule. (The words 'right' and 'wrong' are often used in this sense, as well as in the more fundamental senses of 'correct' and 'incorrect', and 'appropriate' and 'inappropriate', and much confusion has been caused in moral philosophy by a failure to notice, or to pay enough attention to, this distinction. The class of actions which are right, in the sense of 'lawful', may be coextensive with the class of actions which are right, in the sense of correct or appropriate; but the statement that it is is not analytic, and may be open to dispute.)

(ii) We may apply the terms 'consistency' and 'inconsistency' to a man's conduct. One action or decision of mine, for example, may be inconsistent with another, or inconsistent with my declared policy or principles. Again, taking a comprehensive view of a man's life, we may say that he leads a coherent, systematic life, as opposed to a haphazard, random one.

(iii) We may characterise a man's behaviour as intelligent or clever or, conversely, as unintelligent, stupid or foolish. The words 'rational' and 'irrational' are sometimes used to make judgements of this kind.

(iv) We may say that a man's conduct displays some kind of insight into, or discernment of, the requirements of the situation;

and, somewhat similarly, a man who is asked how he knows that a particular action is wrong may reply that he sees directly ('intuits') that it is.

In the next four chapters these four types of assessment are discussed in some detail in their application to both moral and non-moral contexts and situations.

VII

RULES

IT is clearly inappropriate and unreasonable to act in disregard of facts. An action performed in disregard of relevant facts known to the agent is open to criticism, from a rational point of view, just because the facts would be seen on reflection to make it inappropriate. It is stupid to be rude to one's employer in a moment of forgetfulness, failing to realise whom one was addressing. In a different and rather less drastic way, there is something not altogether satisfactory from a rational point of view in acting on beliefs which are in fact false, even though they were not known by the agent to be false. If one has killed one's rich uncle in the belief that he has left one all his money the fact that he has actually left it all to a cats' home indicates that one's action was inappropriate, even if one could not have known it to be inappropriate at the time. More generally, if one is trying to achieve a certain end or purpose it is reasonable to take steps which in one's opinion will, or are likely to, achieve it, and unreasonable to take steps which in one's opinion will not, or are unlikely to; and it is correct or appropriate to take steps which in fact will, or are in fact likely to, achieve it, and incorrect or inappropriate to take steps which in fact will not, or are not in fact likely to.

But it is clear that, when we have learnt all the facts, or as many of them as circumstances permit, and have taken the steps which we think will (or even those which in fact will) achieve our ends, there are still some ways in which we may go wrong, and behave unreasonably or irrationally. For one thing, although knowledge of the relevant facts is necessary, or at least desirable, it is clearly not sufficient for reasonable or correct action; for one can know all the facts and still fail to make proper use of one's knowledge. Moreover, not all our conduct can be regarded as the taking of means to a given end; and even that part of it which can still leaves us with the question, 'Given that this is the reasonable course of action in order to achieve this particular end, is it proper or reasonable to set myself to achieve this end?'

Hume, like many others since, thought that the limits of reasonable behaviour were reached at this point, and that the word 'reason' and its derivatives, when used 'strictly and philosophically', could not be given a wider application. But we have seen that the narrowing of the meaning of a word in this way can be as misleading, through its concealment of connections and resemblances, as it can perhaps be illuminating in drawing attention to distinctions and differences. The purpose of this chapter is to examine one possible method of justifying or defending conduct; a method which consists in showing that the conduct is in accordance with the relevant rules.

An essential feature of rules is that they are to some degree and in certain respects general in their application. The words 'Don't smoke in here', addressed to a particular individual on a particular occasion, do not state or express a rule, whereas the same words exhibited on a notice may perhaps do so. Moreover, just any kind of generality is not enough to constitute a rule. 'All members of the Club must attend the Extraordinary General Meeting to be held on 26 July 1962' is a general instruction, but not a rule: on the other hand, 'All members of the Club must pay their subscriptions by 1 January in each year' is a rule. The distinguishing feature of a rule is that it must, in principle at least, be applicable to more than one occasion; it is not enough that it should be applicable to more than one person. And it is often held that this, or a similar, kind of generality is central to the notion of correct or appropriate action; i.e. that in any situation, moral or non-moral, the correct or reasonable thing to do is to obey the rules that are relevant to situations of that type, and that behaviour which is contrary to the rules is always incorrect and unreasonable. A situation may perhaps be classifiable in two or more different ways, and thus yield different, and perhaps conflicting, rules; the rules of behaviour in air-raids may conflict with the rules of behaviour when playing cricket, supposing that a raid occurs in the middle of a game. It is then a matter of choice which rules to observe. Some may say 'For heaven's sake, stop worrying about the game, and take cover'; others 'Sir, this is a game of *cricket*; be so good as to continue the over'. The question how to settle such conflicts is, however, a subsidiary one.

Since the examination of this thesis in its widest form may throw some light on its validity as applied to morals, I shall, before discussing moral rules, consider four especially important kinds of non-moral rule. These are: (i) means–end rules; (ii) rules of games; (iii) rules of associations; and (iv) rules of courtesy.

(i) *Means–end rules.* There are in many fields of human activity rules which lay down the best, or in some cases the only, means for achieving a given end or purpose; they include, although they are not quite co-extensive with, what Kant called 'rules of skill'. If I desire to have, or to do, something it is obviously reasonable, other things being equal, to take the steps that are necessary to obtain it or to get myself in a position where I am able to do it; and for many such situations there are rules which can be of help in determining the best course of action. Rules of this kind possess varying degrees of generality of application. Some may be such that obedience to them by anyone who desires to achieve a certain end is the best means of ensuring the achievement; others may have a more limited generality in that, while it is appropriate for me to follow them, it might be inappropriate for someone whose temperament differed from mine, or who knew more, or less, about the subject-matter than I. But it is clear that mere obedience to rules of this kind, however general they may be, cannot be a sufficient condition of the absolute rationality or appropriateness of the action which follows them. For they derive what justification they have from the fact, or the decision, that, in the circumstances in which I find myself, action A is the best means of achieving end E. Accordingly, any set of formulated rules may require and receive correction in the light of experience; if someone whom I am criticising tries to justify himself by pointing out that he is obeying the rules I can always reply that the rules are unsatisfactory, and that there is a better way of achieving the desired end than by following them. It is always a mistake to respect rules of this kind for their own sake, though it is a mistake that is quite commonly made (e.g. the slavish obedience to such rules as 'Always play with a straight bat',

'Never end a sentence with a preposition', and 'Never use consecutive fifths').

Nor is obedience to formulated rules a necessary condition of this kind of rationality; for when a situation arises which is not covered by known rules it has to be dealt with in the light of the steps which are required to achieve the desired end in the actual existing state of affairs, without reference to general rules or to states of affairs or ends of this general type. And even when rules have been formulated, it may still be just as sensible to ignore them and trust one's own judgement and opinion about the requirements of the particular situation; judgement is needed, in any case, to decide which rules the particular case falls under. It is owing to this primacy of the particular case that rules of skill tend, in varying degrees, to be more useful for the novice, or at least for the not very advanced performer in any sphere, than for the expert. Their place is in elementary handbooks rather than advanced treatises.

(ii) *Rules of games.* Here the distinction between conduct, or play, in accordance with, and contrary to, the rules is at once more clear-cut and more decisive as a criterion for deciding between correct and incorrect behaviour.[1] It is usually easy to decide whether a given course of action is either prescribed or permitted by the rules, even though there may be occasional difficulties requiring reference to the controlling authorities of the game and perhaps, in extreme cases, a clarification or modification of the rules. More important, as long as one is playing the game, the rules fix categorically and absolutely what one may or may not do. With means–end rules, if I decide that it is too burdensome or objectionable to obey them I can often simply ignore them and pursue my objective by other, more suitable, means; but if I decide that the rules of a game are unsatisfactory in any respect I must still abide by them. I can, of course, take steps to persuade the authorities to alter the rules, or even to persuade my fellow-players to agree to a local, unofficial, alteration;

---

[1] Except, of course, that one can play correctly in one sense (i.e. in accordance with the rules) and still play incorrectly in another (i.e. unskilfully). As we have seen, there is a corresponding distinction between two senses of 'right', 'wrong', and other similar adjectives, as they are used in moral contexts.

but if I ignore the rules I am at worst not playing the game at all, and at best playing it in an unauthorised and improper manner. You cannot play chess at all if you remove your king from the board; but infringing the rule which forbids a player to distract or worry his opponent implies that one is playing chess in an ill-mannered and illegal way, not that one is not playing it at all.

Two kinds of critical question can be asked within the context of a game, when we are concerned with matters of legality rather than skill. We may ask, first, 'Is this action in accordance with the rules?' It is usually easy to discover the answer to this question; if it were not, it would indicate that the rules were badly formulated. And if the answer is 'No', then, as long as we remain within the framework of the game, no further question need arise; the fact that a particular action is contrary to the rules of bridge is a conclusive reason, as reasons in bridge go, for not performing it, even though there may be non-bridge reasons for performing it (e.g. prudential or moral reasons). Secondly, we may ask, 'Is this a sensible, reasonable rule?' This is a question for legislators or would-be legislators of the game, and there are no universal criteria for answering it. Apart from such formal criteria as clarity and consistency, the tests used would for the most part be pragmatic; one would ask 'What disadvantages follow from the existence of this rule, and how can it be amended without introducing fresh, and perhaps greater, disadvantages?' It is clearly understood that the rules can be changed, and in most regularly played games there are recognised procedures for changing them. Some children's games, however, especially those without written rules, are exceptional in this respect; perhaps because children tend to be conservative and because it is often more difficult to change unwritten rules than written ones.

(iii) *Rules of associations*. Clubs, associations and societies are often formed with written sets of rules which prescribe, permit and forbid certain types of conduct to their members. These rules function in many respects like rules of games, but there is one important difference, namely that there is nothing in them which corresponds to the defining or constitutive rules of a game, i.e. to those rules the ignoring of which entails that one is, literally, not playing the game in question. There are some rules of bridge which the players cannot transgress without laying themselves open to the charge that they are not playing bridge at all (as opposed to the charge that they are playing bridge illegally). But, although a club may have some rules which prescribe or restrict the activities of the club as a whole and not merely those of its members, there are no rules which it is logically impossible to break while still remaining a member.

As with rules of games, one can ask of any act, 'Is this in accordance with, or contrary to, the rules?' and, of any rule, 'Is this a good, sensible rule?' The answer to the first question may be complicated by the fact that some clubs have unwritten laws or rules, which are not in the rule-book but which are considered just as binding as those that are. However, these form a problem only for relatively new members; there is usually no difficulty in obtaining agreement among the seniors as to what precisely these rules say. As long as one remains a member of the club it is reasonable to obey the rules, always provided that obedience does not require the transgression of some more important rule; this general principle of obedience can be justified in various ways, for example, by referring to the unfairness of seeking exceptions to any rule in one's own favour and to the inconvenience that would follow any widespread disobedience. Again, if one wishes to change the rules this can be done by a recognised procedure, and the proposed change can be supported or attacked in a reasoned manner; by arguing, for example, that the proposed new rule will improve the amenities of the club or, conversely, that it is contrary to the intention of the club's founders.

For our purposes, at least, the law of the land might be regarded as a set of rules of this kind. The one important practical difference, that one joins a club voluntarily but not, usually, a state, does not affect the logical character of the rules or laws involved. The law, of course, applies to foreigners as well as to citizens; but some of the rules of a club may apply to visitors or guests as well as to members.

(iv) *Rules of courtesy*. These vary from the most formal rules of etiquette, applying perhaps to a very narrow range of activities within a limited society or group, to more general and wide-ranging rules prescribing what is and what is not in accordance with good manners. While some people regard rules of this kind as in some way 'self-evident' or self-justifying, they can in fact be justified or criticised by reference to the general utility of obeying them and, in particular, as ways of expressing one's interest in and consideration for the feeling and welfare of others. There are certain forms of social politeness which, although they are not necessarily helpful in themselves, are regarded as expressing a friendly or sympathetic attitude; actions in accordance with the rules function as signs of such attitudes, even if they are of no direct benefit to anyone, and actions contrary to the rules function as signs of unfriendliness or disrespect, even if they do no direct harm. It is because of this sign-function that rules of courtesy or manners can vary so much from one group to another without losing all their point. In one community the rules which govern the behaviour of a guest towards his host may require him to eat all the food put before him; leaving some on the plate would be taken to imply that the food was bad. In another community a guest may be required by the code to leave a so-called 'manners-bit' on his plate; if one ate all the food this would be taken to imply that the host had not provided enough. Both rules can be justified to a certain extent, and one can see the point behind them. But it is pointless to ask 'Which is the correct rule?' or even 'Which is the better rule?' A custom exists whereby a host will feel insulted at certain kinds of behaviour, and unless one wishes to insult one's host one will refrain from acting in this way (or sometimes, perhaps, explain that no insult or discourtesy was intended—'I had to leave some of the food because I am on a diet'. But some hosts would feel insulted even then.)

Good manners, however, are not confined to the following of a code of rules, i.e. manners are not co-extensive with etiquette. For the consideration and sympathy for the feelings of others which are the justification or foundation of those rules can be, and often are, regarded as of greater intrinsic importance than mere obedience to the rules as such. One may distinguish superficially good manners—by which is meant outward obedience to the rules, however motivated—from genuine good manners, which may care little about rules of 'correct' behaviour, but which exhibit a sincere and constructive desire to respect the feelings and wishes of others, and to take appropriate action according to the circumstances in which one finds oneself. Some actions, one might say, are natural signs of politeness or rudeness, as opposed to artificial or conventional signs; and with the former, unlike the latter, there is no need for a set of rules to connect the behaviour with the politeness or rudeness of which it is a sign.

In all these non-moral contexts in which behaviour may be prescribed or otherwise governed by rules, it is possible to ask questions of the following three types:

(*a*) What are the rules?
(*b*) Is this action in accordance with the rules? *or* What particular action do the rules prescribe in this situation?
(*c*) Is this rule a good, sensible one?

In some cases (those in which the rules are, explicitly or in effect, rules for achieving a certain end) it is possible to ask also:

(*d*) Is the end in view a good or sensible one to pursue?

Question (*a*) is a factual question which is usually, though not always, easy to answer. The answer is discovered, roughly, either by looking things up in the book of rules[1] or, with means–end rules, by calculating what are in general likely to be the most effective means to a given end (or one may sometimes look up rules of skill in handbooks, when one is relying on the calculations of others). One's answer to the question is thus justified or unjustified according as it is shown to correspond or not to correspond to the facts.

Question (*b*), like all questions which involve the subsumption of particular cases under rules, requires the exercise of judgement for its answer; and judging is obviously an activity which can be performed rationally or irrationally, sensibly or stupidly. It requires also a prior answer to some factual question or questions. This may be illustrated by an example from chess. The question 'Has Smith made an illegal move?' may have a two-part answer, first the factual statement 'He moved his king after first touching his queen', and then the judgement 'This move is illegal, because it is contrary to the rule which states that, once a player has

---

[1] In the field of law this is complicated in practice by the existence of common law and judge-made law; but this does not alter the fact that 'Are actions of type T illegal?' is to the outside observer or agent a factual question, even though it may not be so for the court, which has to make a ruling rather than to announce a factual discovery.

touched one of his pieces, he must make a move with that piece'.

Question (*c*) can always be asked in theory, although in some contexts asking it may be held to be somehow improper. The more absurd provisions of some codes of honour retained their influence for as long as they did only because one of the unwritten rules of the code was that it was dishonourable to ask 'What is the point of behaving in this way?'—no man of honour would need to ask. Some types or patterns of behaviour, that is, are essentially non-rational, in the sense that asking for reasons in support of the pattern is ruled out by the very nature of the pattern itself. We may compare the attitude of extreme patriots towards those who ask 'Why *should* we act patriotically?', and notice that, in common usage, to ask 'Why should we do this?' is often interpreted, not as a neutral request for reasons, but as an implied suggestion that no good reasons can be given. Some moralists adopt this non-rational attitude to moral rules.

Question (*d*), where it is applicable, presents no special theoretical problems, though it must be distinguished carefully from question (*c*). 'If you want to get on in your profession, act obsequiously towards your employer' may be a sensible rule, given the desired end (not always, since some employers like independence, or a show of it, in their servants); but if one dislikes the policy of obsequiousness one may be led to question the end itself, that of getting on in one's profession, if it has to be achieved in this way. The question asked will often be, not 'Is this in itself a sensible aim?', but 'Is this a sensible aim when the means necessary to achieve it are taken into account?'

Now a rational attitude to morals, like a rational attitude to non-moral activity, is characterised by a readiness to ask questions of these and similar types. And when we come to examine the thesis that morally proper conduct is essentially conduct which is guided by a set of moral rules we find that this is even more inadequate than a comparable account of correct action in other fields. To begin with, what *are* the rules? If everyone, or at least everyone who was not a complete amoralist, agreed on the answer to this question, the further question, 'How do we know that these are the rules?', would have only academic and philosophical interest. But it is obvious that this agreement does not exist. It is not merely that some are Kantians and some utilitarians; the difference of opinion exists at a much lower level, concerning some quite elementary rules. The extent of this disagreement may be obscured if we regard moral rules as corresponding to Ross's *prima facie* duties, and as laying down tendencies rather than hard and fast laws, although even then not everyone would accept exactly the same set of defeasible 'tendency'-rules, or the same criteria of their defeasibility. But many of the important moral issues arise out of conflicts between such rules; and if we were to try, as of course Ross refuses to do, to lay down second-order rules which give general prescriptions as to the relative importance of the 'tendency'-rules, we should soon find a great deal of disagreement even among morally sensitive people. Many would agree that we ought to keep promises and that we ought to help our friends when they are in trouble. But these rules, if they may be taken as such, are useless as guidance in many cases, viz. in those in which we cannot obey one of the rules without breaking another. For the claim that rational conduct consists in obeying certain moral rules to have any plausibility it is essential that the rules should be such that it is possible to obey them all—we should not think much of the rules of a game or of a club if some of them were mutually inconsistent. And, apart from other difficulties inherent in the notion of a hard and fast set of moral rules, which I shall discuss shortly, it must be obvious that, even among those who accept such a notion of morality, there is considerable disagreement as to what the rules are.

But, even when we are agreed as to the rules, it is not always possible to discover what particular line of conduct the rules require. This is not invariably because the rules are not formulated with sufficient exactness—if this were all, the necessary process of refinement might not be difficult. The trouble is that the rules deal satisfactorily only, if at all, with frequently recurring or previously envisaged situations; there are rules for coping with frequently recurring moral problems, simply because people have seen or decided, from their own and others' experience, that certain ways of behaving are more appropriate than others in situations of that type. But what happens when a new situation arises, one which does not fit into any of the classified types with which the rule-guided morality is equipped to deal? Perhaps, in trying to solve the problem, we ought to adhere to the existing rules (though perhaps we ought not); but obedience to rules is not a sufficient condition of morally correct conduct.[1] The moral problems concerning artificial insemination may illustrate the inadequacy of rules. It is true that some people try to show that A.I.D. is morally wrong by saying that it is a kind of adultery (and there is, of course, a rule against this). But this is to stretch the meaning of the word 'adultery' beyond its normal usage, and the question whether this linguistic stretching is justified cannot be answered without first answering the moral question at issue; hence the proper course is not to try to subsume a new type of act under a classification which does not really fit it, but to consider the act on its own merits or demerits, i.e. to ask whether it is or is not morally appropriate or fitting in some kinds of situation, and to consider the reasons which might be offered for and against it. With morality, as with the taking of means to a desired end, there is what I have called (above, p. 115) a primacy of the particular case; for, as Aristotle says, moral rules are dependent for their validity on the judgement of morally enlightened and well-informed men, and some people at some time have got to think for themselves about moral questions—we cannot always act by rule of thumb, even if some of us at times have to, or at least prefer to. Even if there are any moral rules which it is always without exception proper to obey, this is not an ultimate datum of morality, but can be shown to be true by exhibiting the appropriateness of behaviour which follows these rules to all possible situations in which an agent might find himself.

Can it be held that obedience to rules is, though not a sufficient condition of morally correct conduct, at least a necessary condition? If by 'obedience to rules' is meant the conscious and deliberate following of them the answer is clearly 'No'; for a man can act in a morally impeccable way without having thought about any rules whatsoever. But conduct can be in accordance with rules even if the agent has not consciously used the rules as a guide. In one of his essays[2] F. R. Leavis discusses a criticism to the effect that he is not philosophic enough because he has not

---

[1] For a good general discussion of the inadequacy of rules as a guide to correct conduct, see R. G. Collingwood, *Autobiography* (London, 1939), pp. 102–6.

[2] *Literary Criticism and Philosophy*, in *The Common Pursuit* (London, 1952), pp. 211–22.

formulated in a systematic way the assumptions and general principles on which his literary criticism is based. His answer is, roughly, that his criticism is based on his own perception and sensibility, not on any external norms or principles, and that, while general principles of criticism may be extracted from his work, he is not particularly interested in doing the extracting. Similarly, one does not need to be able to enunciate general rules or principles of conduct in order to lead a good life; but it might be held that the good man's conduct is regular and systematic, in the sense that it follows rules even if it is not actively guided by them, and that one can, on analysis, discover the rules and principles which are embodied or implied in it. The extraction of the rules is an analytic activity which the agent may not care, or even be competent, to perform for himself. Inability to do this may indicate a fairly low level of intellectual attainment, but it does not indicate a low level of goodness, or even of intelligence. One can be a skilful cyclist without being able to explain the rules or reasons behind one's skilful actions, and one can, similarly, be a good man and act morally without being able to give an intellectual explanation of what makes right actions right. One does not need to be a philosopher or have an analytic mind in order to act intelligently, reasonably or in a morally correct way.

Now we saw, when we were discussing non-moral rules, that it is always legitimate to ask of any such rule whether it is a good or a sensible one—that is to say, even though within certain limits the reasonable course of action might be that which is in accordance with the rules, it is still possible to advance beyond this level or stage of reasonableness and to challenge the soundness of the rules themselves. The denial that a certain action is sensible or correct is therefore ambiguous—it may mean either that the action is contrary to the accepted rules or that, although it is in accordance with the accepted rules, these rules are, in some respects at least, invalid or unjustified. This ambiguity and the corresponding distinction between levels of justification are of great importance in moral contexts. If morality is thought, as it is by some, to consist in a rigid adherence to a fixed code of rules, then the question of how to justify the rules may not, in practice, arise; they are sometimes taken unquestioningly for granted, sometimes regarded as the expression of a divine will which it would be impiety to question. And adherence to a code of this kind can perhaps give us an answer of sorts to all our perplexities, although the answer at times will inevitably be unsatisfactory; for, as has already been pointed out, old codes cannot deal successfully with new situations, and if we place our entire trust in them we shall sometimes find that the conduct they prescribe is either irrelevant or unsuited to the circumstances in which we find ourselves, and is therefore to that extent unjustified and unreasonable.

However, the position of one who wishes to depart from a generally accepted code of morals, and to replace it either by a less inadequate code or, preferably, by a more 'open' and less rule-bound type of morality is not altogether analogous to that of the would-be legal reformer or the man who wishes to change the rules of chess or of his club; indeed, 'changing the rules of morality' is a rather strange expression. The reformer can point to deficiencies in an accepted code, by showing, for example, that some of the actions which it prescribes or permits are morally inappropriate, and he can try to persuade people to reject or modify some of their cherished rules; more sweepingly, he can try to persuade them that there are some true moral judgements that cannot be derived from any set of moral rules, however excellent they may be as rules. But the rejection or modification of particular rules, and the rejection of the over-riding importance of moral rules, in general, are matters for individual decision—there is no authoritative individual or committee to make the required change. We talk, admittedly, about moral standards changing; but what we usually mean by this is, not that what was once wrong is now right, and vice versa, but that the moral beliefs or practices of a set or community of people have changed. This difference between moral rules, on the one hand, and rules of games or associations, on the other, can be exhibited in another way. As far as the latter are concerned, a would-be reformer will generally think it proper to follow the existing rules until they are changed, however unsatisfactory he may consider them to be. We ought to play cricket according to the existing rules, even if we think that they are inappropriate or unreasonable in some way, and are engaged in a campaign to persuade the M.C.C. to change them. Similarly with the rules of our club or the laws of our country; moral considerations apart, the sensible thing for the good member or good citizen to do is to obey the rule or law he is trying to have repealed as long as it is on the rule- or statute-book. But the moral reformer will not take this attitude; he will regard himself as obliged to follow his own principles and beliefs where they diverge from the currently accepted rules, and will not, if he is courageous, accept the claim that he ought to follow the custom of the majority until he has persuaded that majority to change it. Indeed, behaving in a way that is contrary to the accepted code, provided that it is done with a serious moral purpose, may be one way of recommending people to change their behaviour—the way of example. There is a parallel here with rules of language or grammar; one way of recommending a new linguistic usage is simply to adopt it oneself—there is no need to persuade, and in some countries no point in persuading, a literary academy to sanction the change first.

There is one other important feature of moral rules that deserves mention. With any other kind of rule there is always, in theory at least, a legitimate way of acting so as to avoid having either to obey it or to disobey it; i.e. there are circumstances to which not merely that particular rule, but rules of that general kind, are inapplicable. If I find the rules of my club irksome I can resign; if I dislike obeying the rules of etiquette prevalent in my social class I can refrain from making the social claims which oblige me to obey them. As for the laws of my country, I cannot, it is true, always in practice go and live elsewhere in order to avoid having to obey them, but at least there are places where those laws do not apply. This does not seem to be true of what is sometimes called 'the moral law'. No doubt its application may vary to some extent from place to place, but its fundamental rules will be regarded as inescapable. I cannot, even in theory, emigrate to a place where they are not binding, except in the trivial sense that some of them will at some times or in some conditions be inapplicable (for example, the rule 'Do not steal' in a community where the institution of property is unknown), and that I can avoid breaking promises by never making any—but not all moral rules can be evaded in this way.

It is open to the believer in the essential rationality of rule-guided conduct to regard moral rules as conditional, i.e. as laying down the best means for achieving a certain end or ends. Some forms of utilitarianism, for example, attach importance to the observance of moral rules because obedience to them is held to be the best way of promoting the general happiness. At first sight this view might seem to be liable to the same objections as have already been made in relation to means–end rules, namely that such rules cannot be completely accurate and that the desired result can sometimes be attained by acting in a quite different way from that which they prescribe. But the moralist may make a reply which is not applicable to means–end rules in general, viz. that obedience to moral rules has additional importance because of men's need to be able to predict and rely on the behaviour of others: even though happiness is the ultimate end, it will be most nearly achieved if there is some uniformity in the means adopted. Nevertheless, the question still arises, 'Why this end rather than any other?'—i.e. rational conduct cannot be held to consist in obedience to rules which lay down, however accurately, the best means of achieving a certain end unless we can first find some justification of the claim that the achievement of that end is ultimately the only, or at least the most, rational human objective.

Before we leave the subject of rules, one further point must be made in order to guard against possible misunderstanding. I have been arguing that obedience to moral rules is not the essence of rational or correct conduct in moral matters, and have suggested in particular that strict obedience to a moral code is in some ways less rational than a morality which treats each situation on its merits instead of as a situation of a certain recognised type (just as, in our serious and intimate dealings with our fellow-men, we should treat them as individuals, not merely as servants or soldiers or Americans or criminals). But none of us has the time or ability for independent thought on every occasion on which action is necessary; and it may be that many men, though morally unexceptionable and indeed praiseworthy, have this ability very poorly developed, even when they have the time. Accordingly, for all of us some of the time and for some of us all of the time, obedience to moral rules can be regarded as the most proper or reasonable behaviour open to us, even though it does not attain to the ideal of rationality. The essential point is that the propriety of obedience to the rules is something that, from a theoretical point of view, requires demonstration by reference to the circumstances of each particular case, even though it may often have to be taken for granted in practice; and it is the job of the independent and rational moralist to see that his reasoned beliefs and decisions are reflected as far as possible in the standards and conduct of his rule-guided fellows.

VIII

CONSISTENCY

CONSISTENCY in some sense, or rather in several senses, is a necessary requirement in any thinking that claims to be rationally conducted. It is possible for someone to reject the ideal of consistency as far as the workings of his own mind are concerned; but if he does, he cannot claim validity for any arguments he employs, however persuasive they may be. Conversely, although one cannot argue directly in favour of logical consistency without begging the question, one can point out the limitations and drawbacks of any steadfast refusal to maintain it. On occasions, of course, the retention of some inconsistency may be the lesser evil; a man may have two very strong beliefs which, as formulated by him, are strictly inconsistent with one another, and nevertheless be reluctant to give up either of them. But in so far as his reluctance is not altogether irrational, it must be due to the fact that each of his beliefs is in some respects true, in spite of the contradiction which exists between his own formulations of them, i.e. it must be possible, in theory at least, to reformulate the beliefs so as to remove the contradiction and still retain what is true and important in them—it is irrational to rest content in a contradiction of this kind. When speaking of beliefs or propositions, we often use the words 'inconsistency' and 'contradiction' interchangeably, for the only relevant type of inconsistency is a logical one; two propositions are inconsistent if, and only if, their conjunction is logically impossible. (We sometimes talk, rather loosely, about a proposition or belief being inconsistent with the facts, but this is simply an elaborate way of saying that it is untrue.) A man sometimes holds two simultaneous beliefs, or makes two simultaneous assertions, which are inconsistent; their inconsistency, and the irrationality of believing or asserting the two propositions, can be shown by exhibiting the contradiction between them.

When we come to consider action, things are not so simple. It is natural, and indeed correct, to see an analogous connection between consistency and rationality of behaviour; but the situation is here complicated by the fact that there are several different ways in which behaviour can be consistent or inconsistent (this is due primarily to the fact that actions may be consistent or inconsistent with a variety of factors). It is the purpose of this chapter to examine some of these ways, and to see what connection, if any, the various distinctions between consistent and inconsistent conduct have with that between morally right and morally wrong conduct. Before we enter on this examination, one preliminary point must be made. In any of the senses in which behaviour may be said to be consistent, this consistency may be of two kinds, which I shall call weak and strong consistency respectively. To take as an example that sense of consistency which denotes a relation between actions, two actions are consistent in the weak sense if, and only if, they are not inconsistent; two actions are consistent in the strong sense if, and only if (*a*) they are not inconsistent and (*b*) the agent in performing them makes deliberate use of some connection between them, such that either the performance of each action in some way facilitates the performance of the other or the performance of one of the actions in some way facilitates the performance of the other. If I go for a walk and, on returning home, have some tea my two actions are consistent in the weak sense; but if I go for a walk in order to work up an appetite for my tea, which I subsequently eat and enjoy, there is a strong, or positive, consistency in my conduct. Philosophers have often used the word 'coherence' when speaking about consistency in the strong sense; it would not normally be said that a relation of coherence existed between two actions, or two desires, merely on the ground that there was no inconsistency between them.

In what follows, I consider four different types of answer that can be given to the question 'With what can an action be consistent or inconsistent?'. These are:

(i) any plan or policy of the agent's;
(ii) previous or simultaneous statements of the agent;
(iii) other actions of the same agent;
(iv) the welfare, policies or actions, both actual and possible, of others.

A considerable amount of overlapping exists between the first three of these categories, but it is convenient to examine them separately as far as possible.

(i) The most elementary situation in which the relations of consistency or inconsistency may occur is in the connection between a plan or policy and its constituent parts or any other action of the agent which may have an effect on the success of the plan or policy. An action is inconsistent with a plan or policy if its performance makes the success of the plan or policy impossible; and in general, an action is inconsistent with any purpose or objective of the agent if its performance makes the achievement of that purpose or objective impossible. A Minister of Foreign Affairs who is pursuing a policy of friendship with a neighbouring country acts inconsistently with that policy if he makes a public speech in which he refers to the inhabitants of the country as a lot of ignorant savages; a student who sets himself to obtain a First Class Honours Degree in order to enter on a particular career acts inconsistently if he fails to devote himself to his work with sufficient energy. An action is consistent, in the weak sense of the word, with a plan provided only that it is not inconsistent with it; it is consistent with it in the strong sense if its performance is either a necessary condition of the success of the plan or at least makes the success of the plan more likely, or easier to achieve.

Inconsistency of this sort, provided that it is known to the agent or that he might reasonably be expected to know it, is a ground of criticism and a sign of irrationality or unreasonableness; we should have no hesitation in describing the behaviour of the Foreign Minister or the student in the above examples as unreasonable. But it is important to notice that the inconsistency, and the unreasonableness of which it is a sign, can be removed in either of two ways: either by the agent ceasing to perform, or refraining from performing, the action that is inconsistent with his policy or objective, or by his giving up, or at least modifying, the plan or objective itself. The latter course is probably as common in practice as the former, although philosophers have perhaps paid less attention to it. A man may indeed set himself an objective, and reject a possible course of action as being inconsistent with its attainment; but we are not all so single-minded as to do this whenever we are aware of inconsistency. What often happens is that we give up the objective or policy, rather than the particular action that is inconsistent with it. In the abstract, and without taking into account the circumstances of the case, it is impossible to maintain that either of these ways of removing inconsistency is more reasonable, or more satisfactory, than the other. Some idealist philosophers seem to have thought that it is always more rational to retain the policy, on the ground that the formation and maintenance of a policy require a higher degree of rationality than the performance of an action motivated by some relatively simple desire. This, however, is a mistake, due to a failure to distinguish two different senses of the word 'rationality'. A plan may be said to exhibit rationality, in one sense of the word, in direct proportion to the complexity and subtlety with which its various aspects are related; and rationality in this sense is exhibited to some degree in the formation of any plan, however rudimentary. But it does not follow that, because one plan is more rational than another in this sense, it is necessarily more rational (or more reasonable) in the quite different sense that there are better reasons for acting on it. In a non-moral case a man may quite rationally, or quite reasonably, reject a highly subtle and complex plan because he sees that carrying it out will lose him the respect of some of his friends (and this does not mean that gaining or retaining the respect of his friends is part of some higher plan). Similarly in a moral case, a man may quite rationally or reasonably reject a highly subtle and complex plan because he sees that carrying it out will cause unnecessary hardship to some innocent people (and this again does not mean that the avoidance of hardship to others is part of some higher plan). In the abstract, all that consistency requires of a man is that, if A and B are inconsistent, he should give up at least one of them; the requirement of consistency cannot by itself show which of the two should be given up.

(ii) Inconsistency between statement and action can take several forms. A straightforward lie, about either one's past actions or one's future intentions, might be regarded as exhibiting a kind of inconsistency, as also might the making of a promise which one had no intention of keeping. Again, the breaking of a promise which one originally intended to keep involves a discrepancy between word and deed, though in this case it is the deed or its absence that creates the discrepancy, and not the original utterance. Where such inconsistency or discrepancy is deliberate, however, it is, at least, not obvious that it is a sign of irrationality of any kind; telling lies and breaking promises are doubtless, in general, morally wrong, but this is because they in some way injure, or are liable to injure, other people, and in particular the people to whom the lies are told and the promises made, not because of a theoretically irrational disharmony between what is said and what is done. The precise nature of the answer one gives to the question 'Why should I speak the truth and keep promises?' will vary according to the type of moral theory one holds; but it has to be treated as a sensible, meaningful question, differing in this respect from 'Why should my actions conform with my plans?'

Statements and actions sometimes conflict without any deliberate intent. A middle-aged man who repeatedly cheats the customs when returning from his holidays abroad may make frequent public complaints about the growing dishonesty of the younger generation; if he fails to see the inconsistency, as often happens, he is guilty of hypocrisy, not of lying. Behaviour of this kind is irrational, paradoxically, just because it is not deliberate. Deceiving other people may on occasions be perfectly rational or reasonable—it may sometimes be morally justified; but deceiving oneself, which is what hypocrisy of this kind amounts to, is irrational, to the extent that it involves a failure to appreciate all the relevant facts. A deliberately chosen discrepancy may not be contrary to reason; but failure to see an inadvertent one is.

Many discrepancies between word and act can be excused on the ground that the agent changed his mind. A man who had announced his intention of voting Labour at the next General Election and who was later seen canvassing for the Liberals would normally be said to be behaving inconsistently; but the charge of inconsistency could be met by his explanation that he had now changed his mind and was a convinced Liberal supporter. There is obviously nothing irrational in principle about changes of this kind;[1] indeed, refusal to change one's mind is often itself a sign of irrationality. We cannot safely regard all a man's actions and utterances as belonging to an abstract, timeless whole, and demand a complete, unbroken consistency throughout. The situations which a man has to face may change drastically, his experience tends to widen and his character to develop; some kind of development in his conduct is therefore not merely permitted but required if it is to remain rational. This seems to be what Emerson was getting at in his famous diatribe against consistency, though in his enthusiasm he obviously presses the attack too far.

> A foolish consistency is the hobgoblin of little minds, adored by little statesmen and philosophers and divines. With consistency a great soul has simply nothing to do. He may as well concern himself with his shadow on the wall. Speak what you think now in hard words and to-morrow speak what to-morrow thinks in hard words again, though it contradict every thing you said to-day (R. W. Emerson: *Self-Reliance*, in *Works*, Riverside ed. (London, 1900), Vol. II, p. 58).

If a man occasionally changes his mind this may indeed be a sign that he is genuinely thinking about the situation as it is and not worrying too much about his own past thoughts or utterances. But a man who changes his mind frequently, however much honesty and freshness of spirit he is displaying, may well be criticised on the ground that he is continually failing to take enough trouble to relate his ideas to the facts; if he was wrong yesterday, the day before yesterday and the day before that, what likelihood is there of his being right today? In other words, although some inconsistency of this kind is rationally defensible, there comes a point beyond which it ceases to be so.

(iii) Adjectives which characterise a man's conduct are sometimes qualified by the adverb 'consistently' to indicate that the

---

[1] Promises, however, are a special case. Someone who refused to keep a promise merely because he had changed his mind and was no longer prepared to do what he had promised would not merely be acting in a morally wrong manner; he would, if he put forward his change of mind as a sufficient justification, show that he did not fully understand the nature of a promise. One of the main functions of the institution of promises is to enable us to rely on other people behaving as they have said they will, even if they should subsequently come to prefer some other line of conduct.

characteristic in question is displayed in all those actions of the agent in which it is possible to display it, the opposite characteristic never occurring. A man may be, in this sense, consistently brave, intelligent or generous; conversely, he may be consistently timid, stupid or mean—and in any field, whether moral or non-moral, he may be consistently right or consistently wrong. This use of the word 'consistently' has little connection with the logical or quasi-logical uses we are considering, being more or less a synonym for 'regularly'. It is clearly not necessarily a term of praise; consistency of conduct, in this sense, is not a virtue unless the conduct itself is antecedently good. It does not even indicate that the agent is acting on a consistent principle; a man who consistently runs away from danger is not necessarily one who runs away on principle—it may be that his fear always conquers his determination to stand fast. And a man who is consistently stupid is not acting on the principle of being stupid.

There is, however, another, more important, sense in which two or more actions may be consistent or inconsistent with one another. To take first a simple example, it is obviously inconsistent for a judge to sentence a thief to two years' imprisonment on Monday, and on Tuesday to sentence another thief with a similar record to five years' imprisonment for a crime with no features to distinguish it from the first (the inconsistency might be caused by the fact that he was feeling particularly happy and benevolent on the Monday, or particularly miserable or ill-tempered on the Tuesday, although neither of these factors would be relevant as justifying reasons). To impose widely differing sentences without any corresponding differences in the crimes or the criminals is inconsistent because there is no rule or principle or policy from which both sentences alike could be derived, or to which both sentences could be shown to be appropriate. A more interesting example is that of the commandant of a Nazi concentration camp who is not himself, in his ordinary life, a vicious or a brutal man (he may be kind-hearted and full of love and devotion to his family and friends), and who nevertheless in his official capacity engages in and authorises the vicious and brutal treatment of the inmates of his camp. There are several cases of this kind on record, showing a readiness to live different parts of one's life in different watertight compartments, as it were, and either a complete failure to see the need for any consistency between the compartments or, more rarely, an explicit denial that such need exists. In general, we may say that two actions are consistent with one another in the strong sense if they are performed by the agent in conscious obedience to a rule or principle or in conscious furtherance of policy, and if they do in fact accord with the rule or further the policy; and that two actions are consistent with one another in the weak sense if they could both be derived from the same rule or principle or be performed in furtherance of the same policy, even if they were not in fact so derived or so performed by the agent.

To what extent is inconsistency of this type a sign of irrationality? In the case of the judge, it is clearly inappropriate for him to pass sentence in radically different ways on different days of the week; but this, it might be argued, is because consistency is something that is especially required of a judge's actions —the passing of sentences on no principle at all, which is what such inconsistency amounts to, is judicially improper, and is also completely pointless (whereas not all injustice need involve inconsistency nor be pointless; it is quite possible for a judge to act on the principle of giving heavier sentences to Jews or coloured people, however unjust that may be). But suppose an ordinary man, not a judge, admits that some of his actions are mutually inconsistent, but denies that this is in any way an objection to them, what kind of comment could be made on this? The crucial point seems to be the extent to which acting according to the feeling or whim of the moment, or as the spirit moves one, is merely non-rational, and how far it is counter-rational. Everyone would agree that there are some fields of choice and action where it is not unreasonable to allow one's actions to be determined by feeling or taste. A man who sometimes takes sugar in his tea and sometimes does not, according to his preference of the moment, is acting inconsistently in a sense, but there is nothing in his behaviour to which exception can be taken on rational grounds. And a great part of our ordinary lives, especially in our relations with our friends and with those we love, is quite properly affected by the way we feel. If a man chose to live the whole of his life in this way he would presumably be unconcerned by any charge of inconsistency; the fact that there was no possible principle or set of principles with which his conduct could be said to accord would not, for him, suggest that there was anything wrong with it.

Such men, however, are found very rarely, if at all. Most of us, however affected by impulses and feelings, make frequent implicit claims in our actions, if not every time we act. Much as a man who makes a statement makes an implicit claim, not merely that the statement is true, but that he has at least some reason to believe that it is true, so a man who performs a particular act very often does so because he thinks it more appropriate than, or as appropriate as, any alternative. And a man whose behaviour is public may be claiming implicitly that it is appropriate, and that reasons can be given for acting in this way rather than any other. To the extent that a man's actions are thought or claimed by him to be rationally defensible in this way, he is vulnerable to a charge of inconsistency, in a way in which the man who lives entirely according to impulse is not; for if one action of his is rationally defensible, it follows that another action inconsistent with it is not—some sort of reasons might be given in support of either, but it is impossible for both sets of reasons to be rationally acceptable.

This point can be expressed in terms of the notion of commitment. It is obvious enough that, if I adopt the principle of helping all those I meet who are in need or distress, I am committed to helping this particular beggar, assuming that he is genuinely in need; in general, the adoption of a principle commits one to certain actions rather than others when circumstances arise in which the principle is applicable. It is less obvious, perhaps, but equally true and important, that the performance of a particular action can sometimes commit me to the adoption of a rule or principle,[1] and so in turn to the performance of another particular action (always provided, of course, that consistency of conduct is something which I value—a man who makes no claim to consistency is not, in this sense, committed to anything). Inconsistency between actions amounts to a failure to act in the way in which one is committed to acting by one's previous behaviour. Every action that a man performs limits his free choice of actions for the future, so long as he wishes to act, or is committed to acting, consistently. Here, of course, as always, a man can change his mind; so that the charge of inconsistency can be met by the

[1] Or, less strongly, to the refusal to accept a particular rule or principle (e.g. my telling a lie commits me to a rule of conduct which permits lying in circumstances which sufficiently resemble those in which I told the lie).

admission that the earlier act was inappropriate or wrong, i.e. the act which commits him to a particular course of action can be rejected. Indeed, both in non-moral and in moral contexts, this is a very common reason for changing one's mind; the realisation, that is, that a particular action, performed or projected, commits one, either to a policy or principle or to another particular action, in a way that one is unable or unwilling to accept.

It might be objected to this account of consistency and commitment that, even if it is correct as far as it goes, it does not take us very far, since, even if the performance of an action commits us to acting for the future in a way that is not inconsistent with it, this restriction on our freedom will often, at least, be extremely slight —so slight as to provide no positive guidance for action. It must be remembered, however, that we have throughout been making an enormous simplification of the facts in the interests of a clear and manageable exposition of them—in particular, we have been talking about the mutual inconsistency of two actions, and so long as we remain at this over-simple level, the criticism has some plausibility. In reality, however, a man's life is far more complex than this account of a relation between two actions would suggest. We all perform a large number of actions, formulate very many plans and policies, adopt many rules and principles; and the requirement that all this great variety of factors should be mutually consistent is not by any means unrestrictive. This indeed is clear from the fact that accusations of inconsistency are so often made, and justly made. It does not follow, of course, that at any given time in a man's life the requirement of consistency is uniquely restrictive, i.e. that a man is always committed to the performance of one act, and one only, in the situation in which he finds himself. Indeed, it is quite certain that this is not so. But men are sometimes so committed; and on many occasions when they are not, the alternatives between which they may consistently choose are clear and limited in number.[1]

I have spoken already of the possible case of the man who rejects altogether the demand for consistency of conduct. But

---

[1] The relations of consistency and inconsistency may exist, not merely between two actual or projected actions, but also between one such action and another to which the agent is committed, whether he intends to perform it or not. No additional philosophical problems arise, however, from this complication.

although such a man might be considered wildly eccentric, it is possible to take a less extreme attitude and, while accepting the general need for consistency, to maintain that there are some types of situation where inconsistent behaviour is better than consistent. It might be argued, for example, that it is inconsistent both to oppose capital punishment and to object that in a certain country a white man is merely sent to prison, not executed, for murdering a negro (when a negro would normally have been executed for murdering a white man). The inconsistency is shown by the fact that one is claiming (*a*) that no one ought to be judicially executed and (*b*) that this white man ought to be judicially executed. Yet someone who held both these positions might naturally be reluctant to give up either of them; for there are strong reasons against capital punishment, and there are also strong reasons against inflicting less severe punishment on one man than on another, merely because the former is white and the latter black. However, although we may agree that the combination of these two attitudes is not improper, we are not thereby committed to tolerating inconsistency, still less to approving of it, since the supposed inconsistency disappears on closer examination. For the person in question is not claiming *tout court* that the white man should be executed (this would indeed be inconsistent with the claim that no one should be executed); he is making two claims at different levels, one that the law ought to be changed so as to abolish judicial execution, the other that, whatever the law is, it should be fairly and equally administered as between black and white. He is saying, in effect, 'Either both black and white murderers should be executed, or none should', and expressing a strong preference for the second alternative; and there is no inconsistency here. In general, there is no inconsistency between urging a change in the law and claiming that, as long as the law remains as it is, it should be properly and fairly applied; to urge a change in the law does not commit one to behaving, or urging others to behave, as if it had already been changed.

A rather different type of case is this. Suppose a man who is not in the habit of giving money to charity is so impressed by the plight of one particular set of people that he does, uncharacteristically, contribute to their relief. Is it not inconsistent to give money to one charity, and yet never to give to others which are less spectacular but equally or perhaps more deserving?

(Complaints of this kind appeared in the correspondence columns of some newspapers over the appeals made on behalf of Hungarian refugees in 1956.) And yet the man who inconsistently gives to one, or a few, charities is surely acting in a more nearly correct way than the man who consistently gives to none. Now if the words 'consistently' and 'inconsistently' are here being used merely to indicate regularity of behaviour then, as we have seen (above, p. 133), regularity is not necessarily a virtue; a man who sometimes does the right thing and sometimes the wrong acts in a more nearly correct way than the man who regularly and consistently does what is wrong. But it might be argued that the inconsistent giver is inconsistent in a stronger sense; i.e. that his conduct is somehow unreasonable, because his decision to give to one charity rather than the other is not based on any rational distinction between the needs and deserts of the two charities. It is true, of course, that a man's choice of charities is up to a point a free one, since unless he is fabulously rich he will be unable to make significant gifts to all deserving charities in proportion to their deserts; but is it not unreasonable to give to charities without taking their relative deserts into account? Given, say, twenty equally deserving objects, it may well be reasonable to give generously to one or two only, rather than make trivial contributions to all; but it cannot be reasonable to give to one without first considering whether it is more deserving than, or at least as deserving as, the others.

Examples of this kind are important because they illustrate the way in which feelings or impulses may lead us to act in one way rather than another without the consequent action being necessarily unreasonable in any way. Different people are emotionally impressed in different ways, and it is quite unreasonable to expect them all to have identical interests. Further, although some charities are more in need or more deserving than others, it does not follow that all our gifts ought to be given to the former rather than the latter, any more than, in general, everyone ought to fulfil the most important tasks that have to be performed, and neglect the less important; the prevention of cruelty to children is more important than the prevention of cruelty to animals, but it does not follow that the latter is unimportant and therefore an unreasonable object of human endeavour. The most severe rationalist must admit that we may derive from feeling or impulse the notion of performing, or the inclination to perform, an action that we should not have considered seriously in the absence of such feeling. However, once we have been led by feeling into considering the action, we may well come to discover good reasons for performing it, and there may well be good reasons even if we do not ourselves discover them. Here, as elsewhere, the fact that feeling is at least partly responsible for initiating an action does not prevent the action from being rational or reasonable—whether it is has to be determined by reference to its relation to the circumstances in which it is performed, and cannot be settled in advance by deciding that it had its origin in feeling.

Before we proceed to discuss the fourth type of consistency/inconsistency relation, two general points are worth making about the types so far dealt with, and their connection with morality. First, consistency, in any or all of the senses which we have been considering, is not a sufficient condition of rational or morally right action. It is clearly possible for a man to act both consistently and irrationally or wrongly; for there are other factors besides inconsistency which make for irrationality—failure to take proper account of relevant facts, for example. This is true even if we are thinking of consistency in the strong sense of the word; the most carefully worked out coherent policy may still be irrational or unjustifiable in some respects.

Secondly, so long as we restrict the application of the notions of consistency and inconsistency to the internal relation between the actions, plans, policies, principles, etc., of a single agent, the extent to which these notions give rise to, or help to account for, moral distinctions is strictly limited. Moral judgements can be derived by means of the concepts of consistency and inconsistency only from other moral judgements; i.e. we must start with a moral judgement before we can arrive at another one. Given that act A is morally required of me, and that act B is inconsistent with it, it follows that it would be morally wrong for me to perform act B. Again, if act C is inconsistent with policy P we can derive a moral judgement from this if either the act or the policy is morally required of us; in the former case it follows that the policy is morally wrong, in the latter that the act is. (It is important to notice the existence of these two alternative possibilities; some of those who hold that 'the end justifies the means' fail to do so. It is, of course, possible, and it is sometimes correct, to reject an otherwise desirable action on the ground that it is inconsistent with a desirable or necessary objective or policy; but it is also possible, and it is correct at least as often, to reject an otherwise desirable objective or policy on the ground that it cannot be achieved without either failing to perform some desirable or obligatory action, or performing some undesirable or morally wrong action.) The mere fact, however, that a man has behaved inconsistently is not sufficient evidence to show that he has done anything that is morally wrong, even though it shows that he has in a sense acted irrationally. For although many of his actions, policies and principles may be mutually inconsistent, it is still possible for him to do all that is morally required of him and to refrain from doing anything that is inconsistent with that.

Whether, indeed, any kind of moral distinctions can be understood or explained as long as we remain at this individual level is extremely doubtful. Some philosophers have, of course, tried to construct moral theories on an apparently individual, as opposed to a social, basis, by explaining morally correct conduct as that which tends best to promote the interests or advantage of the agent or which leads to some other individual end (self-realisation, for example). But to the extent that plausible moral theories are constructed in this way, it is only by the introduction, open or surreptitious, of other factors. It is quite absurd to suppose that a man's duties and obligations could be completely established without taking any account of the needs and interests of other people; and a theory which distinguishes conduct as correct or incorrect solely according as it promotes or adversely affects the interests of the agent is clearly a prudential, not a moral theory.

(iv) It is at this stage that a fourth type of consistency and inconsistency becomes important, in which one man's behaviour is consistent or inconsistent with the actions, plans, policies, principles, needs, interests, wishes, etc., of other people. While behaviour is not called consistent or inconsistent *tout court* in virtue of a relationship of this kind (to behave inconsiderately is not necessarily to behave inconsistently), it is quite natural to speak of a relation of harmony or disharmony, co-operation or conflict existing between two or more people or groups of people, and these relations may be subsumed under the general terms of consistency and inconsistency respectively. We have to ask whether one man's behaviour on a particular occasion is consistent with the needs, desires and interests of others, and this might perhaps be interpreted as asking whether his behaviour could form part of a policy which could be adopted by others, as well as by himself.[1] There is a difficulty, however, in the phrase 'could be adopted by others'. For, in a sense, any policy could be adopted by anyone; it is possible for a slave to agree with his master that he should remain a slave, possible indeed for one man to let himself be injured, and even put to death, by another. If we interpret the phrase as widely as this no action of one man could ever be inconsistent with the actions or policies of another. A possible way of making the necessary restriction would be to make use of the notion of co-operation; we could ask whether an action of agent X was such that it could form part of a joint policy of co-operation between X and some other agent or agents, or indeed all other agents who might be affected by it. If it were objected that this is still not sufficiently restrictive, on the ground that co-operation can in fact take place even where there is a conflict of interests (slaves can co-operate with their masters even when it is not in their interests to do so), it could be replied that the co-operation referred to must, potentially at least, be total; i.e. the notion is one of co-operation between free and equal individuals, without any initial preference or favouritism for the interests or plans of one rather than another (this is sufficient to rule out slavery, since an initial preference for the master's interests over those of the slave, should the two conflict, is built into the relationship). Such a criterion is still somewhat vague, and its application in most cases would require in addition a knowledge of, or agreement on, a large body of relevant empirical facts. For our purposes, however, it is enough to consider the extreme case of the man whose actions are directed entirely by considerations of self-interest or by his appetites and desires as they chance to occur, and who does not concern himself in any way with the desires or the welfare of others. While it is not logically necessary that such a man should ever find himself in conflict with others, it is in practice almost inevitable that he should frequently do so; and when he does he is sure to act in a way that is in principle, and not merely in fact, unco-operative; co-operation with others, if it

---

[1] Compare the somewhat analogous account given above (pp. 133–4) of the criterion for distinguishing between an action which is consistent, and one which is inconsistent, with another action of the same agent.

involves any restriction whatsoever on his own actions, is ruled out from the start. His behaviour may be internally consistent, and objectionable only in its failure to respect the needs and rights of others; in what sense, if any, can it be held to be unjustified and contrary to reason?

Holders of a coherence theory of good, or of morality, have usually proceeded by a kind of analogy from a discussion of coherence between the various desires, actions, principles, etc., of a single individual to consideration of a coherence between a number of individual wills (all those constituting a particular group or society, extending in some cases to the whole of humanity). Now this extended use of the word 'coherence' and a similar use of the word 'consistency' are in themselves unobjectionable; there are clearly enough resemblances or affinities between the internal relations of an individual's desires and actions and the external relations of the desires and actions of a number of individuals to make the use of the same terminology quite proper. To make use of the analogy between the individual and the group or society of individuals is not to commit ourselves to any 'organic' theory of society or to the primacy of the group or society over the individual, as long as we make it clear that we are using such words as 'coherence' in two allied but different senses, not in one and the same sense in both applications. But since there is some difference between the two uses of the word 'coherence', it is theoretically possible that, although internal incoherence is a sign of irrationality, external incoherence (i.e. the inconsistency of one's conduct with the needs and desires of others) is not—a possibility which many defenders of a coherence theory seem to have overlooked.

One important difference between good and bad men, or between law-abiding individuals and delinquents or criminals, is that the latter, although perhaps prepared and able to make some moral judgements, such as 'He ought not to have treated me like that', or 'He was unfair to me', seem to be either unable or unwilling to put themselves into another's place, and to grasp that, if action x performed by A is unfair to them, then quite probably a similar action performed by them is unfair to A. This might be thought a failure of imagination or sympathy, rather than a symptom of irrationality; and it is, of course, a failure of a kind that may be found in people who are highly rational and intelligent in other respects. Moreover, the failure is usually in one direction only; the man who is prepared to complain 'Why should he be paid twice as much as I for doing the same work?—it's not fair' may well fail to take the further step 'Why should I be paid twice as much as he for doing the same work?—it's not fair', although no additional quality of a purely intellectual kind is required in order to be able to take it. Yet it can also be represented as a failure to make a certain kind of valid generalisation—i.e. to generalise from one's own position in the world to the position of all other men who are in a similar situation; and generalisation of this kind, together with the seeing and understanding of such resemblances and similarities, is a reasoning activity. It is clear, moreover, that, whatever the criteria of validity may be, such generalisations can be valid or invalid, in a quite natural sense of those terms. A criminal who complains against the police 'How would they like it if I treated them as they treat me?' is producing a caricature of a rational argument; he is appealing to the principle, reasonable enough in itself, that like cases should be treated alike, but is overlooking or concealing the fact that the cases to which he is referring are really unlike. However, it is one thing to say that such a process of generalisation, if it is conducted at all, must be conducted rationally; quite another to say that it is irrational or unreasonable to refuse to conduct it altogether. We can indeed show an inconsistency in the life of a man who complains about the unfair or wrong treatment which he receives from others and who yet has no compunction in treating others in the same way; yet this inconsistency can be resolved as well by his ceasing to make the complaints, whether privately to himself or publicly to others, as by altering his own conduct. But if a man makes no claim that his way of life is correct or best, and says simply 'This is the way of life I prefer, and I'm going to stick to it' it is difficult to see how his attitude can be shown to be irrational[1] merely because it does not take the needs of others into account.

---

[1] He may, of course, be held to be unreasonable, in one of the special senses of that word; for example, if he refuses to give others their fair share of some joint property, or if he will not 'listen to reason', i.e. will not accept advice which the adviser believes to be good. But neither of these refusals need be a sign of irrationality. It is irrational to refuse to share fairly if you accept the principle of 'fair shares', and equally irrational to refuse what you

L. T. Hobhouse, a believer in a coherence theory, thought that a logically compelling argument could be produced in support of the claim that the refusal to make the transition from concern with one's own needs to concern with those of others as well was irrational—i.e. he held that the transition was required, not merely permitted, by reason. He tried to show that egoism, however internally consistent and systematic, could not be regarded as a wholly rational way of life.

> Ideally, egoism might be internally self-consistent. On the other hand, the principle of universals—as a merely cognitive principle—will at least compel me to admit that you will form a similar system for yourself and that these systems may clash. If, then, both systems are rational, rational systems may be inconsistent, which is contrary to definition. If I hold mine alone to be rational, what is the basis of the difference which I allege between two similar systems? If I assert without ground that what I think or feel is preferable to what others think or feel, that is arbitrary and, therefore, by definition, irrational. It follows that there must be a ground for my preference, and if self-preference is itself a ground, it will justify your self-preference as well as mine, grounds being universal. Thus the principle of self-preference—whether of an individual or a group—involves inconsistencies and is by definition irrational (*The Rational Good* (London, 1921), p. 82).

The chief mistake here is the assumption that, whenever a man prefers one thing to another, he must, unless he is irrational, have some ground or principle on which his preference is based, and must therefore be prepared to claim the objective superiority of what he prefers over what he does not. It is obvious that we all have many preferences which lack such grounds—a preference, for example, for whisky over gin, tea over coffee, blondes over brunettes—but that such preferences are not, because of the absence of a rational ground, thereby rendered contrary to reason;[1] indeed, although some people attempt to justify pre-

---

[1] The fact that my preference for whisky over gin is not rationally grounded does not show that it is contrary to reason, and that I should be more rational if I preferred gin; it implies merely that, as far as reason is concerned, either preference is legitimate.

---

believe to be good advice; but there need be no irrationality if you reject the principle, or do not think the advice to be good.

ferences of this sort by specious arguments about objective superiority, the attempt to justify what neither needs nor can have a justification is itself a sign of irrationality. If the egoist attempts to show that his egoism is justified merely because it is his, whereas that of others is unjustified because they are not he, then he is, of course, arguing inconsistently and irrationally; but if he makes no attempt to justify his attitude at all, then, although his attitude is a non-rational one, it does not follow that it is counter-rational. In asserting and maintaining his attitude, his implicit claim is merely that it is a legitimate one as far as rational considerations are concerned (i.e. that there are no good or conclusive reasons against it), not that any other attitude is illegitimate. This approach to the problem seems to have been rejected by Hobhouse because of his belief that two rational systems could not, by definition, conflict. But the answer to this must surely be to change the definition; to assume in advance that two rational systems cannot conflict is simply to beg one of the questions at issue.

This much at least, however, can be conceded, that a completely ungrounded preference for one's own interests over those of others is non-rational, even if it is not counter-rational, and that the man who does try to justify his preferences by showing that they are at worst consistent with, and at best actively co-operative with, the preferences of others is at a higher level of rationality, in the quite simple sense that he continues to give and consider reasons for his actions and choices after the self-centred man has stopped doing so. An amoralist might remain unconvinced by this, and argue that the alleged reasons were not reasons at all, i.e. that the fact that one's actions are consistent with those of others does nothing to show that they are more correct or more rational than those that are inconsistent—if a man enjoys conflict it is impossible to prove to him that co-operation is superior to conflict (I do not mean merely that it is impossible to convince him, but that it is impossible to produce logically compelling arguments). The most that one can hope to show is that, if one is to have any moral principles, they must be such-and-such or, less strongly, that they must be of a certain stated kind or kinds. Inconsistency of type (iv) cannot be proved to be objectionable; although we can, in Mill's phrase, produce 'considerations capable of determining the intellect either to give or withhold its assent', we cannot demonstrate that the amoralist's withholding of his assent is a sign of error or stupidity or irrationality—the most we can do, and this may in practice be a great deal, is to point out the logical consequences of failure to assent, and ask whether the dissenter is prepared to accept them.

It remains to ask whether, given that we have accepted the requirement that men's actions, desires, etc., should be externally, as well as internally, consistent, we can derive from this requirement any positive rules of conduct, and in particular, whether this requirement is uniquely restrictive or whether there may be alternative, equally consistent, moralities or ways of life. The connection of uniqueness with rationality is sometimes assumed, as it was by Hobhouse; the fact that two systems or ways of life conflict (either in the sense that they cannot both be adopted by the same man without inconsistency or in the sense that adopters of one system are bound in some respects to compete with adopters of the other for the possession of objectives which cannot be attained by both—cp. Kant's example of Charles V and Francis I, who both wanted the same thing, viz. the city of Milan) is taken to indicate that one of the systems, at least, is irrational. This is, however, as we have seen, in general an unjustified assumption. It is theoretically possible, and perhaps possible in practice, that two equally rational systems might conflict. Of course, it might be retorted that the fact of conflict or inconsistency between them showed that they could not be fully rational; but if there was nothing irrational about them except the fact that they did, or might, conflict, there does not seem to be much point in applying the word 'irrational' to them—what grounds are there for assuming a 'monarchical' theory of rationality?

Indeed, apart from questions of theoretical possibility, there is one positive reason for thinking that there may be a number of different, but equally rational, ways of systematically allowing for the welfare and needs of human beings, and so, different, but equally rational, ways of life or systems of morality. Conditions of human life on earth being what they are, it is impossible for all human beings to have all their wants, needs and interests fully satisfied. Consequently, to the extent that we regard moralities and ways of life as means of satisfying human needs and interests, any system, however right and just it may be, is bound to be a kind of compromise between the various needs and interests involved; and there may well be several equally satisfactory ways of arranging this compromise, none of which could be improved upon.

IX

INTELLIGENCE

THIS chapter deals with certain aspects of the relation between intelligence and action, and in particular with the extent to which the distinction between intelligent and unintelligent action runs parallel to, or cuts across, that between morally right and morally wrong action. Philosophers have sometimes used the word 'intelligence' in a very wide sense, in which the question 'What is the connection between intelligence and action?' is identical with the question 'What is the connection between reason and action?' And since this question is the subject of our whole enquiry, it need not form the subject of a separate chapter. But, ordinarily speaking, intelligence is something rather narrower than this; and it is with the ordinary sense of the word that this chapter is concerned.

Within the ordinary sense of 'intelligence', however, an important distinction has to be made between (*a*) the capacity to think or act intelligently which may be possessed in equal or varying degree by all the individual members of a given biological species and (*b*) the degree of intelligence which tends to be manifested by the thoughts and actions of an individual member of a species, all of whose members possess this capacity. We are thinking in terms of the first sense when we contrast men as intelligent beings with amoebas as non-intelligent ones: and in terms of the second when we make J. S. Mill's contrast between Socrates, who is an intelligent man, and the fool, who is an unintelligent or stupid man. Stupidity is not the absence of any capacity for intelligent behaviour—it is absurd to call amoebas stupid—but the tendency to think stupid thoughts and perform stupid actions on the part of a being who has to some degree the capacity for acting intelligently. Intelligent and stupid behaviour alike are possible only in beings who are intelligent in the 'capacity'-sense of the word;[1] and for our purpose we may restrict our consideration of those who possess the capacity for intelligent behaviour to human beings.

Now if we ask what relevance the distinction between intelligent beings and non-intelligent beings, in the 'capacity'-sense, has to that between morally right and morally wrong conduct, the answer is fairly straightforward: a being's capacity for intelligent behaviour is a necessary condition of our ability to attribute either moral rightness or moral wrongness to the behaviour of that being. This, however, does not commit us to the view that morally right behaviour is necessarily intelligent behaviour, and morally wrong behaviour necessarily stupid. The point is, rather, that moral predicates[2] can be meaningfully applied only in situations where some kind of self-directed, purposive activity is involved. For a man to be able to act rightly or wrongly from a moral point of view, he must be able to recognise the situation in which he finds himself, to recognise himself as a potential agent who can alter that situation, and to consider what effects any action of his is likely to have.[3] A man who could not do these things, all of which require intelligence, could not deliberate, decide or choose, and so could not be a moral agent, or indeed an agent of any kind. For the same reason, he would be unable to make any moral judgements about his own behaviour; he would not know, or have any capacity for knowing, the difference between right and wrong. Some degree of intelligence is in fact required for the attribution of any kind of responsibility, legal as well as moral; idiots and mental defectives are either held not to be responsible at all or, in some cases, to be responsible for some of their actions but not for others. Further, the doctrine of diminished responsibility, which is to be found in some legal systems, rests on the principle that a man may be so affected by

[1] There is an analogy here with the notion of illiteracy. Some ability to speak a particular language is required before a man can be illiterate in it.

[2] The word 'predicates' is used here for convenience, and does not presuppose any particular theory about the 'logic' of moral utterances.

[3] That is not to say, of course, that we can make moral judgements only about a man who has thought of all these things; a man can act wrongly through failure to think, but his failure can be held to be morally wrong only if he has the capacity for thought.

circumstances that, although he had the intelligence necessary for fully responsible action, he could not in those special circumstances have been reasonably expected to exercise it. Of course, the behaviour of even a complete idiot could be called correct or incorrect after a fashion, according as it would have been right or wrong if it had come from a fully rational person; but doing this would be attempting to apply to the idiot's behaviour standards which are in fact irrelevant to it. His behaviour may be socially beneficial, harmful or indifferent in its consequences; but it cannot be morally right or wrong.

The question now arises, given human beings with a certain capacity for intelligent behaviour, are there grounds for saying that morally right conduct is indicative of a higher degree of intelligence in the agent than conduct that is morally wrong? Is it the mark of an intelligent man to act rightly, and of a stupid or unintelligent man to act wrongly? Before we can answer this question, however, some account must be given of this concept of intelligence; what is meant by, or what is involved in, saying that someone acted or behaved intelligently, or that his conduct displayed intelligence? All that we have said so far is, in effect, that intelligent beings differ from non-intelligent beings in that they possess the capacity for intelligent behaviour; and we might continue by saying that intelligent men differ from unintelligent or stupid ones in that they tend to think and act intelligently, as contrasted with those who tend to think and act unintelligently or stupidly. But we still need to know what distinguishes intelligent from stupid behaviour. It will not do simply to define intelligent behaviour in terms of its appropriateness, or stupid behaviour in terms of its inappropriateness, to a given situation; for one can hit upon the appropriate act by chance or by guesswork, as well as through the exercise of intelligence. But this difficulty can be avoided if we make use of Ryle's now famous distinction between knowing how and knowing that,[1] and say that intelligent behaviour is that which exemplifies knowing how to act; in this case, the man who acts correctly by accident clearly does not know how to behave in the situation in which he finds himself. However, to explain intelligence in terms of knowing how to act,

---

[1] Cp. G. Ryle, 'Knowing How and Knowing That', *Proceedings of the Aristotelian Society*, XLVI (1945–46), pp. 1–16, and *The Concept of Mind* (London, 1949), Chap. II.

and intelligent behaviour in terms of non-accidental appropriateness (or, as Ryle sometimes suggests, efficiency) still leaves us with some problems, since the concept of knowing how is itself not perfectly clear. Ryle's main purpose was, not to give a complete positive account of the nature of intelligence, but to refute one account of it which he took to be mistaken—a part of the 'intellectualist legend'. 'Intelligently to do something (whether internally or externally) is not to do two things, one "in our heads" and the other perhaps in the outside world; it is to do one thing in a certain manner' (PAS, XLVI, p. 3). With the first part of this statement I should have no quarrel; Ryle seems to me to have made out his case against the view that acting intelligently is just thinking followed by acting in accordance with one's thinking. But the positive claim is less convincing as it stands, not primarily because it is not correct as far as it goes, but because it is incomplete. Ryle, I think, fails to see, or at least to make consistent use of, the distinction between intelligence as capacity and intelligence as tendency to which I have drawn attention.[1] He says 'We do not find in fact that we persuade ourselves by arguments to make or appreciate jokes. What sorts of arguments should we use? Yet it certainly requires intelligence or rationality to make and see jokes' (ibid., pp. 9–10). But from the fact that it requires intelligence or rationality to make jokes, it does not follow that, other things being equal, a man who can make jokes is *eo ipso* more intelligent or rational than one who cannot. Indeed, in any ordinary sense of the words 'intelligent' or 'rational', it would be quite untrue to say that a man who can make jokes is more intelligent, other things being equal, than one who cannot, even though he possesses a certain ability or skill that the other does not. On the other hand, the ability to play chess well might easily be regarded as an indication of superior intelligence; in other words, there is not a one–one correlation between skill and intelligence. Nor is this difference just an inexplicable fact of English usage; if it were, we might agree that the good joke-

---

[1] It is perhaps significant that Ryle says much more about differences such as that between the man who knows how to play chess and the man who cannot play at all than he does about differences such as that between the man who can play chess well and the man who can play, but only badly or indifferently. Both the man who can play and the man who can play well exhibit intelligence, but only the latter exhibits skill.

teller could properly be called intelligent even if he would not usually be so called (because he exhibits the same qualities or characteristics as those exhibited by the man who is normally called intelligent). But there is an important difference between activities of the joke-making type and those of the chess-playing type to which Ryle fails to do justice. In the case of the joke-maker, his ability may be, and usually is, a matter of what may be called 'flair' or 'knack'; he knows[1] how to make people laugh, although he does not know, and does not need to know, why people laugh at some things and not at others.[2] But although the good chess-player may have a certain flair for the game that others may lack, it is clear that this is not his only, or even his principal, distinguishing factor; for whatever has or has not gone on in his mind before he makes a move, it is a necessary condition of being a good chess-player that one can explain the reasons for one's moves after one has made them and, in particular, explain why the good moves are good and the bad or indifferent moves bad or indifferent. Success in the game is not a sufficient proof of skill, any more than it is of intelligence; the retort 'Well, I won, didn't I?' may be satisfying up to a point, but it will not suffice to refute the claim that the winner played badly. Although the playing of chess is a more intellectual activity than many others in which intelligence is displayed, it seems to be a general feature of intelligent behaviour (and not merely a feature of intellectual activity) that the agent can give some sort of account of the correctness or appropriateness of his behaviour; he can answer questions about it, and explain and defend it, though he need not, of course, be willing to give such an account.

To say this is in no way to defend the 'intellectualist legend' that intelligent behaviour is necessarily accompanied or preceded by intellectual activity or a process of reasoning; in the first place, it is the ability to give an account of his action that is in question, not the actual prior or contemporaneous rehearsing of such an account, and secondly, this account need not consist of, or involve, ratiocination or reasoning, even though it does so in many

[1] Even here we might be doubtful about the use of the word 'knows'; he may in this sense know how to do it without knowing how it is done.
[2] As we might expect from the history of the word 'wit', being witty does, often if not always, involve the exercise of intelligence in a way that being humorous does not, or need not.

or in most instances—thinking or reflecting about one's actions, past, present or projected, does not necessarily involve reasoning about them. The joke-maker may need some time to think, consider or reflect before he tells his joke—being good at joke-making is not equivalent to being good at extempore joke-making—but his reflection will not necessarily be, or even include, reasoning (e.g. If this, then that: Not this, because that). The same applies to many activities which we should have no hesitation in describing as intelligent. If someone is shown a series of six patterns and is asked to say which is the odd one out it is necessary, if we are able to infer that his giving the correct answer showed intelligence, that he should be able to give some sort of account of the features in the odd pattern which differentiate it from the others, even though the account might be imperfect in various ways. But this does not mean that he must be able to reason about it, for what is in question here is the seeing, or in the case of the less intelligent person the not-seeing, of certain differences and resemblances; and this seeing does not require the making of inferences.[1] Nor, of course, does it mean that he must be good at describing or explaining his own activities—this is why I spoke of a possibly imperfect account. Ryle is obviously right in saying 'A well-trained sailor boy can both tie complex knots and discern whether someone else is tying them correctly or incorrectly, deftly or clumsily. But he is probably incapable of the difficult task of describing in words how the knots should be tied' (*The Concept of Mind*, p. 56). Intelligent practitioners of an art are not necessarily good teachers of it. But we should still expect even the least facile talker among sailor boys to be able to make such

[1] The ability to see directly, or to infer, resemblances or differences and other relations between objects or characteristics has for long been held by psychologists to be an essential part of the nature of intelligence; and there is no reason to doubt the truth of this, whatever the differences among psychologists when they try to give a more precise account. To explain intelligence in terms of knowing how does not commit one to a thoroughgoing behaviourism; for there is no reason why psychologists should not continue to ask the same types of question about knowing how as they have been in the habit of asking about intelligence—e.g. 'What qualities are principally required for the acquisition of the knowledge how to do things?', the answer to which might include such factors as attention, memory, judgement and the ability to see things in their proper relation to one another, which is itself a kind of knowing how, but is perhaps essential to all other kinds.

observations as 'This is not a proper reef-knot; if you pull it like this, it comes undone'; his ability to discern the difference between a correct knot and an incorrect one when he sees them means that he sees some difference between the two, and we should not be prepared to say of anyone that he saw a difference between two things if he could give no account whatsoever, however rudimentary, of the difference. Of course, we can sometimes say 'I can see there's a difference between A and B, but I can't for the moment see just what it is'; but as long as we remain at this level, we could not at the same time justifiably claim that A was a correct knot and B an incorrect one. For this to be justifiable, we must, at the very least, be able to say 'Although I can't describe the difference between A and B, I can see that A exactly resembles the knots I have been taught to regard as correct, and that B is in some way different from them'; and if this were all that a man could say, we should, I think, be inclined to conclude that he had learnt his knot-tying by rote—by what Ryle calls drill as opposed to training—and that he did not therefore display intelligence in his own knot-tying or in his ability to distinguish correct knots from incorrect ones. There is, as we shall see, an important analogy to this in morals.

To return to the relation between morality and intelligence, it is clear that moral conduct, in the sense of conduct which is, or may be, the object of moral appraisal or assessment, is connected with intelligence in one important respect; for a man to be able to act rightly in a moral sense, to do his moral duty or to fulfil his moral obligations, he must have some knowledge of the difference between right and wrong, and some ability to apply this knowledge in particular situations. And this latter ability is one which involves intelligence and cannot be simply a matter of flair, knack or 'intuition' (in the sense in which people talk about feminine intuition, of just 'knowing' that something is the case, or is right or wrong, without having any reasons or evidence, perhaps even against all the available evidence). It is theoretically possible that a man might go through his entire life without ever acting wrongly even though he never for one moment considered his actions by reference to the distinction between right and wrong—in Kantian language, he might always act in accordance with duty even though he did not know or realise that he was so acting. But, if there were such a man, we should certainly not call him a morally good man, and it is doubtful whether we should use the expression 'morally right' of his actions at all. There is a less extreme type of case: that of a man who knows what is right and what wrong, in the sense that he knows that there are certain types of action which people call 'right' and expect him to perform, and certain types which they call 'wrong' and expect him not to perform. He resembles the man who can see the difference between correct and incorrect ways of tying knots only to the extent that he has learnt this difference by rote and has no understanding of why the correct ones are correct and the incorrect ones incorrect. Becoming a moral agent, however, is not just a matter of learning how people distinguish right and wrong; it involves understanding the distinction and adopting it for oneself. Understanding it does not mean having a philosophical theory about it, nor even being able to teach it to others; it means seeing the point of it, or at least some point in it. The man who, when asked why lying is wrong, says 'Well, if everyone told lies we should all be in a mess' has some understanding of morality, whereas the man who answers 'People say that one ought not to lie, and get annoyed with you if you tell them lies' may well have none.

Could we, then, go on to maintain, as Ryle seems to do, that the difference between the morally good man and the morally bad man is that the former is intelligent, in that he knows how to act in certain contexts, and that the latter is unintelligent, in that he does not? And is the difference between morally right and morally wrong conduct that the former exemplifies or exhibits knowledge of how to act and that the latter exemplifies or exhibits ignorance of how to act? 'Knowing how to behave is exhibited by correct behaviour, just as knowing how to cook is exhibited by palatable dishes. True, the conscientious man may be asked to instruct other agents how to behave, and then he will, if he knows how, publish maxims or specific prescriptions exemplifying maxims. But a man might know how to behave without knowing how to give good advice' (PAS, XLVI, p. 13); and compare 'Moral knowledge, if the strained phrase is to be used at all, is knowing how to behave in certain sorts of situations in which the problems are neither merely theoretical nor merely technical' (*The Concept of Mind*, p. 316).

There are certain kinds of philosophical theory about the

nature of action which give some initial plausibility to this thesis. If it is held that all actions are directed at one and the same end (the good, or one's own happiness, or self-realisation, for example), and that morally correct conduct is conduct which does, or which is likely to, conduce to this end, and morally incorrect conduct, conduct which does not, or which is not likely to, then it is natural to say that it is intelligent or sensible to act in a way that is morally right, and unintelligent or stupid to act in a way that is morally wrong. For whatever theory one has of the nature of intelligence, it is clearly intelligent, up to a point, to act in a way that will achieve one's purpose, and stupid, up to a point, to act in a way that will not (and if the purpose is either the best that one can have or the only one, we can remove the qualifying words 'up to a point'). It is because Aristotle holds a theory of action of this kind that he can reasonably maintain the existence of a close or necessary connection between the moral virtues, or excellence of character, and the intellectual quality of *phronesis* ('practical wisdom'). Morality depends, according to views of this type, on a sort of hypothetical imperative: 'If, or since, you are aiming at a certain end, you ought, as a rational or intelligent being, to act in a way which will, or which probably will, enable you to achieve that end'; i.e. the assertion is both that you ought, morally, to act in a certain way and that it is intelligent to act in that way—the morally right action and the intelligent action coincide. But the view that all men have ultimately one and the same end or objective, or that all our purposive behaviour can be interpreted in the last analysis as the attempt to achieve one and the same purpose, is open to well-known serious objections, and is nowadays held by few philosophers, if any. The manifold variety of human aims and purposes can be given a unity only by the artificial use of a blanket-word, such as 'satisfaction' or 'happiness', to cover a number of different concepts. Nor is it obvious that the achievement of any end or ends in life could be held to be equivalent to the leading of a morally good and proper life; as a Kantian might point out, the fact that I desire something does not make the fulfilment of that desire, or the attempt to fulfil it, morally good or correct, even though it may be good or correct in some non-moral sense of the words.

The situation would not be improved if we were to adopt instead a theory which stated what a man's only aim, or at least his chief aim, ought to be (for example, his own salvation or the general happiness). For it is clear that the advance made in one direction would be achieved only at the expense of a serious difficulty in another. Given the correctness of the claim that there is ultimately only one purpose which a man may have consistently with the requirements of morality, it is doubtless his moral duty to try his hardest to fulfil that purpose; but it does not follow from this that it is intelligent of him to do this, and stupid of him to refrain—for this is the very point at issue. It may indeed be argued that a man who believes in a life after death but who has no concern for his own salvation is stupid; but that is so quite independently of any moral issues, being simply a matter of prudence, and prudence is intelligent and imprudence stupid. But if it is stupid, and not merely wrong, to have no concern for the welfare of others, this must be shown in some way, and not simply taken for granted. And while it is true that a man is stupid if, although he wants something very badly, he acts in such a way that he cannot possibly obtain it, with no compensating advantage, it cannot be shown that a man is stupid not to want something, unless the thing he does not want is a necessary condition of his obtaining something else that he does want; i.e. one could adopt this way of linking morality and intelligence only at the cost of subordinating morality to individual satisfaction or to some other non-moral end.[1]

Leaving aside those attempts to correlate intelligence and morality which require a special kind of moral theory if they are to have any plausibility, could not some attempt be made to assert such a correlation without any moral or theoretical presuppositions? For example, could we not argue that morally right conduct is intelligent conduct in that it exhibits a knowledge of how to behave, quite independently of any theory as to what particular types of conduct did, and what did not, exemplify that knowledge?

As far as general intelligence is concerned, this type of connection with morality would be hard to defend. Certainly we cannot equate intelligence in general with knowing how to behave morally; it is an obvious empirical fact that general intelligence and morality do not always go together. It is obvious that stupid men often act morally (courageously or generously, for example) in the face of great temptation to the contrary, and that an

[1] This price might, of course, be accepted by some.

intelligent man may also be a bad man. But these facts by themselves do not rule out the possibility that there is some close connection between morality and intelligence; a very intelligent man may be a very bad chess-player, even though there is clearly some connection between being intelligent and being a good chess-player, and a man who is in general stupid may be extremely clever at some limited type of activity—mental arithmetic, for example. It is a mistake to assume that intelligence in one field is always readily transferable to others, even though such transfer does occur at times; the tendency of psychologists to make such assumptions vitiated a good deal of early work on the testing of intelligence and allied factors. A man who is good at performing one type of activity will not necessarily be equally good at another, even if the activities are of the same general type; for other factors besides intelligence are operative, especially the factor of interest. A good medieval historian will not necessarily work so well if he enters the field of modern history, even though no additional technical skill is required; the medieval world may stimulate his interest or his imagination in a way in which the modern world does not. In spite of this, some psychologists in the relatively early days of intelligence-testing did produce what appeared to be good evidence for the view that there is at least some correlation between a low degree of intelligence and a proneness towards morally wrong behaviour. In particular, it was for a long time believed that defective intelligence was an important, perhaps the most important, cause of delinquency;[1] but it is now known that many of the early statistics which purported to exhibit this correlation were seriously defective.

> Defective intelligence has usually been overemphasized as a cause of delinquency because of the assumption that a mentally retarded person lacks insight into his problems and is unable to control his impulses. Although poor insight and impulsiveness may be important factors, psychological studies have shown that they are but minor factors in causing delinquent behaviour (M. Sherman:

[1] 'Delinquency' is a term which has legal connotations as well as moral ones, and it is possible for someone to engage regularly in morally wrong conduct without being properly called a delinquent; but this refinement does not affect the main issue, since a person who committed technical breaches of the law which were not considered morally wrong would not be a delinquent either.

Intelligence and its Deviations (New York, 1945), p. 102. The chapter from which this quotation is taken contains a valuable discussion of the evidence.)

But the alternative to correlating morality with general intelligence, viz. the view that the tendency to perform morally correct actions exhibits a special form of intelligence or a special skill is also unsatisfactory. In the rest of this chapter I shall consider three principal objections to it.

(i) There is no special field in which the ability to perform morally correct actions is actualised. To say that correct action exemplifies the agent's knowledge of how to behave may be true up to a point, but it is important to observe that 'behaving' is not a separate, definable, craft-activity on a par with cooking, or playing chess, or riding a bicycle. This is clear from the fact that, whereas it is open to the man who has no skill in a particular art or craft-activity to refrain from performing, or attempting to perform, it, there is no way in which a man can refrain from acting or 'behaving' in general—whatever he does, or does not do, his action or his failure to act may always be the subject of a moral judgement as to its rightness or wrongness. Even if we restrict the field of moral behaviour to those actions which affect the lives and happiness of others besides the agent, a man cannot avoid conducting himself in some way towards his fellow-men, even if he has no settled policy or principles of action, good or bad. Nor does it help if we substitute 'living' for 'behaving' and speak of morally correct conduct in terms of knowing how to live, or living well. Living, in this sense, is not a separate activity which one can choose to perform or not to perform.[1]

It might, perhaps, be maintained that, in spite of this disparity between morally correct action and the skilful or intelligent performance of such activities as cooking and bicycle-riding, there is enough affinity between them to entitle us to say that knowing

[1] The phrase 'knowing how to behave' has an odd sound when applied to moral contexts. We naturally say of a man who repeatedly insults his host that he does not know how to behave; but we are here referring to his bad manners, not to his immorality. It would be artificial to say of a brutal murderer that he did not know how to behave, not because it would not in a sense be true, but because it would be an absurd under-statement, and would have the effect of reducing standards of moral right and wrong to mere rules of etiquette or manners.

how to behave, or to live, does amount to the possession of a skill, but a very special kind of skill—a sort of super-skill or super-craft, the field of activity of which might be unlimited. Could not the logic of 'knowing how to behave' be the same as that of 'knowing how to cook', even though behaving is, as it were, a second-order concept, including in itself all the ordinary first-order activities, both skilled and unskilled? Unfortunately for this proposed solution, there are other essential differences between moral and non-moral qualities to which it does not do justice, and to the consideration of which we must now turn.

(ii) Being brave, and knowing how to handle one's weapons, are both necessary conditions of being a good soldier. It might seem at first as if we could assimilate the first of these conditions to the second, and regard it also as the manifestation of a kind of skill or ability—the ability to face dangerous situations either without fear or, if one is afraid, by keeping one's fear under control. But, although it may be quite proper to use a word such as 'ability' of both conditions, this must not tempt us to overlook an important difference between the two types of ability. Aristotle would explain the difference—and the explanation is clearly correct as far as it goes—by saying that brave actions display a man's character, whereas his ability to use weapons correctly is rather a matter of skill or cleverness.[1] There are difficulties in giving an adequate account of the concept of character, but it is clear that character is not formed entirely by skills and other intelligence-manifesting activities, and that emotional and other factors enter into it as well. So, although we may say that both the brave man and the skilful weapon-user are good at doing certain things, they are not 'good at' these things in the same way. It is sometimes even denied that 'good at' is an appropriate expression in moral contexts.

> I conclude, therefore, that there is one essential difference between those actions that are subject to non-moral appraisals, and those to which moral evaluations are appropriate. Moral evaluations are not expressed in words like 'skilful', 'clever', 'competent', 'good at', etc., but they supervene upon the appraisals in which words of

[1] There are also some qualities (punctiliousness and untidiness, for example) which would not normally be called moral qualities, but which, like them, cannot be explained in terms of the presence or absence of skill or intelligence.

this sort are used. By this I mean simply that the exercise of any skill or capacity is itself subject to moral judgement (C. K. Grant, 'Good At' in *Aristotelian Society*, Supplementary Volume XXXII (1958), p. 187).

But as Grant's fellow-symposiast A. R. White pointed out, we do use the expression 'good at' in some moral contexts. 'A temperate man is good at controlling his desires, a brave man at facing danger.... There is nothing immoral about being bad at mathematics or at remembering names, or, perhaps, at keeping appointments, but there is something immoral in being bad at controlling oneself or respecting confidences' (ibid., p. 206). It should be noticed, however, that although the expression 'good at' can be used in some moral contexts, it cannot there be replaced, as it can in many non-moral contexts, by some expression of the intelligence-family, such as 'clever at' or 'skilful at'; and to this extent Grant is clearly right. It is for most purposes immaterial whether we describe a man as good at mathematics or clever at mathematics (unless we are using 'clever' to indicate that his ability is superficial); but a man who is good at controlling his desires or respecting confidences cannot be said to be clever or skilful at so doing, nor is the man who is bad at facing danger incompetent at facing it. The coward knows what to do, but does not do it; the incompetent soldier who cannot handle his weapons does not know what to do or how to do it (his 'not knowing' may be either permanent—he may never have learnt—or temporary— he may have forgotten what he is supposed to do).

Two subsidiary points should be noted here. First, even in the field of skills and competences, knowing how to do something is not equivalent to being good at doing it, or doing it efficiently. For one may 'know how' without being 'good at', i.e. one may have a capacity without the disposition to display it; a woman may have the ability to cook well (know how to cook) and yet not be good at cooking (a good cook) because she is too lazy to cook at all. One may know how to do something and yet not choose to do it, in non-moral as in moral situations. Secondly, to call someone 'an intelligent x' is not always the same as calling him 'a good x'. Smith may be a more intelligent batsman than Jones without being a better batsman; i.e. he may apply his intelligence more thoroughly to the task of batting and yet, perhaps because he has fewer natural gifts, be a worse batsman. Even in highly intellectual activities, such as bridge- or chess-playing, other qualities besides intelligence are required—the desire to win, for example, and the ability to concentrate at important moments.

The difference between moral virtues or vices and non-moral skills or incompetences may be further elucidated if we consider another example. The man who is a skilful chess-player but who plays badly on one particular occasion (perhaps because he is tired) is, on this occasion, not manifesting the intelligence or skill which he possesses; a skilful player may be trying his hardest and still play badly, or even stupidly. His trouble is that, on this occasion, he cannot see, or does not know, what moves to play, although he can usually be relied upon to have this knowledge. On the other hand, the man who 'knows how to behave' morally but who acts wrongly on one particular occasion may be manifesting as much intelligence as the man who acts rightly; for his trouble is not that he does not know, or cannot see, what to do, but that he cannot bring himself to do it. (The analogous situation in chess would be that of a subordinate who cannot bring himself to play the moves that will beat his employer, because he thinks that winning the game may harm him in his career; and the tactful playing of bad moves need not exhibit stupidity or lack of skill.) The inability to make oneself do something that one knows one ought to do, whether this inability occurs in moral contexts or, as it may sometimes do, in non-moral ones, is a radically different kind of inability from the inability to see or discover what is the correct thing to do. It belongs to the field of what some psychologists call 'personality factors' rather than to the field of intelligence. And it is not necessary to assess the value of the many different psychological definitions of personality in order to appreciate the fact that, while personality may involve, or be affected by, intelligence, there is much more to it than intelligence, whether we are thinking of intelligence in general or of any of its specific forms. There is, for example, some experimental evidence of a fairly close correlation between a high I.Q. and success in certain types of career—those which require intelligence and not much else; but, long before moral considerations are introduced, the correlation between intelligence and ability in many other fields is seen to break down. 'In the employment situation, scores on tests of general intelligence predict success in solving problems encountered in professional, executive, and technical jobs. If the problems are of an interpersonal nature, as in selling jobs, intelligence test scores are of only limited usefulness' (D. M. Johnson, *The Psychology of Thought and Judgment* (New York 1955), pp. 393–4). And, as we should expect, there is no close correlation between high I.Q. and moral goodness; what, after all, could be more 'interpersonal' than morality, involving as it does the personality and character of the agent and of those with whom he comes into contact? In any context, intelligent behaviour is behaviour which is appropriate to the agent's situation, and which is appropriate, not accidentally, but because the agent has appreciated the situation and its demands. But the converse does not apply, for not all behaviour that possesses this type of non-accidental appropriateness is intelligent behaviour; behaviour may be appropriate in that it is determined by such factors as love, sympathy or pity, and these are not aspects of intelligence.

(iii) The third difficulty in the way of connecting morality with intelligence is an epistemological one. The question whether there are objective criteria or standards by reference to which morally right and morally wrong conduct can be distinguished is one on which philosophers still disagree; and among those who agree that there must be some such standards, there is much disagreement as to what they are. But the question whether any particular activity on the part of a particular individual exhibits intelligence, though it may often be difficult to answer, especially in borderline cases, cannot possibly be in principle unanswerable; it must be objectively the case either that intelligence is being manifested or that it is not. If we wish to discover whether a man can ride a bicycle or not we can do so by putting him on one and seeing whether he falls off. Of course, there are practical precautions that need to be taken; for example, he may be trying to conceal an ability that he really possesses. But there is no essential difficulty in devising tests to see whether the *prima facie* answer to our question is the correct one. And there may be borderline cases—e.g. a man who rode for a mile and only fell off once—but the difficulty of classifying borderline cases does not, in general, invalidate the principles of classification which are being adopted.

Some non-moral skills and abilities give rise to complications owing to the existence in different societies or groups of differing standards and customs. If we are trying to discover criteria which will enable us to distinguish good cooks from bad it will be easy enough to state certain minimum conditions which any good cook must fulfil; but difficulties may arise when we try to go further than this. A good cook by English standards might be considered a poor one in France, and vice versa, and the question whether either set of standards could be shown to be superior to the other might have to be answered in the negative owing to irresolveable differences in taste. In general, where there are no universally accepted criteria (as there are in the case of bicycle-riding), or no standards that can be shown to be uniquely valid, even if they are not universally accepted, the question whether, or to what degree, a person possesses a certain skill, or knows how to perform a certain type of activity, cannot always be answered with certainty, not, as might sometimes be the case, because of lack of evidence, but because there is no sure way of deciding what is to count as evidence. It should be noticed, however, that a first-rate cook according to one set of standards and a first-rate cook according to a different set of standards may well be equally intelligent and equally skilled, even in the judgement of someone who rejects one of the two sets. It is true that what is a delicious crème brûlée to one man may be an unpalatable burnt custard to another; nevertheless, culinary skill has been exhibited in producing it if the effect is what the cook intended, and culinary incompetence has been exhibited if it is not. So the cooking of an expert Englishwoman and an expert Frenchwoman may be equally skilful and intelligent, in that the former may cook perfectly according to the principles of Mrs. Beeton, and the latter perfectly according to the principles of Mrs. Beeton's French equivalent, if there is such a person. Intelligence is here displayed in the successful achievement of what the agent is trying to do, or to produce; and, although in general people may act unintelligently in choosing their objectives, and not merely in choosing the means to them, there is clearly no such lack of intelligence in this case—there is nothing unintelligent or stupid in cooking according to the standards of the people for whom one is cooking, however open to question those standards may be.

The importance of factors other than intelligence becomes even greater when we come to the question of behaviour in moral situations. In a conservative society all the rules of conduct may be clear and relatively fixed, and in any society there will be some such clear and fixed rules; and one can, of course, conduct an empirical investigation into the behaviour of any given person to see whether it is in accordance with those rules or not. But to make an investigation of this sort is not to ask how far a person's behaviour manifests intelligence of any kind; for it makes no assumptions about the validity, propriety or suitability of the rules, and it is impossible to hold that intelligence is exhibited in obeying a set of rules without making some such assumption—at the very least, it must be shown that obeying the rules is in some way more reasonable than failing to obey them. The alternative would be to assume that any moral rules or standards which are generally accepted within a given society are ultimate standards, in that it is logically improper (not merely morally improper) to ask critical questions about their goodness or badness or their correctness or incorrectness. We should not be able to say of anyone 'He knows how to behave according to the standards of his society, but he doesn't really know how to behave, for those standards are themselves corrupt'. But criticism of rules and standards does frequently occur, and is bound to occur. No one has to accept all the standards of his immediate neighbours, and the non-conformist can, and often does, defend his non-conformity with intelligent and sensible arguments. In any society, old-fashioned people often fail or refuse to distinguish two quite different types of behaviour, referring to them indiscriminately as immoral. We may instance the breaking of the old code of sexual morality, first, by those who, in general, accept the code or pay lip-service to it, but who fail, always or frequently, to live up to it and, secondly, by those who deliberately reject this code and replace it by another set of standards. People in the first group have clearly gone wrong, by their own standards, although even their 'going wrong' may be due in very small degree to lack of intelligence. They 'know how to behave' in a weak sense of that expression; i.e. they know how they should behave,[1] even though they do not always exhibit this knowledge in their actual behaviour. But the members of the second group can be shown to be acting wrongly only by showing that the old standards, which they are rejecting, are better than the new ones, which they are observing. We may say that this group, unlike the first, claim to

[1] This, is, perhaps, not true of those who merely pay lip-service to the standards they fail to live up to; but even they know what the standards are, although their claim to accept them is hypocritical.

know how to behave, in a strong sense of that expression; i.e. they claim to know how they should behave, and that their behaviour exhibits that knowledge. In other words, there may well be a fundamental difficulty in moral contexts in deciding between rival claims to possess moral knowledge; a difficulty which, borderline cases apart, does not occur in those non-moral activities in which there is an indisputable connection between correctness and intelligence, incorrectness and stupidity.

X
INTUITION

WE may say of an ethical proposition or principle that it is reasonable to accept or believe it, or to live by it, and we may defend our statement by producing some sort of evidence or using some kind of argument. Alternatively, we may say that accepting it or deciding to live by it is a matter of faith or non-rational commitment.[1] But these two alternatives do not exhaust the possible answers to questions about the epistemological status of moral principles. For some philosophers have held that some moral principles are such that (i) they cannot be rationally justified, (ii) they do not need rational justification, and (iii) nevertheless reason enters into our apprehension of them, in that we know directly, by a kind of moral intuition, that they are true; their truth is self-evident to anyone who fully understands their meaning. Within this group of philosophers some, like Sidgwick, have, though that only one, fundamental, principle was apprehended in this way, all other moral judgements and rules being testable by reference to the fundamental principle; others, like Ross, have thought that there were a number of intuited principles, none of which could be derived from any higher principle. For our purposes, the difference between these views is not important.

An intuitionist theory of morals has, on occasions at least, had the merit of stressing the impossibility of demonstrating the truth of all one's moral beliefs or principles; and it might seem to have,

[1] 'Non-rational' in the sense that no reasons can be given in support of this commitment rather than another. Such faith or commitment need not, of course, be contrary to reason.

even though it does not in fact have, some support in the common use of such words as 'vision', 'insight', 'discernment' and 'blindness' to stand for certain types of moral knowledge or, in the case of the last, ignorance. It is, however, radically unsatisfactory as an answer to the question 'How, if at all, do we know that we ought to behave in certain ways, and not in certain others?'

Consider, in the first place, the claim that there is at least one moral principle of which no proof or justification is needed—we just 'see' it to be true, provided that we understand it, and are not being misled by our emotions and desires into a kind of wishful, or otherwise distorted, thinking. One difficulty here is that the question whether a proof of any proposition is needed is a subjective question, the answer to which will depend on various factors, notably psychological and sociological ones. This is seen as soon as we become, rightly, suspicious of the passive voice in 'no proof is needed', and ask 'Who needs, or does not need, proof?' If a man does 'see' that something is the case, then there is, of course, a sense in which *he* does not need proof that it is (provided that it really is the case, and that his 'vision' is not distorted, a point to which we shall have to return later). But it does not follow that it is unreasonable for anyone to ask for proof, or that no one could need it. For I might not have enough insight to see that it was true, and yet be able to follow and accept a proof that it was. Both in theory and in practice, this contrast often occurs. A scientist who is good at generalisation may 'see' the explanation for a group of phenomena, whereas a less perceptive one may fail in this respect, and yet be able to follow, or indeed to provide, a proof that the proffered explanation is correct. Similarly, an expert strategist may 'see' that a certain plan is unsatisfactory, whereas a less brilliant planner may have to ask for, and obtain, proof that it is unsatisfactory. Moreover, even though I can 'see' something to be true, I can still quite sensibly look for proof that it is; a prudent man will not trust his intuitions too far. And even though I 'see' intuitively that a certain course of action is the best, I can still, and will, if I am sensible, look for confirming (or refuting) evidence. It may be said that there are some propositions which no one can doubt—no one, at least, who understands them; is it not really absurd to demand proof of these? The reply to this is twofold. In the first place, even if we are absolutely certain of the truth of a proposition, and if its denial does not even make sense to us, we may still try to prove it in order to make our beliefs, or our knowledge, as systematic as possible. A mathematician can in this way prove that $2 + 2 = 4$, given certain axioms and definitions, even though most of us cannot imagine what it would be like for it to be false. And secondly, it is in any case doubtful whether any non-tautologous ethical proposition is such that no one could help believing it; moreover, many propositions which people have not been able to help believing have in fact turned out later to be false. Some remarks of C. S. Peirce are apposite here, even though they were originally directed by him at those who claimed that the first principle of induction could be intuitively known:

> To say that we cannot help believing a given proposition is no argument, but it is a conclusive fact if it be true; and with the substitution of 'I' for 'we', it is true in the mouths of several classes of minds, the blindly passionate, the unreflecting and ignorant, and the person who has overwhelming evidence before his eyes. But that which has been inconceivable today has often turned out indisputable on the morrow. Inability to conceive is only a stage through which every man must pass in regard to a number of beliefs—unless endowed with extraordinary obstinacy and obtuseness. His understanding is enslaved to some blind compulsion which a vigorous mind is pretty sure soon to cast off (*The doctrine of necessity examined*, in Collected Papers Vol. VI (Cambridge, Mass., 1935), pp. 37–8).

Even where we may not wish to dispute the correctness of a belief, further reflection may lead us to conclude that its apparent self-evidence is deceptive, and that it owes its truth to its dependence on some other proposition or principle. It is worth noticing in this connection some remarks of Sidgwick about deceptive self-evidence.

> Each individual in any society commonly finds in himself a knowledge not obviously incomplete of the rules of Honour and Etiquette, and an impulse to conform to them without requiring any further reason for doing so. Each often seems to see at a glance what is honourable and polite just as clearly as he sees what is right; and it requires some consideration to discover that in the former cases custom and opinion are generally the final authority from which there is no appeal (*The Methods of Ethics* (London, 1930), pp. 340–1).

Sidgwick goes on to say that there are often conventional elements in our apparent moral intuitions, which need therefore to be tested to see whether they are genuine intuitions, i.e. genuinely self-evident. But what sort of tests could possibly be of use here? Of the four necessary conditions of a genuine intuition laid down by Sidgwick, three (all self-evident propositions must possess clarity and precision, they must be mutually consistent and they must be generally accepted by those who understand them) are tests (whether good or bad does not concern us) of truth, not of self-evidence; and the one test that is a test of self-evidence (that the proposition concerned must be ascertained to be self-evident by careful reflection) is unworkable and useless. For, as Sidgwick's own remarks quoted above should have shown him, any moral proposition which some men accept without proof or argument or reason may be thought by others to require proof or reasoned support; and the fact that after a great deal of careful reflection a man finds a moral proposition to be self-evident means no more than that he is not prepared to consider the possibility that it might be false—and this is in no sense an objection to anyone else who is prepared to consider it.

Some further defects of intuitionism appear as soon as we subject the notion of intuition to a careful analysis. The word 'intuition', like the companion word 'insight', is a metaphor drawn from the sense of sight, a metaphor which is repeated in the common intuitionist expression 'We see (directly) that something is the case'; and a person who fails to 'see' what others do may well be called 'blind'. Now the verb 'to see', in its literal sense, is used in two different ways. Ordinarily, to say 'I see an x' or 'He sees an x' is to imply that the thing seen is real, that it has some sort of objective existence outside the optical and nervous system of the man who sees it. Sometimes, however, the verb is used without this implication. 'I see stars' may be used by a man who is looking up at a clear night sky and seeing real stars (or what he takes to be real stars, even if they are not); alternatively, it may be used by a man who has received a severe blow on the head and is describing his visual sensations without claiming that the stars which he sees are real stars. Similarly, a man who says 'I see a coloured patch' may be referring to a real coloured patch on an otherwise white wallpaper; alternatively, he may be describing the after-image which he sees when he shuts his eyes after he has been looking for some time at a brightly coloured object. Now we may make a comparable distinction within the philosophical use of the word 'intuition'. Most ethical intuitionists have used it and its corresponding verb in such a way that a false intuition, like a non-existent seen thing (according to the first way of using the verb 'to see'), is a contradiction in terms. 'He intuits [or 'sees'] that p' implies the truth of p. So we could not say 'I intuited p, but I was mistaken' (any more than we could say 'I saw a cat, but I was mistaken'); we should have to say 'I thought that I intuited p, but I was mistaken in thinking so'. Others, however, of whom Ewing is perhaps the most prominent, have been prepared to speak of true and false intuitions, much as one might speak of veridical or illusory visual experiences.

Now if one uses 'intuition' in the former way intuiting is certainly a guarantee of the truth of what is intuited, just as knowledge is a guarantee of the truth of what is known. But the guarantee is worthless. If we are not sure whether a certain proposition is true, or whether we ought to act on a certain moral principle, an intuitionist friend may say to us, 'Don't worry. The proposition is true, for I see directly that it is so: the principle is correct, for I see directly that you ought to act on it. In neither case are evidence, argument or, in general, reasons necessary.' But it would be absurd to attach any weight to this sort of remark, unless we had independent evidence of the accuracy or penetration of our friend's intuitive powers. With this use of 'I intuit, or see directly, that . . .', as with a similar use of 'I know that . . .', a claim is being made which, if valid, does, of course, entail the truth of the proposition intuited, or known. But the claim to possess intuition or knowledge is not self-justifying; contrary to what some intuitionists suggest, it requires justification and defence before it becomes reasonable to accept it. It is sometimes held that the phenomenological nature of the intuition or apprehension provides this justification, and that we can discover by phenomenological investigation or by introspection whether a given mental activity or process is properly called an example of intuition or not. But this is a mistake. There is no discoverable difference, *qua* state of mind, between the state of mind of a man who thinks he intuits that something is the case, or ought to be done, when this is in fact not the case, or ought not to be done, and the state of mind of a man who genuinely intuits that something is the case, or ought to be done.[1] The same subjective certainty, the same inability to conceive that one may be mistaken, the same rejection of the need for proof, may be equally present in both cases.[2] In his famous article 'Does Moral Philosophy Rest on a Mistake?' (*Mind*, 1912, reprinted in *Moral Obligation* (Oxford, 1949), pp. 1–17) H. A. Prichard accused moral philosophers of absurdly trying to justify our knowledge of moral truths—as if my knowledge that I ought not to break a promise could be, or needed to be, justified. But while it is, of course, absurd to talk about justifying knowledge, it is by no means absurd to talk about justifying someone's claim to know, or someone's belief that he knows; for a claim to know, or a belief that one knows, is not rendered self-justifying simply because the knowledge claimed or believed is direct or intuitive, rather than mediate or discursive. If a man says that he saw me in London on a certain date I do not have to investigate his state of mind or his optic system in order to refute him; I may be able to produce reliable evidence which shows that I was in St. Andrews at the time. Similarly with 'seeing that' or 'intuiting that'; a claim to see intuitively that promise-breaking is always wrong may be challenged, not by trying to find out directly whether the mind of the man putting forward the claim is really in a condition of intuiting or not (and how could one try to find this out anyway?), but by arguing, independently of anyone's 'intuitions', actual or alleged, that promise-breaking is sometimes morally permissible. We still need, and may sometimes have, a way of distinguishing, among putative intuitions, those which really are intuitions, and therefore, by definition, true, and those which are not really intuitions, and which may therefore be false. Using Ryle's concept of 'achievement-word', we may say that 'intuiting' (in *this* sense), like 'seeing' in the parallel case, stands for an achievement, not a task or activity; and, unless the word is to be used quite arbitrarily, a criterion is required in order to decide

---

[1] Just as there is no difference, *qua* state of mind, between the state of mind of a man who knows something and is aware that he knows it, and that of a man who mistakenly believes that he knows it.

[2] In a rather similar way, there may be no phenomenological difference between the genuine inspiration of the poet and the bogus 'inspiration' of a mere versifier—they may have the same 'feel', and the difference between them lies in their products.

whether the achievement has in fact been made. If I won the race, of course I receive the first prize; but I won the race only if I reached the tape before any of the other competitors.

But if, on the other hand, one uses the word 'intuition' as a purely psychological or phenomenological word, referring to the way in which one comes to believe or think something, and thus allowing the existence of false, as well as true, intuitions, then of course these particular difficulties are avoided. Now, however, it becomes hard to see the point of intuitionism as a theory, at any rate in the field of ethics; in fact, it becomes difficult to see any difference of principle between intuitionism and a 'moral sense' theory such as Shaftesbury's. For while one can say that people intuit, or see directly, that something ought to be done, saying this is now not to imply that it really ought to be done; if one says 'He intuits, or sees directly, that p' this is now analogous to a literal use of the verb 'to see' in which it is not clear whether the real existence of what is seen is implied or not ('I see a red patch' used without any indication of whether it was a physical red patch or an after-image, for example). Hence the question 'How do you know that you ought to do this?' can no longer be answered by saying 'I intuit, or see directly, that I ought to'. It is obvious that, on this view, one cannot even begin to argue that no proof or justification of intuitions is required. Since the intuitionist still holds that no proof of them is available, one is thus left with intuitions which are no more, from the point of view of logic and justification, than assumptions or postulates; and intuitionism then shades over into a quite different type of theory or attitude.

The intuitionist might try to avoid this objection by claiming that the intuitions of certain types of men are more likely to be true than those of others. After all, the military insights of experienced and intelligent generals are more likely to be sound than those of ignorant amateur strategists; similarly, the moral insight of the wise and good man is, though not infallible, more likely to produce correct judgements than that of the man who is bad or stupid or ignorant. One difficulty about this is that wise and experienced men may be very bad men, with a thoroughly distorted moral vision; and while the vision of the good man is likely to produce correct judgements according to his own standards of goodness, complications are caused by the existence of differing standards. Within a closed and narrow community, the intuition of its best members may lead them to make judgements which are acceptable in the light of the more or less fixed standards of the community; but what happens when one's 'good men' themselves disagree? (This disagreement does clearly occur as soon as we widen our frame of reference and leave our narrow community.) The parallel with the professional insight of the experienced general is inexact; for the correctness of his insight can be tested in action, whereas no such independent test is, even in principle, possible for moral intuitions if this kind of intuitionism is correct. This form of the theory, in fact, leads to a kind of ethical subjectivism which the intuitionist is usually anxious to avoid; if one is prepared to be a subjectivist there seems to be little point in talking about intuitions in this way.

A. C. Ewing, in his British Academy lecture on *Reason and Intuition* (PBA, XXVII, 1941, pp. 67–107), denied this subjective implication on the ground that the difficulty of conflicting intuitions, or apparent intuitions, is not confined to ethics, and is therefore no argument for ethical subjectivity.

> There is frequent disagreement about matters of fact as to what has happened or will happen or concerning the causes of something, and when we have exhausted the arguments on a given point in these matters there still remains a difference between the ways in which the arguments are regarded by the antagonists. . . . These are genuine differences between competent researchers as to the force of arguments even about matters of fact where we are estimating probabilities, even in historical studies. . . . Again we are confronted with a situation in which we either see or do not see and cannot logically prove that what we seem to see is true (ibid., pp. 93–4).

Ewing seems to forget, however, that in factual matters argument and intuition are second-best methods of discovery. In principle, factual questions can be answered by direct observation or experiment; and where this is possible it is the best and most certain method of answering them. Sometimes in practice it is not possible, and theorising becomes necessary. We may have to speculate as to the present plans of the Russian or Chinese political leaders, or whether there will be a nuclear war within the next ten years; and in the course of such speculation we shall no doubt make use of ratiocination and intuition (or guesswork). But everyone would agree that this speculation may be extremely hazardous; and the more nearly complete our answers to the questions, the more assumptions we may have to make. In all factual matters, however, we may construct an ideal observational situation in which the answers to our questions could be discovered by direct observation; i.e. in theory we should not have to rely on speculation, which is required only when observation is impossible. Even though we cannot in fact observe the deliberations of the Russian leaders, we know that there is a set of objective facts which are in principle open to observation; all our arguments and insight into the facts depend for their validity or truth on the nature of the facts as our ideal observer would directly observe them. And here, the parallel with ethical intuition breaks down; for there is nothing in moral matters corresponding to an ideal observational situation, by reference to which our ethical intuitions could be tested—it is not merely that they cannot be tested in practice, but that they cannot be tested even in principle. One might perhaps, remembering Adam Smith, say that correct moral intuitions are those that would be intuited by an impartial observer or spectator of the situation. But this would be unhelpful, since not all moral disagreement is attributable to the partiality of one or both of the parties to the disagreement, unless one defines 'impartial' and 'partial' so widely that 'an impartial observer' simply means 'an observer whose decision as to the moral requirements of the situation is correct'; and then all one is saying is that correct moral intuitions are those moral intuitions which are correct—i.e. one is not providing a criterion at all.

I have been arguing that the concept of intuition, however interpreted, is unhelpful in the solution of the philosophical problems of ethics. Similar considerations cast doubt on the claim made by many, at least, of the intuitionists, that ethical intuition is in some way connected with reason. The claim, in traditional language, is that reason works in two ways, intuitively and discursively; and, in more everyday language, that when we rely on moral intuition (as, it is claimed, we must do in the end) we are putting our trust, sensibly, in reason and not, stupidly, in feeling, emotion or assumption. Ewing, for example, claims to be helping to provide a 'rational basis for ethics' (*The Definition of Good*

(New York, 1947), p. 212). Now in that book Ewing stresses the importance of coherence as a test of the correctness of our supposed moral intuitions; and there is, as we saw in Chapter VIII, an obvious connection between coherence and rationality. But the concept of coherence does not help the believer in one fundamental moral intuition; and in any case, the mutual coherence of one's moral intuitions is only a necessary, not a sufficient, condition of their truth. And if moral intuitions are supposed to provide a rational basis for one's moral beliefs or decisions, then we are entitled to ask 'On what grounds do you claim that the basis is rational?' In other words, the claim to intuit or to have insight, discernment or other direct apprehension of moral truths is an arbitrary, and therefore non-rational, claim unless it can, in principle at least, be supported with reasons. Hence, if it can be so supported, intuition is not the last word: if it cannot, it has no claim to be called rational, in any of the senses of that term.

The question may be put in this way: 'Why is it reasonable to rely on moral intuition?' If the word 'intuition' is used in the first of our two senses it is obviously reasonable in a sense to rely on it, since it is by definition true; the man who has it knows what to do, how to act. But this is a misleading answer; for if we use the word 'intuition' in this sense the question should really be formulated as 'Why is it reasonable to rely on a putative moral intuition?' And the answer to this clearly is 'Unless we have independent grounds for believing the putative intuition to be a genuine one, it is reasonable only to the extent that it is sometimes reasonable to make assumptions which cannot in any way be tested'. Reliance on assumptions may indeed be reasonable if there is no alternative; but to say this is to say no more than that one must sometimes make up one's mind to act in one way or another, even if there appears to be no reason why one should adopt one course rather than the other—it is stupid to behave like Buridan's ass. If, on the other hand, the word 'intuition' is being used in our second sense, then, since intuitions may now be true or false, it is reasonable to rely on them only if we have independent evidence for supposing them to be true; and thus intuition is no longer the last word, as its defenders claim it to be.

XI
THE LIMITS OF JUSTIFICATION

I BEGIN this chapter with a reiteration and development of two points that have already been made briefly.

(i) The first of these concerns the distinction between the antecedents of a belief, act or decision and its justification. Epistemology has all too often either failed to make this distinction or, having made it, failed to observe it consistently. Some seventeenth- and eighteenth-century writers, in particular, confused psychological questions with questions of justification, although the confusion is by no means unknown in more recent times. The question how a particular belief arose in an individual's mind, or in the minds of a number of men, is logically quite distinct from the question whether it is reasonable to hold the belief on the evidence available. This is not to say that questions of origin are always entirely irrelevant to questions of proof or evidence; the fact that my belief that horse X is going to win the Derby came to me in a dream, and is not based on an examination of form, is a relevant consideration to anyone who is wondering whether to back the horse or not. The point is, rather, that, even if the belief has been arrived at in some such non-rational way, it may still turn out to be true, whereas a belief arrived at after a careful and intelligent examination of all the available evidence may turn out to be false. The importance of the parallel distinction in the field of conduct can hardly be overestimated. Questions about reason and morals are often posed in a form which suggests a distinction between a rational and an irrational method of making, or arriving at, decisions; we either sit down in a cool hour and reflect, taking note of all the relevant facts, and making a series of inferences, or we act without reflection, on impulse, or at the behest of our feelings or emotions. But this distinction, though a perfectly fair one as far as it goes, is subsidiary to the distinction between an action or a decision which can be justified (i.e. shown to be either required or permitted) and one which cannot. One method of arriving at decisions is better than another only to the extent that it generally leads to better decisions. Hence, although it is perfectly legitimate to use the words 'rational' and 'irrational' (in the sense of 'non-rational') as synonyms for 'reasoned' and 'unreasoned', as these terms are applied to decisions, the claim that rational decisions, in this sense, are better than non-rational ones, or that rational methods are better than non-rational, requires justification. This justification can, in part at least, be provided. In the field of belief one is more likely, as a rule, to arrive at a correct opinion if one studies the facts carefully according to the normal rules of evidence than if one makes random guesses; though it does not follow from this that it is always better to study the evidence carefully than to follow a hunch (one may not be good at examining evidence, one may not have enough time, there may be evidence that one's hunches often turn out to be right).[1] So with decisions, one is doubtless more likely in general to make correct or reasonable decisions if one studies the facts and thinks rationally about them than if one tosses a coin or acts impulsively; although there are more exceptions here, since many of our actions are the result of habit or training, and may not require, or admit of, previous reflection —many of the situations that arise when we are driving a car or riding a bicycle are of this kind. It is much less obvious that acting on a previously reasoned decision is always better than acting from some feeling or emotion; for many actions, particularly those arising out of personal relationships, are often thought to lose some of their value if they are performed as a result of

---

[1] This may be illustrated by the example of football pools. Some people have argued that one is as likely to make winning predictions by the random method of shutting one's eyes and sticking a pin into the list of teams as by the method of studying form and making a reasoned judgement of probabilities. If this is true it is obviously just as reasonable or sensible to adopt the random method.

deliberate calculation rather than an immediate feeling of, say, friendship or love. And in any case, the question of justification still remains. Whether an action or a decision is impulsive or calculated or purely arbitrary, it can still be either appropriate or inappropriate to the agent's situation; and in deciding whether it is appropriate or not many factors may have to be considered which, up to the time he acted, never entered the agent's head at all. Even when we act in the belief that we are acting rightly, we are not necessarily ready or able to produce an immediate justification for our action. We may need time to work out a justification, we may, through some lack of dialectical skill, be unable to produce one; the important question is not whether the agent has justified, or can justify, his action, but whether a justification can be given, no matter by whom.

The kind of distinction of which we have been speaking is sometimes described as a distinction between the logic or order of discovery and the logic or order of proof. But the use of the word 'discovery' here can be misleading, for, like the word 'know', we are not entitled to use it in any particular case unless what we are claiming to have discovered, or believe we have discovered, really is so. What often happens in practice is that if someone is inspired to formulate or propound a certain hypothesis (for example, that blood is circulated through the arteries by the pumping action of the heart), and if he subsequently proves that this hypothesis is true, his discovery is dated back to the original formulation of the hypothesis. But although this is perhaps natural enough, it is strictly illegitimate; discovery, in this sense at least, is an achievement, not an activity or process. The proper contrast with proof or justification is provided by such words as 'inquiry' and 'investigation' and, in the case of action, 'deliberation'. The point I have been trying to make can thus be summed up by saying that rules for the conduct of deliberation, however important they may be, are distinguishable from, and logically subordinate to, criteria for assessing the correctness or incorrectness and the appropriateness or inappropriateness of actions. It follows that any attempt to construct a set of universally applicable rules for deliberating, or for moral deliberation in particular, is bound to fail, since differences of capacity and intelligence between individuals will mean that rules suitable for one type of individual will not always be suitable for another type. One cannot, of course, justify a line of conduct merely by appealing to one's feelings; but if a man's feelings usually lead him to act rightly, and if he is not particularly good at formulating reasons for and against projected actions, or at seeing inconsistencies, he may often be well advised to let his feelings guide him. It may indeed be reasonable for him to do this rather than try to think things out for himself, in the sense that the reasons for doing it are better or stronger than the reasons for doing anything else; the reasonable procedure to adopt is not always a reasoned procedure.

As one would expect, there is a similar distinction to be made in the field of moral judgements about, or moral attitudes towards, actions. When a man makes a moral judgement or adopts a moral attitude he may make it or adopt it after a long process of thinking or as an immediate reaction to a situation (whether by a kind of insight, in a neutral sense of the word, or in a purely emotional manner). But however he has come to make the judgement or to adopt the attitude, the question still arises 'Is the judgement true or false, or the attitude appropriate or inappropriate?' And this question can be answered only by asking whether there are good or sufficient reasons for making the judgement or adopting the attitude.[1] An intuitionist might claim that the way in which a judgement has come to be made is a, or even the only, test of its truth; but we have already seen the difficulties of this position.[2]

This distinction has one important corollary. So long as we consider the use of reason as a method of conducting an enquiry or of deliberating, it is natural to think of it as one method among several, and to argue that it is better or worse, as the case may be, than the others. Most philosophers who have discussed the nature and limits of rational methods have had one particular alternative chiefly in mind—reliance on divine revelation, in the case of Locke, for example, and on feeling or inclination, in the case of Hume or Kant; reliance on authority, human or divine, in the case of Cudworth. Methods of a rational kind have often been

[1] Cp. the comment of Sir Winston Churchill in a letter to the then Dominions Secretary written on April 3rd 1945: 'You say you can "only trust to your own instincts". I have offered you reasons at the end of a long day' (W. S. Churchill, *The Second World War*, Vol. VI (London, 1954), p. 637).

[2] Unless intuitionism does take this illegitimate step, it has to be regarded merely as an account of the way in which moral judgements are actually made, and thus cannot be regarded as a rival to any theory about the justification or criticism of such judgements.

recommended by philosophers who have been disturbed by the prevalence of irrational methods and attitudes. C. A. Campbell, for example, defends the life of reason against competing claims, especially those on behalf of a life based on faith; and the life of reason is defined by him as 'the life in which the practice is habitual of founding belief upon critical examination of the appropriate evidence, and of guiding action, save where the urgency of a situation calls for a more immediate response, by reflective comparison of the merits of alternative courses in the light of considered principles' ('The Claims of Reason', in *Philosophy*, XXV, 1950, p. 121). Whatever view one takes of the limitations of the rational approach, as defined in some such way as this,[1] it is clear that it can be regarded as an alternative to other approaches (to a reliance on faith, or a Lawrentian 'thinking with the blood', for example) and that the relative merits of the various approaches can be discussed. But when we come to consider justification and criticism of actions, the use of reason cannot be regarded as the best method of conducting this justificatory or critical process among a number of other methods, for there can in the nature of things be no other methods. Any attempt at a justification or criticism of an action purports to be rational, since it inevitably consists in the giving of reasons for or against the performance of the action or the truth of the belief. And once the process of reason-giving is begun, one is committed to rationality in the sense that one cannot without absurdity put an arbitrary and dogmatic end to the critical process; the reasons one gives are open to challenge or to supplementation, and, equally important, one's readiness to stop at a particular stage and accept something as true without further justification may itself be challenged. Even the giving of so dogmatic a reason for holding a belief to be true as 'Aristotle hath said it' at once allows an objector to ask whether this really is a valid reason, and perhaps to argue that it is not, by pointing out some statements of Aristotle which are indisputably false. Of course, occasions may arise in which there is room for doubt, and in which nevertheless no further reasons can be given; the critical process has its limitations, and we shall be discussing some of them later in this chapter. But when such occasions arise, faith, or feeling, or authority cannot take over

[1] One might doubt, for example, whether 'reflective comparison' can help us to a rational preference for one set of principles rather than another.

from rational methods of discussion as the providers of justification; the most that can be said is that, if we cannot decide on rational grounds between two alternatives, we are entitled, if we wish, to rely on feeling or authority or some other non-rational factor in the making of our choice.

In the rest of this chapter, then, the discussion of the nature of rational or reasonable conduct and the limits within which these and other comparable epithets can be applied will be concerned primarily with questions of rational justification or rational criticism of actions, actual or projected, and with the extent and limitations of such justification and criticism. This is not because methods of deliberation and decision are unimportant—in actual practice they are obviously of enormous importance—but because such questions are logically subordinate to justificatory or critical ones.

(ii) The second point which I wish to reiterate concerns the importance of facts. It is clear that a great deal of stupid or otherwise inappropriate behaviour is due to ignorance of, or failure to pay due attention to, the facts of the situation; this is because, in any context, moral or non-moral, the rightness or wrongness of an action depends on its relation to the situation or circumstances in which it is performed. Actions, unlike theoretical speculation or imagination, must come up against a world of brute fact—a world that can be changed to a certain more or less limited extent, and which for the rest has to be accepted, and cannot be ignored. Action which attempts to ignore facts ceases to belong to the sphere of the practical, and escapes into a visionary world which has no contact with reality. This is indeed so obvious that it might be thought superfluous to say it, were it not for the fact that its importance has often been overlooked. It may well be an exaggeration to say that all differences of opinion about what ought to be done arise from differences of opinion about the facts (that, in Stevensonian language, all disagreement in attitude is rooted in disagreement in belief); but so many practical, and especially moral, differences do arise from this source that its importance requires to be stressed. Due regard for relevant facts is a necessary feature of a rational approach to the making of any decision; and an action may be subject to rational criticism on the ground that it is inappropriate to the circumstances as they are, even though it may be appropriate to the circumstances as the agent thinks them to be. Indeed, reasoning with someone, with a view to persuading him to do something he has decided not to do, or not to do something he has decided to do, often takes the form of pointing out facts unknown to, or unappreciated by, him; there need be no ratiocination, in the sense of the drawing of inferences. Parents may reason with a girl who is set on marrying a man they think unsuitable by asserting that he is only after her money. There may be no need for inferences here; the girl might well agree that she would be foolish to marry the man if her parents' assertion about his motives were true, and that its truth or falsity is the only question at issue.

The extent to which some philosophers have made morality an irrational matter of whims and feelings has been exaggerated by some of their critics who have failed to pay proper attention to this aspect of moral deliberation and decision. Hume and Stevenson, for example, have both been criticised by rationalists on these grounds; but some of the criticisms are unfair, to the extent that they fail to take account of the ways in which Hume and Stevenson allow, consistently with their general position, that having correct beliefs about the situation in which one is acting is important and, as far as it goes, a sign of rationality. To say that reason reaches the limits of its application to conduct after logical validity of argument and knowledge of all relevant facts have been achieved may be, in the end, unsatisfactory; but an insistence on the importance of logical rigour and factual accuracy can hardly be claimed, without gross hyperbole, as an opening of the flood-gates to the waters of unreason.

Although I have from time to time referred to the distinction between moral and non-moral judgements or contexts, I have said very little about the nature of the distinction. An adequate account would require a whole book in itself, and I do not in any case feel confident of my ability to provide one. Moreover, the exact nature of the distinction is still a matter of considerable controversy among philosophers; and an account of the connection between reason and morals will be more satisfactory if it is consistent with any plausible theory of the distinction than if it is consistent with only one. Most of the accounts so far put forward are defective, either because they omit certain important features or, more seriously, because they build into their definition of morality certain of their authors' positive moral opinions. Fortunately, whatever theory one has about the distinguishing features of moral judgements, and whatever difficulties might be provided by borderline cases (Are we here talking about morality or about manners?), there is a very large class of judgements which are indisputably moral judgements and a very large class of situations in which we indisputably ask ourselves what is morally required of us, or what is morally permitted to us, in them. Even if we cannot give an exact definition of a moral judgement in terms of necessary and sufficient conditions, we can thus still profitably ask to what extent it is possible to engage in rational justification and criticism of actions on moral grounds (to find moral, as well as non-moral, reasons for and against them); for the most part, the question which reasons are moral and which non-moral is not in dispute. Moreover, it is clear that the procedure, here adopted, of regarding moral assessment and non-moral assessment of actions as in important respects similar is justified by the facts. The so-called moral words (good, bad, right, wrong, duty, obligation, etc.) are all used in non-moral contexts as well as in moral ones; and it would be surprising if their moral use took an entirely different form from their non-moral use. And of course it does not; even if we do not agree that 'good' in 'Jones is a good man' functions in exactly the same way as 'good' in 'Smith is a good doctor', we must admit that the two uses are not entirely disparate. There are resemblances, as well as differences, between moral rules and various kinds of non-moral rule; resemblances, as well as differences, between the moral appropriateness of an action to the agent's situation and the appropriateness of an action in terms of manners or prudence.

There is, however, an important distinction to be made within the field covered by the word 'morality'. Sometimes we speak of actions being right or wrong relative to a particular code or system (much as we speak of actions being permitted or forbidden by a particular legal system): the morality, in this sense, of one society or group may differ in important respects from that of another. As long as we remain at this level, the questions that arise take the form 'What does the morality of society S prescribe, permit or forbid in situations of type s?'; and these are questions for the social anthropologist or for a casuist working within the moral system concerned. The question 'How ought a man to behave in this situation?', when asked at this level, must be expanded to read 'How, according to the morality of this society) ought a man to behave in this situation?' Any answer to this question can, of course, be supported or attacked with reasons; but the reasons will be limited to considerations of the content of the society's moral rules, and judgements as to which rules cover the situation in question, and in what way (there is an exact analogy here with the extent to which rational criticism or justification may be provided for an answer to the question 'Does the law of this country permit me to do X?'). Difficult cases might arise which would defy the giving of a simple answer, just as legal situations sometimes arise in which it is not easy to decide what the law is; but there are no questions of philosophical principle involved, and the philosophical problems about the origin or foundations of moral judgements (reason, feeling, revelation, etc.) simply do not arise. It is important to notice that a great deal, at least, of moral deliberation does take the standards of conventional or accepted morality for granted and, in asking 'What ought I to do?' asks in effect 'What do the standards of accepted morality require me to do?' This is often obscured by the fact that the deliberating agent's attitude to the morality of his society or group is internal, as contrasted with the external attitude of, say, the investigating anthropologist; we may make a similar contrast between the internal attitude of the member of a club to the rules of that club and the external attitude of the social researcher or journalist. Both may want to know what conduct the rules require; but in the internal situation one thinks of the rules as binding on oneself and on others, whereas in the external situation one thinks, not of the rules as binding, but of the rules being thought of as binding by members of the society or club. The internal attitude accepts the rules, even while examining them; the external attitude merely examines them.[1]

Contrasted with this sense of the word 'morality', in which different groups can have different moralities, there is another sense which has nothing to do with any kind of relativism. It is exemplified by the man who says 'I do not want to know what I ought to do according to the moral code accepted by present-day Englishmen (or Germans, or Chinese); I want to know what I

[1] It is worth noticing that it is natural to speak of morality at this level in terms of recognition of and obedience to a code or a set of rules.

really ought to do'. Here existing moral codes or systems are no longer taken for granted, but are open to rational criticism. One of the defects of conventional morality is that, like every kind of convention, it tends to be conservative;[1] rules and practices which once had point or value continue to be followed even when their point has disappeared or, worse, when their observance has become positively harmful. Rules and prescriptions, if they are to be valid in terms of absolute, as opposed to conventional, morality, must prescribe conduct that is appropriate to human beings as they are and to the situation as it is; much of the moral controversy which recurs between older and younger generations arises from the belief of the latter that the former have failed to notice changed facts and circumstances that lead to changed moral requirements.[2] This conservatism is enhanced by the important part which is played by feelings and emotions in the reinforcement, if not the formation, of moral attitudes. The feelings which accompany moral approval and disapproval are apt to be strong, even when the attitude of approval or disapproval has been adopted on rational grounds; and altering one's feelings is not something that can be done directly and immediately by taking a decision. Even those who have decided that a particular rule of conventional morality has no justification may still feel uncomfortable when they transgress it, however unreasonable they may think this discomfort to be.

It is with what I have called 'absolute morality' that we are principally concerned; the important question for us is not 'How far is it reasonable to accept the conventional morality of one's society or group (or, indeed, that of any other)?', but 'How far is it reasonable to accept the demands and ideals of a corrected morality?' It is not simply a matter of suggesting reasons for altering or retaining particular features of an accepted code; for, as we have seen, rational considerations may indicate that one's conduct cannot properly be governed entirely by reference to

[1] Many conventional moralities have a built-in resistance to rational enquiry, in that too close an investigation into the foundations of the system is thought to be immoral, as evincing a potential willingness, or an insufficient degree of unwillingness, to behave in a morally wrong way. The same is true of some codes of honour.

[2] Reasoned discussion can enter in here, at least to the extent that it is possible to argue about the exact nature of the facts and about their implications for practice.

a code or system of rules, however enlightened that code may be.

The notion, which I have been using, of an alteration in moral rules or moral beliefs, requires a word of elucidation. It is, of course, impossible to alter moral rules directly, by agreement or by the decree of some authority, in a way analogous to that by which the law of the land can be repealed, amended or extended by legislative act.[1] Although an individual can, sometimes with difficulty, give up his early adherence to the accepted morality of his society in one or several respects, a society cannot change its moral rules in the same straightforward way as that in which it can change its laws. Changes in moral thinking and practice, whether rationally motivated or not, are usually gradual and are strongly resisted by many. They are brought about, not of course by any kind of moral legislation, but by the slow and steady effect on people's minds of the actions of those who have, as individuals, decided that the existing standards are defective. Moral changes occur either as the result of deliberate persuasion by reformers or by men following the examples set by those who have adopted new standards, even though they are not in fact setting out to recommend their adoption by others.

I have in some previous chapters dealt with the limitations of reason in the establishment and criticism of moral standards and beliefs. We have now to bring together some of the factors previously considered in isolation, and to try to give a more positive account of the situation.

Conduct, actual or projected, can be the subject of rational discussion and assessment to the extent that reasons can be offered in its favour or disfavour. Sometimes the giving of reasons will consist simply in the provision of logical or factual arguments which can be tested by the normal rules of deductive or inductive logic, or in the making of factual assertions, which can be tested, in principle at least, by means of observation and

---

[1] Even the notion that the law of the land can be radically changed by legislative acts is far from being universally accepted in civilised societies. It has often been held that the legislator's task must be confined to discovering what the Law is, and applying the resulting knowledge to situations which have arisen since the last relevant act of legislation. The view that the legislator has, legally speaking, a completely free hand is a comparatively recent development, and is still rejected by some jurists.

experiment. The logical and factual parts of ethical argument provide no special problem for the moral philosopher. It is with the arguments, or those aspects of them, that are not confined to strictly logical inference or to the asserting of observable facts, that this type of ethical enquiry is principally concerned.

An inference which is not formally valid may sometimes be expressible in valid form if the rule in accordance with which it is made is used as a premiss. For example, a man who, when asked for a reason for a particular action of his, said that he had to do it because he had promised to, would not be giving a formally valid reason; but a formally valid argument could be constructed after this fashion:

Whenever a man has promised to perform an action, he must do it.

I have promised to do x.

Therefore I must do x.

The conclusion here follows from the two premisses, but the truth of the first premiss may itself be questioned (so, of course, may the truth of the second, but this does not as a rule give rise to philosophical difficulties, however hard it may be in practice to establish the facts in question).[1] An argument of a similar kind might be constructed in support of the first premiss; but the effectiveness of all such arguments in justifying their conclusion inevitably depends on some premiss or presupposition which cannot be justified within the framework of the particular argument. Even if we construct[2] a complicated system of ethical arguments which would justify or refute any conceivable moral judgement by reference to a single fundamental moral principle

---

[1] It is worth noticing, however, that attempts to model ethical systems on mathematical ones are bound to include some factual material before any particular moral judgement or prescription can be arrived at. We cannot get from 'All promises must be kept' to 'I must do x' without making use of the factual premiss 'I have promised to do x' (and perhaps, indirectly, of other factual premisses or presuppositions as well). Without some such factual reference, any ethical system must remain entirely hypothetical.

[2] Such a construction would in fact be extremely artificial; for in morals, unlike mathematics and logic, we sometimes regard as ultimate or fundamental a principle or proposition that is of a relatively low logical order. We sometimes reject an action because a rule or maxim forbids it; but we sometimes reject a rule or maxim because it requires of us an action that we cannot bring ourselves to perform.

(taken in conjunction with the relevant facts), this principle itself could not be proved in the same way. In any system of proof, moral or non-moral, one has to accept some proposition as unproved within the system.[1]

What, then, are we to say about the unproved principle (or principles, if there should be more than one unproved principle in the system)? There seem to be three possible views: (*a*) one or more moral principles are self-evidently true, and therefore no proof of them is needed; (*b*) one or more moral principles must be taken as postulates (as opposed to axioms); i.e. the presuppositions of a moral system are not rationally defensible except by reference to the nature of the ethical system which they generate; and (*c*) one or more principles in any ethical system cannot be proved in the system, but may be susceptible of some kind of rational justification or defence which falls short of proof. I shall discuss these three views in turn.

(*a*) The Cartesian model, according to which all particular moral judgements are derivable from one or more self-evident first principles, is open to all the criticisms that have previously been directed against intuitionism. Even if it makes no use of the word 'intuition', similar difficulties and confusions arise in the notion of self-evidence. In particular, we shall find that the power of a presumed self-evident first principle to generate positive and concrete moral prescriptions will vary in inverse proportion to its self-evidence, i.e. to the likelihood that it will be accepted by all those who understand it.[2] We might, perhaps, succeed in formulating some principles to which it might be difficult, or even impossible, to take exception; but we shall find that they will be so vague that it will be impossible to make use of them to justify one moral alternative rather than another. The moment we try to remedy this state of affairs by giving a clear content to the first principles we shall find that they are no longer self-

---

[1] This requirement is logically necessary; but the facts about morality and human nature might, as many philosophers would insist, make it necessary to accept more than one such unproved proposition. What is said here about the limitations of rational justification in respect of a single fundamental moral principle will apply even more strongly to any theory which holds that there are several irreducible principles.

[2] Of course, a statement might be universally accepted and still be false. We cannot make the self-evidence of a proposition into a guarantee of its truth without making the concept of self-evidence entirely vacuous.

evident, i.e. that it is possible for them to be rejected by people who understand their meaning perfectly well.

The fact that a theory leaves room for legitimate disagreement about first principles is not necessarily fatal to it, for the possibility of such disagreement might have to be allowed for in any correct account—at least, our argument has not yet shown the contrary. But it is fatal to a theory which asserts the self-evidence of the fundamental principle or principles; self-evidence, whatever account one gives of the concept, can allow neither doubt nor disagreement (except, of course, on the part of those who do not understand the meaning of the proposition which is claimed to be self-evident). The attempt to save the theory by claiming that where there is disagreement one party at least must be mistaken in saying that the principle or proposition is self-evident inevitably fails. It is pointless to say that someone is mistaken in thinking a proposition to be self-evidently true unless one can support one's statement with reasons; and the only valid reason for saying this would be the fact that he had not understood the proposition. But this sort of misunderstanding is clearly not the source of all ethical disagreement about first principles—a man who rejects the proposition that one should treat others as one would wish to be treated by them is not necessarily failing to understand the proposition. And the attempt to give any other kind of reason why the person with whom one disagrees is mistaken will clearly be inconsistent with the theory of self-evident principles; for to give reasons why a principle should be accepted is to admit that it is not, what it had up to now been regarded as being, a fundamental principle, and to admit that one's theory is not, as it purports to be, a theory based on the existence of self-evident first principles.

(*b*) It might seem a natural step, after the inadequacy of a theory based on self-evident moral principles has been pointed out, to try to retain some kind of hierarchical system of moral principles and judgements, but to regard the first principles of the system as assumptions or presuppositions rather than self-evident truths—the model would be, *mutatis mutandis*, that of non-Euclidean rather than that of Euclidean geometry.[1] The value

---

[1] For a good account of this view, see D. C. Williams, 'Ethics as Pure Postulate', *Philosophical Review*, XLII (1933), pp. 399–411. At the end of his article, Williams suggests certain criteria by which we might be led to prefer

of the model, however, seems doubtful as soon as we ask 'Why these postulates, rather than any others?' Of course, the postulates of any system must be such that they do not generate any contradictions or inconsistencies, otherwise it would not be a system in the required sense, but this limitation is not sufficiently restrictive, for it would still allow the most absurd sets of rules or principles to be laid down as assumptions. The difficulty is not merely that there would be no way of distinguishing morally acceptable principles from morally unacceptable ones, but also that there would be no way of distinguishing a moral principle from an entirely non-moral one. There is, in fact, an important difference between ethics, on the one hand, and mathematics and logic, on the other, which makes any attempt to construct an ethical system on this type of mathematical model a vain one. For although many logical and mathematical systems can be applied to the world, or to various aspects of it, it is quite possible, and perfectly proper, to construct such systems for their own sake, as a kind of intellectual exercise; and the fact that some systems of this kind might have no application would be no objection to them, considered purely as logical or mathematical systems. But an 'ethical system' which could not be applied would not be an ethical system at all;[1] for this much at least can be said about an ethical system or way of life, that its function is to guide conduct— the notion of such a function is built into it, as it is not into the notion of a logical or mathematical system. Someone might still, of course, construct a practical system of conduct as a *jeu d'esprit*, not taking it seriously himself; but it could be considered an ethical system only to the extent that it could be taken seriously as a guide to conduct, however frivolous the attitude of its author might have been.

(*c*) Given that, within an ethical system, some propositions or principles are bound to be unprovable, what room is left for

---

[1] It might, of course, be a system of ideals, some, or all, of which could not be lived up to absolutely; however, as long as the ideas could be taken as guides to conduct, the system would have a practical application in the required sense.

---

some suggested first principles or postulates to others; to the extent that a 'postulational' theory allows for this, it does not rest entirely on assumptions and is not open to the objections brought against such theories in this section. It becomes, rather, a theory of the type discussed in section (*c*) below.

rational discussion and argument about them? In speaking of ultimate or fundamental principles, have we not, it might be asked, ruled out any such discussion from the start? The answer to this, of course, is that the principles are ultimate only within the system, and that we can still ask ourselves whether or not to accept the proposed system. The question now arises whether, and if so, what, reasons can be regarded as relevant to the solution of this deliberative problem. We have already seen some of the objections to supposing that the adoption or rejection of an ethical system can be a completely arbitrary matter; yet to argue that one ethical system is morally better than another requires some point of reference outside both systems (provided that both meet the requirements of consistency and feasibility). It is impossible, I think, to establish such a point of reference in any way that is both unambiguous and indisputable; the most that can be done is to try to see how well or badly the rival systems fulfil the function that such systems must[1] perform, and the more precise we are in defining these functions, the more room for legitimate disagreement there is likely to be.

The philosophy of morality is tied to, or dependent on, certain kinds of fact in a way in which many other branches of philosophy are not. For although it is doubtless impossible to deduce moral judgements from purely factual propositions about human nature, human desires and biological needs, moral principles and truths are nevertheless in a sense rooted in such facts. The rightness or wrongness of an action depends on its relation to a situation or to circumstances; and the nature of the human situation in general is therefore highly relevant to any determination of moral rightness or wrongness. An important consequence of this is that many theses which might be put forward either frivolously or as exercises in philosophical scepticism can be dismissed as absurd, whereas analogous theses in some other branches of philosophy cannot. There is no point, to take some obvious examples, in announcing the existence of a moral obligation either to do something that no sane human being could ever bring himself to do, or to do something that no sane human being could ever have any conceivable motive for doing, or to do something that everybody

---

[1] This cannot, of course, be a moral 'must'; we cannot solve a moral problem by referring to a higher principle if the higher principle cannot be established without first solving the lower-order problem.

is inevitably going to do anyway. The paradoxes to which a process of Cartesian doubt may lead in respect of, say, the existence of other minds or physical objects cannot arise in moral philosophy in the same extreme form. It is sometimes said (whether truly or not need not concern us) that solipsism cannot be disproved by theoretical argument, but is open to objection merely on pragmatic grounds—i.e. that no one can live his life systematically believing that there are no other human beings besides himself. But it would be absurd to say of a comparable rejection of a moral attitude which a philosophical sceptic adopted, or professed to adopt, that it was a merely pragmatic refutation. The derogatory use of 'merely', suggesting as it does that some superior type of refutation might conceivably be available but unfortunately is not, is inappropriate; for what better refutation of an alleged moral principle could there be than a demonstration that it was impossible for anyone to use it as a guide to conduct?

But one can, I think, go further than this very modest statement about the function of moral principles, or sets or systems of such principles. Before we can do this, however, some attention must be paid to the notion of function itself. 'Function' is a word about which philosophers do well to be suspicious. It has often been used in a loose and question-begging way, especially by some biologists and psychologists. But it has some uses that are both legitimate and important. We can quite properly and strictly speak of the function of a thing that has been designed explicitly to fulfil this function (or purpose); the function of a set of traffic lights is to regulate the movement of cars, motor cycles, pedestrians, etc. If someone doubted, or professed to doubt, whether this was the function of traffic lights, in this sense of 'function', the question could be settled by referring to certain historical facts about the purposes of their inventors and of those who had set them up.[1] In a different sense, we can legitimately speak of the biological function of an organ in terms of the role it fills in the working of the whole organism of which it is a part—the function of the heart is to circulate blood through the body.[2] If

---

[1] Note, however, that this use of 'function' is liable to slide over into the third, 'sociological', sense; we can ask what part traffic lights play in the life of the community.

[2] The word 'purpose' is sometimes substituted for 'function' in both this sense and the next. There is no harm in this substitution as long as we do not

someone doubted, or professed to doubt, a functional statement of this kind the question could be settled by comparing the results of the action of the heart as it affects the life and working of the organism as a whole with an assessment of the results that would occur if its action did not take place. In this extreme case we could say that the action of the heart is a necessary condition of the working of the human body; in other cases we could say that the activity of the organs concerned (the eyes, for example) made a useful, if not an essential, contribution to the working of the body.

Now we may extend the use of the word 'function' into the social sphere, and suggest that there are certain factors—institutions, for example, or practices—which make either an essential or a useful contribution to the working of social relations[1] between human beings. We may then proceed to criticise any human action on the ground that it is neglecting the function of the institution or practice of which it is making use. It would not be enough, of course, to criticise someone on the ground that he was using an institution for a purpose which it had not originally served—there need be nothing objectionable in innovation of this kind. The argument would be, rather, 'The practice or institution in question cannot be of the nature which you, explicitly or implicitly, claim it to be; for if it were, it could not do the work which it is the function of that practice or institution to do.'[2]

---

[1] It is tempting to say 'to the working of society'; but this can be misleading, for the relations in question can exist between any two human beings who have some kind of contact with one another, whether they would naturally be called members of the same society or not. For a fuller account of the social sense of the word 'function' see D. Emmet, *Function, Purpose and Powers* (London, 1958), especially Chapters III and IV.

[2] A sociologist is primarily concerned with the function that a practice or institution actually fulfils. In theory, it is always possible to say 'I agree that X does have this function; but I think that it ought to fulfil a different one'. Any such claim would, of course, have to be considered on its merits; but, where any fundamental sociological phenomenon is concerned, its initial implausibility is very great. What could be the point of saying 'Language, or morality, ought to have a quite different function from that which it actually has'?

---

make the mistake of arguing from 'The purpose of X is . . .' to 'X was deliberately created for the purpose of . . .'.

Before we discuss the application of this idea to morality, it is worth considering a non-moral example, and that of language provides some useful analogies. Consider the following quotation:[1]

> It is a strange fact that people rarely appeal to the purposes of language when defending the correctness of a piece of language or defending the doctrine that there is some correctness in language. The reason why Humpty Dumpty cannot do what he says he can do, namely make words mean what he likes, is that that would prevent him from communicating with other people, which is the main purpose of language.

In other words, our linguistic activities must, within certain limits, obey the rules of language because language or talk that does not obey the rules cannot perform the main function of language, i.e. it cannot do the main job that language has to do. Of course, if Humpty Dumpty does not want to communicate he can use language as he pleases (though we might have some scruples about calling it 'language' if his activities were sufficiently idiosyncratic); but if he does want to communicate—and it is a very odd human being who does not, at some time or other—he must obey the rules which make communication possible. It is no use adopting a completely new set of rules of your own on the ground that the new ones are better than those generally accepted; for communication will not be possible except with others who use the new rules—agreement is essential. Now suppose that someone took a more radical line than the merely eccentric Humpty Dumpty, and challenged the whole claim that the main function of language is to enable people to communicate with one another, how could his challenge be met? We could point, in the first place, to some relevant empirical facts: that men's ability to communicate with one another is a necessary condition of any kind of civilised, indeed of recognisably human, life, and that communication by means of language is, for an enormous variety of purposes, far more effective than any other kind. Secondly, if anyone had an alternative view as to the function, or the main function, of language we should have to consider it on its merits and examine the reasons which he produced

---

[1] R. Robinson, 'A Criticism of Plato's *Cratylus*', *Philosophical Review*, LXV (1956), pp. 333-4.

in its support;[1] and our agreement or disagreement with him would depend in the end on our views as to the correctness of his claim that language did have this function, and, if it turned out to be correct, on our views as to the relative importance of the two functions.

This example from the field of language may suggest a reason why we cannot adopt just anything as a moral principle. If any rule of action whatsoever, however arbitrary, could count as a moral rule the resulting state of affairs would make it impossible, or at least appallingly difficult, for us to 'get on' with other people; and this 'getting on' with other people is a function (and, I think, the main function) of moral rules and of morality in general.[2] A moral rule or principle must not merely fulfil the condition, mentioned earlier, that it can be acted on, or adopted as an ideal; it must also fulfil the more restrictive condition that it can be adopted as a means of initiating or preserving or extending some kind of co-operation or social activity between human beings. Human nature being what it is, and the limitations of life on this planet being what they are, some sort of restrictions on the free play of appetite and impulse, as well as on the calculations of self-interest and aggrandisement, are necessary if any kind of peaceful co-existence is to be achieved.

Now suppose someone disputes a functional account of this kind, what sort of arguments could be offered in its defence? The same sort in general, I think, as were relevant in the case of language. If a man (some moral equivalent of Humpty Dumpty, perhaps) disputed the need for, or the value of, co-operation and social activity, or the claim that it was the function of morality to promote these ends, he would be committed either to attempting to show that certain ends which he and his opponents agreed in valuing could be better achieved in some other way (and it is difficult to see how he could even begin this attempt, let alone

---

[1] Relevant considerations, analogously to those appropriate to the establishment of the biological function of any organ, would be the social effects produced by the existence of language, and the consequences for human relationships that would result from its extinction.

[2] We are speaking here, of course, of the function of moral principles outside the particular moral system of which they may form a part; i.e. in effect, of the function of a moral system or way of life as a whole. Any moral rule or principle may have a much more specific function within a particular system.

succeed in it); or to rejecting the ends for the achievement of which some sort of social life and some sort of morality are essential conditions—and to do this would be to reject any kind of recognisably human life altogether. A really tough-minded rejection of all moral standards of any kind cannot, in the end, be proved wrong by logical methods. The most one can do is to exhibit the implications of such a rejection; and it is worth noticing that most so-called amoralists have, whether openly or surreptitiously, had some standards of behaviour which they were not prepared to transgress, however unconventional those standards might be. One cannot show, without making some assumptions or presuppositions, that men ought to co-operate with one another in the business of living; what one can try to show is that the adoption of certain rules, principles or standards of behaviour (called 'moral' rules, principles and standards), or less strongly, the adoption of rules, principles or standards of a certain general type, is necessary to the attainment of any such co-operation.[1]

If someone, as opposed to denying that moral principles had any function, produced an alternative theory of their function, which included a reference to social co-operation, but which went beyond this (i.e. which held that the facilitating of co-operation was only one function of morality, and perhaps not the most important), one would again have to consider the alternative account on its merits. The theory which I have sketched cannot be given a direct and conclusive proof, and so alternatives cannot be ruled out in advance (this is no more possible than with the claim that the facilitation of communication is the main function of language); but it can be defended by rational arguments against objections. Two fairly obvious possible objections may be briefly examined here. The attempt to make morality depend solely on relations between human beings overlooks, it might be said, that men have duties also to God, and to, or at least in connection with, animals. The objections, however, are not seriously damaging. As far as animals are concerned, the wrongness of causing them unnecessary pain can be derived, by a kind of analogy, from the wrongness of causing unnecessary pain to human beings,

---

[1] It is no part of my purpose in this book to construct any kind of 'applied ethics'; I am here merely sketching, in a most rudimentary way, the form which an applied ethics would have to take if it claimed to be rationally based.

together with the empirical fact that animals, like humans, are sentient beings with a capacity for feeling pain; i.e. the resemblance in this respect between humans and animals is sufficiently great for us to extend the moral rule which originally applied only to the former to the latter as well. And if it is held that a man has some duties to God which are not fulfilled in terms of any behaviour towards his fellow-men we should, I think, naturally say that these form no part of morality, even though they do form part of religion. Worshipping God is a religious, not a moral, duty; conversely, helping one's fellow-men is a moral duty, even though it may be a religious duty as well.

Although I have been arguing that the function which moral principles and systems have to fulfil restricts the number of alternative, mutually inconsistent, systems that can be rationally defended, I have not attempted to show, and I do not think it can be shown, that there is only one rationally defensible system; i.e. only one rationally defensible set of moral principles, rules, standards and precepts which will do the job that such things have to do. When all allowances have been made for differences of culture and degrees of civilisation, and for the considerable amount of real uniformity that is to be found behind the wide variety of moral standards that exist and have existed in different times and places, the approach in terms of the functions of a moral system will not provide us with conclusive reasons for saying that one system is better than any other, actual or conceivable, although it will sometimes enable us to say that System A is in certain respects, or on the whole, better than System B. There may sometimes be cases in which there are no moral reasons whatsoever, and not merely no conclusive reasons, for preferring one system to another. This is less awkward for practical purposes than it might at first seem, however; for although we may describe the situation by saying that a man must choose or decide between alternatives, even if there are no moral reasons for choosing one rather than the other, the use of such words as 'choose', 'decide' and 'adopt' may be misleading unless we are careful to observe just what kind of choice or decision is involved. 'Choosing' one way of life, one morality or one set of moral principles rather than another, although it is analogous in some respects to ordinary common-or-garden choosing, is in other ways very different. In the first place, it is not a choice that can be made as the result of a momentary whim, liable to change as soon as a contrary impulse is felt. Although we may change our moral principles or standards, or decide to live in a different way, the change cannot be made every five minutes when a whole way of life is in question; some kind of steadiness and stability is part of the meaning of such expressions as 'principles', 'system' and 'way of life'. Secondly, to the extent that our adoption of a way of life or a set of standards is the result of deliberate decision on our part, it is often brought about by decisions to perform particular actions which are seen, at the time or subsequently, to commit us to the adoption of certain rules or principles. For example, in order for a man to adopt the principle of helping those in distress, it is not necessary that he should explicitly formulate to himself the general principle of helping others; it is enough that, whenever the occasion and opportunity arise, he decides to help people because they are in distress. Thirdly, and perhaps most important, all of us are to a greater or lesser degree under the influence of many non-rational factors, such as social pressure or custom or our unconscious desires, and as a result we do not always have a completely free and unlimited choice in these matters. Moreover, as a result of his upbringing and social environment, a man will have at any given time some standards and principles which he has not chosen for himself, but which he accepts because he has been taught them and it has not occurred to him to reject them. Hence sometimes at least, the fact that one moral system is not in the abstract rationally preferable to another does not entail that a particular man in a particular environmental situation has no reason to prefer it. If a man has been taught a set of standards which are shared by his neighbours this is a good reason for him to resist any attempt to exchange these standards for a set that cannot be shown to be better, even though they may be as good. Agreement on standards of morality is important; other things being equal, it is better for all members of a community to agree on standards than for there to be two conflicting, though in the abstract equally reasonable, sets. For agreement is one of the aspects of co-operation which it is the function of any set of standards to promote.[1]

[1] There is some point here in an analogy with diplomatic practice, for which at times the fact that an agreement has been reached is more important than the exact nature of the agreement.

In general, however, the main implication of the foregoing discussion is this: that there may be some moral disagreements (just as there may be some non-moral disagreements about actions) which cannot be settled by any rational procedure, in the sense that there are no conclusive grounds, of any kind that can without linguistic distortion be described as rational, for preferring one of the two suggested courses of action to the other (even though there may be grounds for preferring either of these to any third course). This is a fundamental impossibility, and must be distinguished in this respect from two other, apparently analogous, kinds of impossibility which present no theoretical difficulties. These are (i) the impossibility of discovering all the relevant facts and (ii) the impossibility of showing that action x is better or worse than action y according to an agreed set of rules or standards, simply because, when assessed by these standards, the two actions are equally good (an example would be the inability of a crude utilitarian to find any grounds for preferring either of two actions, each of which will produce exactly the same quantities of pleasure and pain). The impossibility in our case is one of principle, because there is nothing that would count as an agreed correct solution, since it is an essential feature of this imagined case that the two parties have not agreed on any prior assumptions or decisions. Moral argument, in fact, is essentially dialectical, in the sense that it requires one to have some common ground with one's opponents or fellow-disputants; without this, rational discussion with others is impossible. The same is true, *mutatis mutandis*, of moral deliberation. In the asking of the deliberative questions 'What shall I do in this situation?', 'What principles shall I adopt?', 'Shall I lead this kind of life rather than that?', there is bound to be a theoretical limit to the cogency of the reasons with which one may in one's thoughts support or rebut the various alternatives. The model here is not a mathematical one (it is not, as we have seen, a matter of quasi-Euclidean, or even quasi-non-Euclidean, axioms or postulates), and the limit does not have to come at the level of the highest or most general principle; but at some stage or other, if a man's way of life is to be governed by rational considerations, he has to recognise the need to make at least one decision or choice for which conclusive reasons cannot, in principle, be given. Although there may be conclusive reasons for making this decision rather than many possible or conceivable alternatives, there cannot always be conclusive reasons for making this decision rather than any possible or conceivable alternatives. Whatever factors enter into a man's preference for one way of life over another, this preference cannot always be shown to be correct or incorrect by purely rational arguments or considerations of the kinds which we have been discussing in the last few chapters.

The account which I have given of the moral rightness and wrongness of actions does not provide a short and simple answer to any of the stock philosophical questions such as 'Is morality based on reason?' or 'Can reason distinguish between right and wrong?' This, however, is not an objection to it (except perhaps from the point of view of those who are required to write short examination answers to such questions); for there is no reason to suppose that any full and useful philosophical account of anything can be fairly and unmisleadingly summarised in a few sentences. Certainly the concept of morality and, more especially, the concept of reason are too complicated for a simplification of this kind to be possible without distortion. If I were forced to give a 'Yes' or 'No' answer to the question 'Is the difference between right and wrong a matter of reason?', I should personally regard 'Yes' as rather less misleading than 'No'; but there are many philosophers who will think that my affirmative answer is half-hearted and hedged around with too many qualifications. I have already dealt, directly or by implication, with some objections; but there is one general type of objection which must be considered before we bring this discussion to a close. This is that an account of this kind overlooks the objective element in morality, and that, in particular, in stressing the element of choice or decision in morality it fails to do justice to the fact (or at least the strongly held belief) that the rightness or wrongness of an act, or the existence of a particular duty, are things that a man discovers rather than creates, and are thus not dependent on his own decisions, choices or preferences. Granted that many subjectivists have overstressed the emotional, or in general the non-rational, factors in the making of moral judgements and decisions, and have paid too little attention to the various ways in which such judgements and decisions can be subjected to rational criticism and assessment, and that the account I have given perhaps avoids this particular error, it may still be claimed that it implies a limit to the objectivity of moral decision; if the starting-point of morality is subjective, is not all the rest in a sense subjective, however rational its derivation from that starting-point may be?

It is a mistake to allow the emotional and evaluative overtones of a word to extend their attachment from uses of the word to which they are appropriate to uses to which they are not. 'Subjectivity' is a bad thing in so far as it indicates acting or thinking according to arbitrary whim or feeling where accurate and unbiased examination of the facts of a situation is called for; and in such contexts, conversely, 'objectivity' is a good thing. But the element of decision or choice about which I have spoken is not subjective in this pejorative sense, if indeed it is subjective in any proper sense at all. It is not a matter of whim or feeling, nor is it arbitrary; the choice between two equally reasonable ways of life cannot be made on the ground that one is more reasonable than the other, but this does not mean that it can be made by tossing a coin. Indeed, the whole controversy between subjectivists and objectivists in ethics is, I think, based on a confusion. The objectivist, in insisting on the objective truth or falsity of moral judgements, does not see that what he insists on is true only given certain principles, standards or decisions (however natural or reasonable, in the sense of 'rationally defensible as far as rational defence will go', those principles, standards or decisions may be); while the subjectivist does not see that moral decisions are not necessarily mere matters of feeling or emotion or non-rational 'attitude',[1] but can be argued about or discussed in a neutral, non-partisan spirit. The point I am trying to make may perhaps become clearer if we compare two different kinds of value-judgement with reference to the subjective and objective elements contained in each. Objectivity of a kind is clearly involved in certain types of non-moral value-judgement, notably in judgements about skill. 'X is a better carpenter, or chess-player, than Y' is more or less equivalent to 'X is a more skilful carpenter, or chess-player, than Y'. And, to take a particular example 'Botvinnik is a better chess-player than Kemp' is not the expression of a subjective, Stevensonian attitude; it is undeniably and

---

[1] They may, of course, be mere matters of feeling for some people. Conversely, we can if we wish use the word 'attitude' of a moral position that has been worked out by its holder in a highly intellectual and subtle way.

objectively true. Its truth is, however, dependent on the acceptance of certain chess-playing standards and might to that extent, I suppose, be called 'subjective'; but it is important to notice that the acceptance of these standards is not arbitrary—indeed, the statement in question is true relative to any conceivable set of chess-playing standards.[1] Now consider the statement 'X is a (morally) better man than Y'. Given that, if this is to be straightforwardly true or false, it must have an implicit reference to some moral standards, need it refer solely to some set or sets of accepted or conventional standards, or could a statement of this kind ever be true, given any conceivable set of moral standards? The answer is not so clear-cut as in the chess example, because there is nothing in morals exactly analogous with the notions of winning and losing, or with the notion of skill in general. Yet although, because of the conflicting standards adopted by different people, a man may be called good by some and bad by others for one and the same decision or choice (e.g. for preferring the interests of his family to those of his country), there are still some matters over which disagreement would be absurd. By any conceivable moral standards, a man who goes around killing people merely because their continued existence is a bar to his financial enrichment is, to that extent, a worse man than one who waits for them to die a natural death, however great the temptation to the contrary. And in general one cannot make completely arbitrary moral judgements about the goodness or badness of any particular aspect of a man's character. For to call someone morally good is to indicate that there is some feature of his character or conduct that makes it reasonable or appropriate to commend it; it is not simply to commend it, if 'commend' stands for the performance of some act of commending or the adoption of some attitude of commendation, for one can perform such an act or adopt such an attitude in a quite arbitrary way, for no reason at all, whereas to say that someone is a morally good man and then to admit that one had no reason for saying it would be to undo the logical effect and point of saying it in the first place.

---

[1] On the other hand, the question whether Alekhine was a better player than Capablanca cannot be answered with the same degree of certainty; for one's answer to it might well have to depend on one's preference for a certain style of play, and although this preference might be rationally defensible up to a point, it could not be conclusively shown to be correct.

Now let us suppose that two different ways of life have been adopted by two men, and that both ways meet in an exemplary fashion all the various criteria of reasonableness that have been laid down. There will almost certainly be many points at which the two men's moral judgements on various issues will coincide, in spite of their differences of principle. Certain types of killing, for example, are regarded as wrong by people of the most diverse moral principles and standards; and agreement of this kind often obscures the relation which such moral judgements have to the different standards or principles or ways of life which have been adopted by the people who make them. But where the two ways of life diverge there is no possibility of further rational comparison of their merits.[1] It is, however, irrational to feel quite satisfied with an 'objective' account of fundamental moral preferences, while at the same time feeling some emotional dissatisfaction with a theory which allows the existence of some preferences which cannot be conclusively defended, even in principle. With morality, as with chess, the fact that some preferences cannot be conclusively shown to be correct does not entail that all preferences are arbitrary; and there is no difference, as far as their implications for conduct are concerned, between a utilitarian or an intuitionist theory, on the one hand, and a theory of the kind I have put forward, on the other. Let us consider, for the sake of clarity, an exaggeratedly simple example, and suppose that a particular man's choice between two rival ways of life amounts in the end to a decision whether his duties to his family and friends are, in case of conflict, to take precedence over those to his country, or vice versa. A utilitarian would say that the correct decision is the one which will in the end have the better consequences as far as the greatest happiness of the greatest number is concerned; but this statement, however true it might be, would in a case of this kind be completely useless as a guide or criterion, even in principle, since there would normally be no way of deciding which choice would have the better consequences.[2] An intuitionist might say that one preference or the

---

[1] Except, of course, that as time goes on and circumstances change one way of life may come to possess defects not possessed by the other, in a way that could not have been foreseen earlier.

[2] It is not merely that one could not be sure what the consequences would be, but that even if one could be sure of this, there would be no objec-

other is correct, and that the correct one will become clear on reflection, there being no relevant arguments or evidence to aid us in our reflection; though unfortunately some people, not being very good at reflection of this kind, will not arrive at the correct answer even when they think they have done so, and though there is in any case no way of telling who has the correct answer and who has not. The account of the dilemma which I am suggesting is of the following kind: since the preference for family and friends over country, or vice versa, cannot be regarded as positively right or wrong, correct or incorrect, either is legitimate provided that it has been assessed and found appropriate in the light of the various reason-providing factors (consistency, what sort of life does the choice commit me to? and so on) that have been mentioned. It is clear that some people feel an emotional dissatisfaction with the 'subjectivity' of the third way of speaking, and an emotional satisfaction, or at least an absence of dissatisfaction, with the 'objectivity' of the first two; but this difference of emotional reaction has no rational justification. I said earlier (p. 145) that some people are at a higher level of rationality than others because they continue further than others in the process of giving, or considering, reasons for their actions and decisions. But it is no sign of a higher level of rationality to seek for reasons at a stage where no further reasons can in fact be given, or to seek for conclusive reasons where only partial or inconclusive reasons are available.

---

tive way of deciding which of the alternative sets of consequences was better.

INDEX

Abstraction, 18–20, 35
Actions, appropriateness/inappropriateness of, 103–4, 122, 135, 179–80, 205
Actions, correctness/incorrectness of, 104–5, 110, 115, 179, 205
Animals, 197–8
Aristotle, 103–4, 122, 156, 181

Bentham, 16
Berkeley, 21
Butler, 73

Campbell, 181
Churchill, 180
Clarke, 7, 27–38, 45, 65, 95, 96
Codes of Morality, 123–5
Coherence, 128, 142, 144–7, 176
Collingwood, 122
Commands, 10–11
Commitment, 135–6, 199
Communists, 31
Conceptions, clear and distinct, 11–14
Consistency/Inconsistency, 37–8, 90–1, 110, 127–47
Co-operation, 140–2, 145, 196–8, 199
Cudworth, 7–14, 180

Decisions, 177–9, 198–9, 200–1

Deism, 27, 29
Deliberation, 178–82, 185, 200–1
Delinquency, 158–9
Demonstration, 15, 18, 20–6, 27
Descartes, 2, 3, 7, 11, 15
Disagreement, 31–2, 34, 89–90, 182, 200
Discovery, 2–3, 11–14, 43, 179, 201

Emerson, 132
Emmet, 194 n.
Enthusiasm, 24, 46
Epicurus, 7
Euclid, 31
Ewing, 171, 174–6

Facts, 44–5, 112–13, 182–3, 192–3
Faith, 181
Feelings, 62–3, 134–5, 138–9, 178–80, 181–2
  moral, 11, 57–8, 60, 61–3, 70, 202
Freedom, 65–6

Geometry, 11, 12, 19, 21
Gibson, 15
God, 3, 7, 8, 10, 11, 21, 23–6, 28–9, 33–6, 68, 70, 74, 197–8
Good, 36, 48–51
Grant, 160–1

INDEX

Hegel, 65
Hobbes, 7, 27, 31, 50, 67
Hobhouse, 144–6
Hume, 39–63, 64–5, 67, 68, 95, 96, 113, 180, 183
Hutcheson, 47

Impartiality, 62–3, 175
Inconsistency, see Consistency
Injustice, see Justice
Insight, 110, 168, 170, 173–4
Intellect, 64–5
Intelligence, 49–50, 110, 148–66
Intuition, 111, 167–76, 204–5
Irrational, see Rational
Irrationality, see Rationality

Johnson, 162–3
Justice, 34–5, 91
Justification, 22, 56, 83, 100, 102, 105, 106–11, 167–9, 171–2, 177–205

Kant, 19, 64–91, 96, 114, 146, 180
Knowing how, 150–2, 155–66

Language, 194 n., 195–6
Lawrence, 181
Leavis, 122–3
Liberal Democrats, 31–2
Locke, 7, 15–26, 27, 29, 35, 45, 46, 180
Lying, 130–1

Mathematics, 3, 11–14, 15–19, 21, 29–31, 35, 37, 103, 188, 190–1, 200
Mill, 145–6, 148
Molyneux, 20
Moore, 2
Moralities, 146–7, 184–5

Morality, 183–7
    function of, 193–8
    objective standards of, 8–11, 174–5, 201–5
Mossner, 3
Motives, 40–3, 47–51
Murder, 31–3

Nazis, 31

Obligation, 9, 28–9, 33
Ockham, 7

Passmore, 7
Peirce, 169
Policies, 129–30, 133–4, 136, 139–40, 141
Postulates, 190–1
Prichard, 172
Principles, 8–12, 23, 24, 26, 31, 34, 71, 72, 77, 191–2
Promises, 9, 79–83, 88–9, 131, 132 n.
Protagoras, 7

Rational/Irrational Behaviour, 51, 86–7, 99, 100, 101, 125–6, 131–2, 139–40, 143, 144–7, 177–9
Rationality, 1, 66–7, 130, 146, 175–6, 183, 205
Reasonable/Unreasonable
    actions and decisions, 51–56, 98–100, 101–2, 104–5, 129–30, 143 n., 167, 176, 204–5
    beliefs, 52–5, 59, 97
    feelings, 42, 46, 51–2
    men, 109–10
Reasoning, 40–1, 45–6, 47, 59–60, 152–3
Reasons
    for acting (justifications), 54–6, 97–8, 104–5, 106–7, 135, 181, 187–8, 205

INDEX

Reasons, (*contd.*)
  for acting (motives), 54n., 97–8
  for moral beliefs, 104, 107–9, 181
  for non-moral beliefs, 54–6, 96, 105–6
Reid, 48–53
Responsibility, 149–50
Revelation, 2–3, 23–4, 180
Robinson, 195
Ross, 121, 167
Rousseau, 65–7
Rules, 110, 113–26, 134
  of associations, 73, 116–17, 121, 125, 185
  of courtesy, 117–19, 125
  of games, 115–16, 119–20, 121, 124
  of morality, 19, 22, 24, 71–4, 77, 110, 120–6, 164–6, 184–7, 188
  means–end *rs.*, 114–15, 119
Ryle, 150–6

Seeing, 170–1, 173

Self-evidence, 22, 29, 31, 33, 118, 169–70, 189–90
Shaftesbury, 173
Sherman, 158–9
Sidgwick, 167, 169–70
Skill, 151, 159–64
Smith, 175
Spinoza, 27
Stevenson, 107–9, 182, 183, 202–3

Thinking, 98–9, 101–2
Threats, 82–3
Truth, 11–14

Universalisability, 75–91
Unreasonable, *see* Reasonable
Utilitarianism, 204–5

Voluntarism, 7, 10–11,

White, 161
Williams, 190 n.
Wollaston, 45

For Product Safety Concerns and Information please contact our EU representative GPSR@taylorandfrancis.com
Taylor & Francis Verlag GmbH, Kaufingerstraße 24, 80331 München, Germany

www.ingramcontent.com/pod-product-compliance
Lightning Source LLC
Chambersburg PA
CBHW052112300426
44116CB00010B/1635